THE EVOLUTION OF GREAT WOR
URBAN WEALTH AND ECONOMIC GROWTH

Seville was once the unofficial capital of Spain's opulent New World empire, but it failed to become a financial metropolis. The former colonial backwater Hong Kong, however, defied the odds by growing into a major trading centre. Why is it that some cities seemingly destined to become financial capitals fail to realize their potential? What are the key factors distinguishing cities that become wealthy from those that don't?

In *The Evolution of Great World Cities*, Christopher Kennedy examines how geography, technology, and especially the infrastructure of urban economies allow cities to develop and thrive. His investigation revolves around case studies of large cities – including Venice, Amsterdam, London, and New York City – focusing on important junctures in their histories. Kennedy weaves together insights from urbanists such as Jane Jacobs and economists such as John Maynard Keynes, drawing striking parallels between the functioning of ecosystems and of wealthy capitals. *The Evolution of Great World Cities* offers an illuminating introduction to urban economies that will change the way you think about cities.

CHRISTOPHER KENNEDY is a professor in the Department of Civil Engineering at the University of Toronto.

CHRISTOPHER KENNEDY

The Evolution of Great World Cities

Urban Wealth and Economic Growth

UNIVERSITY OF TORONTO PRESS
Toronto Buffalo London

Rotman-UTP Publishing
University of Toronto Press
Toronto Buffalo London
www.utppublishing.com
Printed in Canada

ISBN 978-1-4426-4273-7 (cloth)
ISBN 978-1-4426-1152-8 (paper)

∞

Printed on acid-free, 100% post-consumer recycled paper with
vegetable-based inks.

Library and Archives Canada Cataloguing in Publication

Kennedy, Christopher, 1969–
The evolution of great world cities : urban wealth and economic growth /
Christopher Kennedy.

Includes bibliographical references and index.
ISBN 978-1-4426-4273-7 (bound)   ISBN 978-1-4426-1152-8 (pbk.)

1. Urban economics.   I. Title.

HT151.K46 2011   330.9173′2   C2011-903097-7

University of Toronto Press acknowledges the financial assistance to its
publishing program of the Canada Council for the Arts and the Ontario
Arts Council.

 Canada Council   Conseil des Arts
for the Arts   du Canada

 ONTARIO ARTS COUNCIL
CONSEIL DES ARTS DE L'ONTARIO

University of Toronto Press acknowledges the financial support of the
Government of Canada through the Canada Book Fund for its publishing
activities.

To Denise, William, and Clarisse

Contents

Foreword

RICHARD FLORIDA

Trust me, I read a lot of books on cities. This one is different. *The Evolution of Great World Cities* is one of the most truly original takes on cities and their economic development that I've read in quite a while.

I met Chris Kennedy several years ago, via our colleague Eric Miller, who heads the University of Toronto's Cities Centre. I had only recently arrived in Toronto to lead a new think tank, the Martin Prosperity Institute, dedicated to studying what makes cities and regions succeed. In our first get-together, Kennedy outlined his ideas on the role of infrastructure – and by that I mean infrastructure broadly defined – in the growth and development of cities. He told me he had just finished a manuscript on this issue, and I asked if he would send it over to me.

When I read the early drafts of what would become this book, I was blown away. Here's a work that builds on the insights of figures from Adam Smith to Jane Jacobs and considers the recent findings from civil engineering and physics to construct a new perspective on cities and their economic development. Stories from London to Detroit to Hong Kong to Toronto help illustrate the common threads that weave together great cities through the ages.

Kennedy is a systems thinker in the best sense of that phrase: he's able to analyse and interpret the data and the on-the-ground dynamics, but he also sees the bigger picture and takes the longer view. His greatest contribution lies in showing the role that infrastructure plays in the growth and development of cities, especially the world's great cities. The economies of cities and their infrastructure systems are so closely intertwined that it is often difficult to tell where one ends and the other begins. Wise additions to a city's infrastructure lead to new growth, and smart growth provides the prosperity and impetus for fresh waves of investment in infrastructure. And, while scholars have identified key relationships between infrastructure investment and economic activities in general, they all too frequently fail to consider the bigger picture.

Kennedy's definition of infrastructure goes far beyond roads and bridges. It also includes rules and codes and ways of doing business. London laid the groundwork for its later commercial dominance by changing its building code and widening its streets after the catastrophic fire of 1666. The rebuilding process stimulated demand, increased densities, and led to the adoption of new technologies that set London and England on a new growth trajectory. The United States rose to economic pre-eminence by periodically developing entirely new systems of infrastructure – from canals and railroads to modern water and sewer systems to federal highways. Each played a major role in seeding and shaping long eras of growth. The new age of creative capitalism likewise requires a new infrastructure broadly construed. The cities that put in place that new infrastructure will achieve broad first-mover advantages that power growth well into the future.

Kennedy's book also is an important contribution to our understanding of the way cities and even nations respond to and recover from major economic crises. Major shifts in infrastructure power growth and enable economies to recover from severe economic crises and resume rapid expansion. These will be important considerations in the coming decades. What kind of infrastructure should we build today? How can government best invest its precious resources in projects that support growth, put people back to productive work, and undergird a more sustained prosperity? Understanding the historical and urban processes Kennedy lays out can help us generate better answers to these questions, and better policies to restore growth and achieve a more lasting prosperity.

The Evolution of Great World Cities marks a major contribution to our understanding of economic geography, urban engineering, infrastructure, and the underpinnings of why cities grow and develop. It will be influential and highly cited. And it will change the way you think about cities.

Acknowledgments

First thanks go to Jennifer DiDomenico, acquisitions editor at the University of Toronto Press, who made this happen, and to my editor, Curtis Fahey, who helped tighten and polish an ambitious text. Thanks also go to copy-editor John St James and the production team at the Press. Several students, family members, and friends provided helpful feedback: Sybil, Dave, Gaurav, and Joanna, even Mum and Dad. Special mention goes to colleagues Barry Adams, Eric Miller, and Richard Florida, who read early versions of the text, provided commentary and enthusiastic encouragement, and, in Richard's case, a masterful foreword. Farther afield, individual chapters were read by scholars such as Sir Peter Hall, Henry Regier, and Robert E. Wright, and the whole text was critiqued by three anonymous reviewers. Any mistakes that remain are mine. Useful advice on the publication process was received from Chris Madsen, Rodney White, and my sister Fiona. I am also very grateful to all those who provided photographs: my sister Kathy's friends Patricia Moore and Steve Ingham, Moon Lee, Anton Foleros, Lance Rosol, David Gregory, and Temple University Libraries.

THE EVOLUTION OF GREAT WORLD CITIES:
URBAN WEALTH AND ECONOMIC GROWTH

Introduction

The twenty-first century has been hailed as the *urban century*. As the global economy is transformed by waves of green, bio, and information technologies, cities are at the vanguard of the new post-industrial age. The coming of this era was well described in 1998 by scholar Allen J. Scott, who wrote that 'a new global capitalist economy is coming into existence, with regions constituting the fundamental building blocks or motors of the entire system.' Scott also recognized that cities lie at the heart of these economic regions.

Of course, the most significant economic phenomenon of the first decade of the century has been the continuing rise of China's economy, but even this has primarily to do with cities. Over the past thirty years, China's economy has grown at a remarkable rate, averaging close to 10 per cent annually. This growth is driven by city building. The country's urban population has increased from 34 per cent to 43 per cent in just ten years.[1] In any given year, nearly half of all the new buildings in the world are constructed in China.[2] The Chinese economy might grow to be the largest on the planet by mid-century. Perhaps the greatest questions, however, concern the country's cities. Will Shanghai or Hong Kong rise to be an elite financial centre on a par with London or New York City? Will Beijing emerge to be as politically significant as Paris or Washington, DC?

A plethora of books has welcomed the age of the city. For a general readership, books such as Jeb Brugmann's *Welcome to the Urban Revolution: How Cities Are Changing the World*[3] appropriately capture the new urban vibe. Academic publishers have been no less busy with a surge in studies, by economic geographers in particular, on the rise of the urban service sector, the cultural transformation of cities, and the growth of creative cities and the new economy. Taken together, this literature is important and exciting, and it has perhaps inspired this book in a small way. Essentially, however, my focus is different.

Long before the advent of the post-industrial city, there was a long history of wealthy cities playing significant roles, beginning in ancient times and extending to the twentieth century. Accordingly, the goals of this book are deeper, and arguably more fundamental, than the contemporary literature on the modern global city. In the following chapters, I aim to explain why certain cities are wealthy and how they have grown so over time. These are clearly important questions for professionals involved in local economic development, as well as urban planners and infrastructure strategists. But local politicians, business leaders, and other members of civic society who are involved in fostering the well-being of their cities also make decisions that influence the growth of urban wealth, and they too, I hope, will find something useful in my analysis. Through it, the reader may come to a better understanding of why it is that cities such as London and New York City are so wealthy, and why, in spite of huge entrenched advantages, it is possible for other cities to rise and challenge the current global financial centres.

A further word about the book's focus. My subject is *great world cities*. Here I am not strictly following John Friedmann's definition of the world city as a control centre in the global economy,[4] nor, for that matter, Saskia Sassen's notion of the global city as a service centre,[5] although there is a strong relationship between control and wealth. My focus, rather, is on cities that, based on the value of citizens' assets, are wealthy – which typically tend to be financial centres that host major banks and financial markets. I seek to understand, first, how cities evolve to become financial centres – and thus wealthy cities – and, second, how economic growth, measured by output or income in the conventional economic sense, occurs in cities in general.

My central thesis is that physical infrastructure substantially underlies the wealth and economic growth of cities. Two definitions are in order here. First, by 'infrastructure' I primarily mean transportation systems, which determine land use in cities, and other physical assets such as water pipes, sewers, and buildings. It can be rightly argued that other factors such as culture, education systems, or institutional capacity also contribute to the wealth of cities; I recognize this to the extent that these factors influence infrastructure, for example, through building codes, but my main interest is how the wealth of a city is tied to its physical shape. Second, whereas urban economic growth is typically measured or understood in terms of increases in the output, or income, of a city, I define 'wealth' as the value of tangible assets owned by citizens, though, clearly, growth in wealth and growth in output and income are interrelated. Wealthy cities, in my view, are those that are home to citizens with highly valued holdings of financial, real estate, and other assets. In such cities, infrastructure contributes to wealth in several ways, from asserting the power of an urban market over its surroundings to influencing the balance of consumption and investment by citizens. Moreover, fundamental changes in infrastructure have caused huge increases in the wealth of cities, increases that parallel the changes that occur in ecosystems as they pass through stages of ecological development. My final claim, in fact, is that cities mirror ecosystems as they develop and grow, and, just as an ecosystem can be unhealthy, so can cities. Factors that can constrain the growth of some cities or spur the growth of others – such as location, diversity, and physical structure – have parallels in the ecological model.

This book is a multidisciplinary undertaking. It is primarily an exploration of economic theory through the lens of urban history, but it also follows a few economists in its concern with the field of ecology. A rich variety of case studies from urban history are deployed to support arguments about how urban growth and development occur. Most of the economic theory used is conventional microeconomics and macroeconomics, though considered in the context of cities. As the conventional economic theory becomes overstretched, however, I turn to the field of ecology and evoke basic scientific concepts of how ecosystems function in order to understand more comprehensively the evolution of urban wealth. Insights are occasionally drawn from a few other disciplines, such as architecture, business management, geography, physics, and urban planning. These and other disciplines may not be drawn upon as much as certain readers might like, but the fault – if such it is – should be attributed less to the disciplines concerned than to the tastes, interests, and, perhaps, limitations of the author.

Some of the scholars mentioned will be household names: the likes of Aristotle, Thomas Aquinas, Adam Smith, and John Maynard Keynes, for example. Others may be less well known, and will need to be introduced. Among those whose works have touched substantially upon cities, and whom I draw upon in this book, are Jane Jacobs, the brilliant seer of American cities, who became a political activist and local icon upon moving to Toronto; Fernand Braudel, the great French historian whose works include *The Mediterranean and the Mediterranean World in the Age of Philip II* and *Civilization and Capitalism, 15th–18th Centuries*,[6] the first of which was written inside a Second World War prisoner-of-war camp; and the economic historian Norman Gras, whose categorization of four phases of urban development is key to my own understanding of how cities grow.[7]

Throughout, this book explores a diverse range of economic theories and conceptual frameworks. In some respects these theories are competing, perhaps conflicting, yet each plays its part in providing understanding of the wealth of cities. Much of the dynamics of real estate markets – exemplified by the spiralling towers of Hong Kong – can be understood in terms of microeconomics. New York City's outmanoeuvring of Philadelphia to become the financial centre of the United States in the nineteenth century can be explained by economic geography, with a touch of political intrigue. New insights into the economic effects of sprawling auto-based suburbs in places such as Chula Vista, California, or the Greater Toronto Area can be gleaned from Keynesian macroeconomics. Weaving the chapters of this book together is an exploration of what various theories can and cannot explain about the growth of cities.

Many influences have come to bear in giving rise to this multidisciplinary project. These include a long-time personal interest in urban history; training in 'integrated thinking' during my MBA studies in Toronto at the Rotman School of Management, which prides itself on examining business issues from multiple perspectives; over a decade studying sustainable cities and urban metabolism during my current day job at the Department of Civil Engineering, University of Toronto; and a long association with the interdisciplinary International Society for Industrial Ecology. Of particular significance in the evolution of my thinking has been a course I developed, building on my training in economics, which introduces various subfields of economics to graduate engineering students. In this course, formally titled 'Infrastructure Economics,' I employ a variety of perspectives, from microeconomics through macroeconomics, evolutionary economics, and ecological economics, as they relate to infrastructure systems.

The order of material in this book follows a logic similar to that in my course, moving from microeconomics to macroeconomics and beyond, interlaced with examples and insights from urban history. Chapters 1 to 4 aim to understand what the wealth of cities is and how it comes about. The focus is primarily on the wealthiest cities of all – the financial centres. These chapters also generally draw on a microeconomic perspective, whereas chapters 5 and 6 take a broader macroeconomic perspective, focusing on how economic growth, as measured by output or gross metropolitan product, occurs in cities. In these last two chapters, technological advancement leading to increased efficiency in industrial production will be recognized as important, but so will the consumer demands that are largely related to the ways in which urban infrastructure is laid out. Macroeconomics can be brought to bear in understanding many aspects of urban economic growth, but cities change in messy, complex ways. Hence, we will eventually turn from a physical perspective to a more biological one in order to understand the *evolution* of cities.

Such is the broad picture of the book's structure. As for the individual chapters, chapter 1 sets the stage by studying the works of two scholars, Peter Hall and Fernand Braudel, who have had the greatest influence on my thinking about why the wealth of cities is important and why some cities become wealthier than others. Next, chapter 2 addresses the fundamental question of how to define the wealth of a city. The chapter is essentially an exploration of value theory – the philosophical branch of economics concerned with measuring the value of a *thing* – only in this case the thing is a *city*. It concludes with the argument that the wealth of cities should be measured by the assets of citizens, as reflected by real estate and financial markets. Following this, chapter 3 sets out to understand how real estate markets and financial markets really work – revealing what microeconomics can explain about the functioning of markets. Chapter 4 argues that the wealthiest cities of all are those that host and control markets, that is, the financial centres. It explores how financial centres compete with each other, recognizing, as in economic geography, the importance of spatial relationships. Chapters 5 and 6 seek to understand how economic growth occurs in cities. Chapter 5 establishes that there is a connection between the physical shape of cities and economic growth; in short, households become locked in to consumption patterns determined by the ways in which urban infrastructure – particularly transportation systems – develops. In searching for a fuller theory of how the wealth of cities grows, chapter 6 adds a twist; it argues that the evolution of cities can be understood in a way parallel to how ecologists make sense of ecosystems. Because this book presents a multifaceted, complex, and sometimes subtle argument that builds from chapter to chapter, there is clearly a need for a summary of its main points. That is the purpose of the concluding chapter 7.

At a more detailed level, each chapter starts out with a vignette of a particular city – Seville, London, New York City, Toronto, Hong Kong, and others – which helps to frame and inform (I hope in an entertaining way) the analysis that follows. Each also delves, accessibly, into economic theory, explaining topics such as real estate markets, capital accumulation, and other aspects of macroeconomics. To fully understand how the wealth of cities evolves, however, requires broader insights into the role of the built environment, and technological innovation; it also requires a dose of ecology. Only with all these ingredients can we understand how the wealth of great world cities has evolved.

Following the historiographical discussion in chapter 1, with its reflections on why urban wealth has mattered in history and how it has come to be concentrated at certain places at certain times, this book will build towards a richer understanding of cities by first asking, in chapter 2, how the wealth of a city can be measured. This is no easy task. Joan Robinson, the inheritor of John Maynard Keynes's chair at Cambridge, wrote: 'Economics is the scientific study of wealth, and yet we cannot measure wealth. This seems a sad state of affairs.'[8] Robinson was particularly concerned with the difficulty of establishing measures of wealth that are comparable over different periods, thereby avoiding the problems posed by changes in the relative prices of goods in consumer price indexes and the emergence of new types of goods. With this in mind, the reader will have to be content with a measure of wealth that is valid at a single point in time.

Different perspectives on the meaning and underlying nature of wealth can be seen in the works of the great philosophers and economists such as Aristotle, Aquinas, Richard Cantillon, Adam Smith, and Alfred Marshall. Some have considered wealth to be based on natural resources, others on industrial machinery, and yet others on inventiveness or social capital. The importance of these last two is exemplified by the case of twelfth- and thirteenth-century Paris, which was a truly creative city that spawned the magnificent Gothic style of architecture. One of the scholars to grace thirteenth-century Paris was the Dominican priest Thomas Aquinas. Once we start probing into the economic theory of value, in part through Aquinas's eyes, it is apparent that there are potentially conflicting theories suggesting that the value of a *thing* may reflect its scarcity, its utility, or its labour of production. Chapter 2 will argue, however, that all three dimensions can be simultaneously included in quantifying urban wealth when the spatial context of cities is recognized.

The case of the value of residential homes is particularly pertinent, since much of the wealth of cities is reflected in such properties. Homes provide a good deal of utility – warmth, shelter, security, and comfort. The value of a home also reflects embodied labour, not just to construct it but also to provide all the raw materials and infrastructure to service it. Scarcity of location – such as proximity to an alluring downtown core, or a posh, sought-after neighbourhood – is another important attribute of housing value. Indeed, all three dimensions of value are apparent in our homes.

Expanding the perspective beyond residential homes, I argue that the value of all assets owned by residents of a city is a potential means of quantifying the wealth of the city. This proposition is tested at some length in chapter 2; it means that the value of commercial enterprises is reflected in the wealth of cities where shareholders live. Moreover, the value of municipal infrastructure and other assets – even Philadelphia's $6.4-billion city hall – is not counted as an extra component of urban wealth. This is because the presence and function of such municipal infrastructure is already reflected in the value of residential homes in the city.

Recognizing that the measurement of wealth can really be achieved only via markets, I shall then explore in chapter 3 how markets work, uncovering some surprising findings about their ability to conserve wealth. The wealthiest cities of all are those that operate or control financial markets, but to reach such a status means competing with other cities.

Markets are often the most lively, sometimes exhilarating parts of a city. Whether a simple street market selling fruit and vegetables, a pungent fish market, or a mysterious Middle Eastern bazaar full of wondrous treasures, there is something exciting about visiting such markets. Perhaps it is the expectation of finding a bargain, or uncovering some unique or unusual merchandise. Of course, there are many different types of markets in cities – and some are more mundane. Shopping at the local grocery store can become routine. Yet the sustenance that such stores provide to cities is clearly important. In fact, markets of all varieties are fundamental to civilization; without them, society would arguably collapse into a state of oppression or war.

It is also through markets that the wealth of cities is mediated. Through various institutions, systems, and procedures, markets help determine the value of goods and services that cities rely on. The markets for real estate, financial products, and commodities are extremely powerful. Some, such as the dynamic Hong Kong real estate market, the splendid gold market of Dubai, or the almighty Wall Street, are simply breathtaking.

Markets, though, are prone to rise and fall on a whim. The bursting of some market bubbles has made deep marks in history: for example, the Dutch tulip-bulb bubble of 1636, the Mississippi and South Sea bubbles of 1720, and the Wall Street collapse of 1929 that began the Great Depression. In more recent memory, there was the dot-com bubble of the late 1990s and the financial crisis of 2008, the latter precipitated by a collapse in the US housing market. How can the wealth of cities be based on such flimsy, temperamental markets?

Emerging from the discussion in chapter 3, however, is a recognition that total wealth is more steadfast. Indeed, the wealth of cities is typically less prone than that of individuals to the whimsy of stock markets or bubbles in property markets, because of the interaction between the markets. Data from 1970 to 1999 show that peaks in equity markets tend to correspond with troughs in property markets and vice versa. When market bubbles burst, wealth is generally redistributed, rather than lost. In other words, capital is approximately conserved. The financial crisis of 2008 was quite unusual, in that both property markets and equity markets fell together. This was in part because of the securitization of real estate mortgages in the United States, which tied the property and financial markets together. The response to both of the main markets collapsing was a flight to gold, a time-honoured tradition when all other opportunities seem too uncertain. Capital was still conserved in the midst of such a crisis; moreover, cities such as Dubai, home to the world's largest gold market, flourished.

With its world record-breaking Burj-Khalifa tower, exotic Gulf island communities, and spectacular gold market, Dubai is competing with other cities of the Middle East to become the region's financial centre. This is an example of a phenomenon seen all around the globe. In an increasingly urbanized world – and one that is carbon-constrained to boot – governments at all levels are recognizing that the competitiveness of cities is key to economic prosperity.[9] There is a long history of competition between cities, however; several examples are reviewed in chapter 4, examples that make plain that the development of commercial activities, industry, and transportation infrastructure are key steps prior to the emergence of a city as a financial metropolis. Before the 1830s, Philadelphia was home to the first central bank in the United States and was regarded as the nation's financial centre, rather than

New York City. There are examples in Germany and Italy, too, of the country's financial capital moving between cities. In Switzerland, Zurich emerged as the financial centre only after the opening of the Gotthard tunnel in the late nineteenth century. The historical evidence, as Gras observed, shows that cities progress through three early phases – as centres of commerce, centres of industry, and then transportation hubs – before becoming financial centres. This is an important insight for competing cities, for the greatest and wealthiest cities are those that host and operate markets themselves, in particular financial markets.

Moving beyond financial markets, chapter 5 turns to the broader question of how economic growth occurs in cities. The question arises in part because Gras's description of financial-centre formation is based on historical evidence, rather than economic theory. More broadly, though, when the wealth of cities is measured by the assets of citizens, it is clear that the value and amount of such assets – property and financial holdings – increases with the income of city residents. Income, or more specifically per-capita income, is closely related to economic output and thus can be used to describe the economic growth of cities.

Several theories of economic growth, old and new, are reviewed in chapter 5, but even the great works of Adam Smith and Jane Jacobs are found to overemphasize the production side of the economy, with little attention paid to consumption. Smith saw the division of labour through industrial capital investment as key to economic growth, while Jacobs, writing in an urban context, stressed the importance of developing new kinds of work. Both are right, but neither really asks why consumers would have heightened demands for the greater quantities of goods and services provided by increased productivity or new work. Others, such as David Hume, William Petty, and John Maynard Keynes, gave more recognition to the role of consumption in economic growth.

The argument I shall make in chapter 5 is that urban economic growth occurs through increased consumption associated with a lock-in to new technologies. The application of technology to achieve higher productivity of firms, or to increase the size of markets, is necessary, but not sufficient, to explain economic growth. For a new technology to contribute to economic growth, it must increase the competitiveness of firms but also pass on additional costs to consumers such that their overall expenditures increase. Moreover, while the increased expenditure is often for desirable, luxury items at first, society evolves to become locked in to the new technology, such that it becomes indispensable. A recent example is the information-technology revolution of the 1990s, through which the combination of the Internet and personal computers created substantial new industries. While accessing and exchanging information with millions of websites around the globe, the PC surreptitiously became part of households' autonomous, or indispensible, consumption.

The technology that has arguably become the most indispensible for cities, however, is the automobile, a fact that Henry Ford recognized. Largely through the laying down of infrastructure and other aspects of urban design, many cities have grown to be dependent on automobiles. The role of urban design is clear when comparing the low automobile ridership of Freiburg, Germany, with its pedestrian-friendly city centre, tram lines, and cycle paths, to the car culture of Chula Vista, in San Diego County, California, with its six-lane arterial roads and neighbourhoods with few points of access and limited internal connections. Many cities have evolved to become auto-dependent like Chula Vista. This has provided jobs for innumerable people, from road-construction workers to parking attendants to body-shop repair workers – and, moreover, has substantially increased the consumption of cities.

The concern is, though, that citizens of these automobile cities, especially in North America and Australia, may be over-consuming at the expense of capital investment. Household savings rates in nations with the most sprawling cities dropped to around zero in recent years. By contrast, the great city-state of Singapore, with its substantial public-transit system and deterrents to automobile ownership, has the highest savings rate in the developed world. Citizens of Singapore accumulate capital through real estate investments. Macroeconomics, thus, provides some insights into the growth of cities, but chapter 5 is left clutching for a fuller theory of growth that can capture phenomena such as capital formation, capital maintenance, technological change, and evolving urban form.

Ultimately, urban history poses a number of examples that are hard to explain with conventional economics. How did London's economy grow so rapidly after the city was burned to a cinder in the Great Fire of 1666? Why did New York City emerge as the leading economic powerhouse of the twentieth century at a time when 25 per cent of its workforce was unemployed? How did the economy of such an innovative and successful city as Detroit undergo such spectacular decline? To explain such developments, this book eventually arrives at an ecologically based theory of urban economic development.

In chapter 6, inspired by insights from Alfred Marshall, Peter

Mirowski, and others, I turn to the field of ecology and develop an organic theory of urban growth. Following Richard Nelson and Sidney Winter,[10] I argue that firms operating in an urban economy can be seen as analogous to organisms in an ecosystem. Firms are the basic units of an economy – independent and typically surviving based on their ability to be competitive or collaborative, yet also dependent on the overall state of the economy, just as organisms are dependent on their host ecosystem. Moreover, the distribution of firm sizes in an urban economy has similarities with organisms in an ecosystem. As with a food web, there is a structural relationship between firms in an economy, with capital goods and services generally passed upwards through a structural hierarchy. Capital in the urban economy is approximately conserved just like mass in ecosystems. It also comes in several forms: physical capital such as buildings and machinery is like organic biomass, while human capital, such as technical knowledge and management skills, is in a sense the nutrient of firms. Meanwhile, money flows through the urban economy, conserved like energy but degrading in quality with each transaction, as per the second law of thermodynamics.

The power of the ecosystem analogy to urban economies is its ability to interpret some of the most spectacular transformations in cities observed in history. When London was destroyed by the Great Fire of 1666, its economy behaved analogously to an ecosystem being brought back to an early stage of ecological development, with a phenomenal rate of recovery. London was rapidly rebuilt like an early-stage ecosystem with large quantities of energy being used to produce new biomass. Similarly, New York City in the 1930s found itself with an excess supply of workers that it put to use by constructing urban highways, which ultimately defined the new urban form of the twentieth century. Accumulating capital, New York moved to a higher level of development, like the growth of a great forest. An opposite occurrence – the death of the economy of Detroit akin to a dying ecosystem – occurred in part because of a lack of economic diversity and growing infrastructure that strangled the city.[11]

Chapter 7 integrates the material from the previous six chapters into a new understanding of urban wealth. It first tells another of the book's many tales – this time about the changing fortunes of two great rival Canadian cities, Toronto and Montreal. Three contributions of the book are then highlighted as being particularly important: the measurement of wealth through the assets of citizens; the association between consumption in cities and urban form; and the conceptual understanding of urban economies based on analogy with ecosystem theory. Together, these provide a deeper understanding of the evolution of the wealth of cities.

Cities, in short, are complex, adaptive systems with multiple agents determining the course of their development – businesses and households interacting in changing ways yet always influenced by the historical shape, form, and culture of the environment in which they operate. Somehow, in this mix, certain cities emerge to be exceptionally wealthy – a process that I try to understand, and explain, in the chapters that follow. Let the story now begin.

1 Where the Streets Are Paved with Gold

Standing on Highgate Hill, Dick heard the bells ring out
'Turn again Whittington, three times Lord Mayor of London.'

Every British schoolchild is brought up learning the fourteenth-century tale of Dick Whittington. As a poor country boy, Dick hears that the streets of London are paved with gold, so he sets out to the great city to seek his fortune. Arriving cold and hungry, he is taken in by a rich merchant who employs him as a scullery boy. Dick's small room in the merchant's basement is overrun with rats, so he earns a penny by shining shoes and uses it to buy a cat. Later, because of the cruelty of the merchant's cook, Dick decides to leave London, but, after setting out, he hears the Bow Bells ringing. Regarding this as a sign, he turns around and returns to his employer's house, where he learns that the merchant has sold his cat at a great profit in a far-off land. This transaction makes Dick a wealthy man and he even marries the merchant's daughter, Alice.

The real Richard Whittington, on which the character Dick was based, was actually the youngest son of a minor noble from Gloucestershire; he indeed came to London and became a wealthy merchant, a moneylender to kings, and eventually lord mayor of London on four occasions (1397, 1398, 1407, and 1420). Among his exploits was arranging the financing for the building of Westminster Abbey. Whittington was well known as a philanthropist; he provided donations for the construction of London's Guildhall and for repairs or extensions to various churches, hospitals, libraries, and prisons. Dying without an heir, he left his considerable fortune to charities that he had established.

What is quite remarkable about Whittington's tale is the endurance of the wealth of London. In the fourteenth century, the city's trade with faraway lands produced sufficient wealth for the construction of magnificent buildings and the blossoming of philanthropy. Whittington's city was one where the streets were indeed paved with gold. In 2005 the square mile of the city of London alone accounted for over 2 per cent of the United Kingdom's gross domestic product (GDP) and witnessed some $1109 billion per day in foreign-exchange turnover. In 2009 London was home to twenty-six billionaires, second in the world only to New York City, which had fifty-five.[1]

Of course, London is not the only city where the streets are paved with gold. The same has been said of New York City; and in sixteenth-century Seville, the streets were paved with gold *and* silver.[2] No doubt there are others, but why is it that some cities, such as London, have maintained their wealth, while others have faded? This is a question that scholars have wrestled with at least as far back as Xenophon of Greece. In writing on how Athens could continue to increase its revenues, he suggested several possibilities, one of which was the avoidance of war. A similar observation was made in a celebrated speech by the ruler of Venice, the doge Mocenigo, upon his deathbed in 1423. The old doge impressed upon his people the importance of remaining at peace if the wealth of Venice was to be maintained. If the citizens followed his advice, he promised that they would be 'the masters of the gold of Christendom'[3] – and so they were, for a while.

Other factors such as geography and development of technology also underlie the wealth of cities. In his famous book the *Wealth of Nations*, Adam Smith noted that there was something special about the geography of cities. Smith observed that cities situated on seacoasts or navigable rivers were not constrained by their hinterlands and could trade with the remotest corner of the world. 'A city might in this manner grow up to great wealth and splendour, while not only the country in its neighbourhood, but all those to which it traded, were in poverty and wretchedness.'[4] In more recent times, other writers, such as Jane Jacobs, have pointed to creativity and inventiveness as being fundamental to the wealth of cities. This may be so, but we shall find that there is more to it.

Many scholars have written on the great cities of world history, among them the prolific Lewis Mumford, author of the classic *The City in History*,[5] Paul Bairoch, who wrote on economic development,[6] and Spiro Kostof of urban-architecture fame.[7] Naturally, there have also been numerous historical studies of specific cities – far too many to list here, though several will be drawn upon as the book progresses. But, for my purposes, the works of two scholars – Peter Hall and Fernand Braudel – provide the most relevant beginning. Hall's collection of histories of great cities[8] highlights in particular the role of wealth in the cultural, technological, and physical transformation of cities, while, from a different perspective, Braudel identifies wealthy cities that became financial capitals of the West.

Cities of Culture and Innovation

Hall's *Cities in Civilization* tells the stories of several great world cities at key junctures in history. In his analysis, some cities are noteworthy because they were centres of cultural revolution, some because they produced fundamental technical innovations, and others because they redefined the very shape and form of urban environments through their development of infrastructure. I will start by briefly recounting a few examples and insights from this great work. Not only do Hall's findings provide material for better understanding the wealth of cities, but the three major factors he emphasizes – culture, invention, and infrastructure – are fundamental components of economic growth.

Hall tells the tales of six great cities which experienced cultural – though by no means tranquil – golden ages.[9] Athens in the age of Pericles stands out among all Greek cities for its creativity – in philosophy, science, architecture, art, poetry, and drama. Fifteenth-century Florence lay at the heart of the Renaissance, while Elizabethan London, thanks to Shakespeare and his contemporaries, experienced a golden age of poetry and drama. Vienna is more complex; the city of music at the turn of the eighteenth century spawned, one hundred years later, a society of art, science, and literature in the midst of an 'aging imperial order.'[10] Paris too, in the era from 1870 to 1910, experienced a golden age of painting. Lastly, Weimar Berlin in the short space of the 1920s reached new heights in art, theatre, music, and cinema – and invented much of the cultural style of the twentieth century. What is noteworthy about all six cities is that they reached cultural peaks at times of great social transformation, as conservative, aristocratic, or conformist values gave way to open, rational, and sceptical ones. As Hall explains, 'Creative cities, creative urban milieu are places of great social and intellectual turbulence, not comfortable places at all.'[11]

The wealth of these cities also played a role in their creativity. Hall notes that all six were rich by the standards of their time, but also exhibited large discrepancies in quality of life between rich and poor. It could be said that such discrepancies occur in all cities. Yet it seems to have been particularly the case in these 'cultural crucibles,' where individual patronage was essential. What would have happened to the creative genius of Leonardo de Vinci had it not been for the riches of families like the Medici? Unlike the next group of cities, however, these cultural crucibles were largely dominated by well-established 'old' wealth.

The cities known for major technological innovations experienced, in contrast, an explosive generation of new wealth.[12] Hall reviews six such cities, from the nineteenth century to the present day: Manchester, Glasgow, late-nineteenth- and early-twentieth-century Berlin, Detroit, Tokyo-Kanagawa, and San Francisco and environs. Manchester, as the centre of the cotton industry from 1760, was the quintessential city of the Industrial Revolution, according to Hall. Glasgow, another significant Industrial Revolution city, was where James Watt first tinkered with steam engines, and it later came to be the world's most prolific centre of shipbuilding. Berlin, with rivalry from New York, was entrepreneurial in electrical engineering, starting around 1890; it was there that Werner von Siemens first set up his telegraph firm. Across the Atlantic, Detroit, of course, is well known for its automobiles. Silicon valley, the legendary innovative centre of the San Francisco Bay area, achieved many significant advances in semi-conductor technology. Tokyo-Kanagawa was equally innovative in advanced electronics.

These innovative cities have some remarkable commonalities. All were fringe cities or settlements at the time of their flourishing. They possessed traditional skills by which innovations could be exploited, but were not well-established industrial cities. Lacking old wealth, they were unstuffy, non-hierarchical places. A few key individuals, such as Richard Arkwright and Henry Ford, featured in entrepreneurial successes, but the development of local networks of highly skilled labour was also important. In some cases, the entrepreneurial workforce itself, if not the regional population, provided much of the demand for the new products. A final similarity between the innovative cities – at least the first four – was that all experienced spectacular industrial decline once their central invention (cotton manufacture in Manchester; shipbuilding in Glasgow; electrical engineering in Berlin; and automobiles in Detroit) became commonplace.[13]

A further group of cities considered by Hall were also entrepreneurial – not in manufacturing new products but in the evolution of their very own infrastructure.[14] Rome under the emperors Trajan, Augustus, and Claudius made advancements in water supply. To serve their population of one million, the Romans, around 300 BC, built a system of 14 aqueducts, 317 miles in length and regulated by 247 reservoirs delivering 220 million gallons of spring water per day. From 1850 to 1870, Paris, under Baron Haussmann, doubled in size, added sewers and water supply, and constructed its famous boulevards, parks, and gardens. Meanwhile, Victorian London adopted a free-market approach to developing major urban infrastructure. From 1880 to 1940, New York grew at an unprecedented rate and overcame technological challenges, consistently breaking records in the construction of buildings, bridges, tunnels, and electric traction. From the early 1900s, Los Angeles constructed a system of streetcar lines and later urban highways that allowed the city to disperse with seemingly limitless bounds; congestion was a problem from about 1920, by which time most households owned a car. In sharp contrast, Stockholm, from the middle of the twentieth century, developed into the model socialist city, providing one of the greatest examples of integrated land use and transportation planning. Such cities fundamentally changed the physical appearance of urbanity.

Hall offers a range of explanations for why innovation in urban infrastructure occurred in these cities. The simplest and possibly most apt is that the cities had no other choice: 'A Rome growing unprecedentedly in a dry climate, a London faced with cholera, a New York grappling with hopeless tenement congestion, a Los Angeles finding itself gridlocked, these cities acted because they were under the threat of urban breakdown.'[15] Other factors are also apparent, such as social/moral order, vested interests, key individuals, and, perhaps, business cycles. Ultimately, Hall suggests a pluralistic explanation for innovation in infrastructure: 'some conjunction of a general socio-economic stage of evolution, a particular political response ... and a suitable cultural ambience.'[16]

What is noteworthy in Hall's analysis of innovation in urban infrastructure is the relative insignificance of economic expectations held by innovating cities. No doubt, costs, of huge proportions, were calculated for all these great urban infrastructure projects; and some individuals may also have foreseen economic benefits. Yet the cities did not necessarily set out to build grand aqueducts or super-transportation systems for the sake of achieving economic or financial reward; it was done for much more pressing humanistic reasons.

Financial Centres

While Hall's work certainly discusses economics, he opts not to use financial power – or, more bluntly, wealth – as a major category for grouping his city case studies. Financial historians might argue that Hall could have paid more attention to cities that made innovations in methods of finance, such as Italian city-states for bonds, Amsterdam for joint-stock companies, and Edinburgh for modern insurance.[17] A broader approach, which shall be pursued here, is to study particular cities during the era when they were arguably the dominant financial centres of the Western world.

The lineage of powerful cities that were at the centre of world economies[18] is skilfully traced by the French historian Fernand Braudel. In his analysis, Venice, following on from the ancient capitals of Athens, Rome, and Constantinople,[19] held primacy over the rest of Europe by the late fourteenth century. Subsequently, a handful of cities in the West – Antwerp, Genoa, Amsterdam, London, and New York City – have achieved financial supremacy. Braudel does not venture much in time beyond the eighteenth century, but Youssef Cassis has partially picked up his baton by describing the financial activities of London and New York City – among other cities.[20] Cassis, though, is primarily focused on the financial history of banks and stock markets; this is important and valuable, and we shall draw upon his work in a later chapter. Yet the story of hegemonic cities remains incomplete.

What follows is a short history of the West's hegemonic cities from the time of Venice, drawing initially upon Braudel's work.[21] This is useful for two reasons. First, it will acquaint the reader with several cities which reappear later in the book. Second, the history of the hegemonic cities offers an alternative perspective on world history, one that is rarely seen in the multitude of books on warring nation-states. The prolific twentieth-century urbanist Lewis Mumford defined the city as 'a point of maximum concentration for the power and culture of a community.'[22] If that definition is correct, and I believe it is, a better understanding of the wealth of cities should result from looking at the most powerful cities. More to the point, however, studying the points of maximum concentration of power – that is, cities – must surely lead to a greater understanding of world power. After all, where else but in cities do nation-states get the funds to conduct their wars, or repair the damage afterwards?[23]

Venice was established at the heart of Europe's economy in the early fifteenth century. Between 1405 and 1422, it had annexed a ring of towns on the Italian mainland – Padua, Verona, Brescia, and Bergamo – thus providing itself with hinterlands. More significantly, in 1383, Venice had occupied Corfu, the gateway to the Adriatic, to which it later added a string of smaller ports and islands stretching towards Constantinople and the Islamic world. In so doing, Venice established itself as the key trading centre and dominant economic hub, not only of the prosperous Italian city-states, but of a wide array of European cities, from Vienna to London and Hamburg. As Europe's main entranceway to Constantinople and the Near East, Venice controlled the trade in all major commodities – pepper, spices, Syrian cotton, grain, wine, and salt. In 1423 Venice and its territories had an annual revenue of 1.6 million ducats. This was far greater than the revenue of any other Italian city-state, greater than the revenues of England and Spain, and even greater than the one million ducats of France, which had ten times the population.[24] Venice had a huge fleet of ships – so large that almost the whole of the city's capital was wrapped up in them. It ensnared the surrounding economies, including that of the German people, forcing all trade to take place through its port – to its own great profit.

The Venetians pursued a deliberate economic policy to ensure that much of Europe's trade took place in their city. German merchants, for example, were assigned compulsory, segregated residences in the Fondaco dei Tedeschi, opposite the old Rialto Bridge.[25] There the visiting merchants had to deposit and sell their merchandise under strict surveillance – and purchase Venetian goods with the proceeds. These foreign merchants were excluded from the highly profitable long-distance trade with the east, which was reserved for citizens of Venice only. Moreover, the Venetian state forbade its own merchants from buying and selling goods in Germany. Thus, the German merchants had to come to Venice to trade. Of course, they could have traded at other ports, such as Genoa, but Venice dominated – it was Europe's warehouse.

The Venetian state, furthermore, established a system of protected convoys to provide security for its merchants and thereby reduce their risks and transportation costs.[26] The system of the *galere da mercato* included a number of state-owned ships operated by private merchants. They provided archers, slingsmen, and later canon to protect groups of Venetian vessels sailing on various routes throughout the Mediterranean and for a time to northern Europe. By pooling their resources together within the system, Venetian merchants were able to reduce their transportation costs relative to those of foreign rivals.

With the wealth that came from dominating Europe's trade, the Venetians created a beautiful city.[27] Thousands of oak piles were sunk into the sand and mud of its lagoon. These supported masses of stone brought by ship from Istria at great expense. Thus, the earthen streets were paved and many of the wooden bridges were rebuilt in stone. The great Doge's Palace was restored and many smaller palaces were constructed along the banks of the Grand Canal.

By 1500, however, owing to the unexpected rise of Portugal, the mantle of economic leadership had passed to Antwerp in Belgium. When Vasco da Gama sailed around the Cape of Good Hope, a new route to the east was opened, signalling the beginning of Venice's slow decline. Lisbon or perhaps Seville might then have become Europe's financial centre, given the concurrent opening of the Americas. But the Spanish and Portuguese needed capital and equipment for their American activities. By the act of opening a bank branch, the Feittoria de Flandre, the king of Lisbon essentially made Antwerp his financial centre.[28] Antwerp was already established as a port for the importing and dyeing of English woollens. It now became the location where German silver and even Hungarian copper were traded for Portuguese spices.

A further boost to Antwerp's fortunes occurred around 1535. By then, Spain was overflowing with gold from South America and King Charles V needed the established Antwerp money market for his financial dealings all over Europe.[29] A multitude of other goods were traded through Antwerp too: timber, tar, and wheat from the Baltic, and linens, woollens, and household manufactures from the Netherlands, Germany, England, and France. The economy of Antwerp blossomed. By 1570, its population had reached 100,000, having more than doubled since 1500.[30] Building sites covered the city, new streets and squares were designed, and new industries such as sugar and salt refineries and soap-making and dye works were established. The wealth of Antwerp, however, having been established by the Portuguese, was now tied to Spain – and when the Spanish state went bankrupt in 1557, Antwerp's short era of financial supremacy ended.

Europe's financial centre then returned to the Mediterranean, this time to the city of Genoa. The ancient sea port set against barren hills had for centuries tussled with Venice. Yet it was not through its ships, merchants, or industry that Genoa came to dominate Europe. It was through its investments. The Genoese were great bankers, with establishments throughout Europe, which made them sufficiently versatile that they were able to shift their interests from waning to rising states as the need arose, surviving many financial crises in the process. In 1557 it was Genoese bankers who stepped in to aid the bankrupt Spanish king, establishing a complex international financial system to provide regular income from irregular receipts.[31] Although it is hard to be specific about Genoa's period of dominance, Braudel suspects that the city remained Europe's leading financial power until 1627, when yet another Spanish bankruptcy occurred!

Genoa was succeeded by Amsterdam, which had been on the rise for several decades. Amsterdam was the principal city of a group of cities in the United Provinces – a region that was notable for a lack of natural wealth and the extent of urbanization (50 per cent of the population lived in cities).[32] The strength of Amsterdam had been boosted by the migration of merchants and other wealthy citizens from Antwerp, which was besieged in 1585. To these were added French Protestants and wealthy Jews from Spain and Portugal. Like most world-dominating cities, Amsterdam had a great tolerance for cultural diversity along with a laissez-faire approach to government which allowed commerce to prosper.

Also of significance were maritime skills. The Dutch operated large whaling operations, producing oil, and had a massive herring fishery. They were great shipbuilders, too, inventing the highly efficient flyboat and employing sufficient modern technology to produce one warship per week.[33] As early as 1560, Amsterdam controlled 70 per cent of the heavy Baltic trade and five-sixths of the trade between the northern Atlantic and Iberia.[34] By 1669, the Dutch fleet was equivalent to that of the rest of Europe combined.

Upon this base, Amsterdam flourished into a financial powerhouse with a global presence. The bourse, that is, stock exchange, was rebuilt in 1592, just as large-scale shipping of grain to the Mediterranean had begun. In 1602 the Vereenigde Oost-Indishe Compagnie (VOC) was founded with a capital of 6.8 million florins, equivalent to sixty-four tons of gold.[35] It was ten times larger than its English rival formed two years earlier. The VOC did far more than just bring spices to Europe. It opened up a vast intricate web of trading relationships, exchanging textiles, cottons, coral, gold, pewter, copper, deer pelts, silk, rice, sugar, pepper, wheat, elephants – the list goes on – between an array of ports.[36] Vast amounts of goods sailed into Amsterdam to be sold, stored, and resold. Like Venice and Antwerp, Amsterdam gained a monopoly over the trading activities of nearby economies, England, France, and Scandinavia being subservient to it.[37] Accompanying the trade, great masses of money constantly circulated through the bourse, and so, taking over from the Genoese, the men of Amsterdam became suppliers of credit to the whole of Europe.

During the eighteenth century, however, London caught and surpassed Amsterdam in wealth and power. There are several possible reasons why. One early factor was perhaps the Glorious Revolution of 1688–9, which saw the Dutchman William of Orange and his wife Mary become king and queen of England.[38] With William and Mary came expertise and institutional reforms to a city that was already on the rise. Other potential causes include a lack of Dutch technology for further capital investment, corruption of the VOC, and the English switch to paper money.[39] England's defeat of Holland in their fourth war of 1782–3 might have been a minor factor. The Dutch financial crises of 1763, 1772–3, and 1780–3 and subsequent civil revolution were certainly hard on Amsterdam markets. Yet in many respects Amsterdam's control over English trade had waned by 1730, because the Dutch had found themselves at home in London and were seduced, as Braudel puts it, by the English national market.[40]

London's growth in power corresponded with the rise of the English nation-state and the expansion of the British Empire. It is challenging to separate London's growing wealth from that of Britain as a whole in the age of the Industrial Revolution. London was and still is far larger than any other British city. The population of Greater London grew spectacularly through the nineteenth century, from 1.1 million in 1801 to 7.2 million in 1911.[41] In 1900 London housed one-fifth of England's population.[42] In some respects it was four cities all in one: the city core, the heart of London's financial power; the West End, home of Parliament, royalty, and high society; the port of London; and the south bank, which had grown around the seventeenth-century theatres. Although it is often overlooked in discussions of the Industrial Revolution, London had the largest and most diverse industry in the country. Much of its industry was traditionally conducted by small, often single-proprietor, businesses, and yet, when large multinational companies set up in Britain from the 1850s, the majority chose to locate in London.[43] Moreover, much of the growth in industry elsewhere in Britain was fuelled by London, if not via investment from the wealthy city then through the shear size of London's consumer market.[44] Probate returns between

1809 and 1914 showed that twenty out of forty British fortunes of over £2 million were held by Londoners.[45] Given also London's focal point in Britain's transportation system, the city in many ways created the national market.

London developed substantial transportation infrastructure and fostered technological change. It was by far the most significant port in Britain. In 1841 the registered coastal tonnage of three million tons arriving in London was three times higher than that into Liverpool – the next highest.[46] Although London's percentage share subsequently declined, it grew in absolute terms, reaching twenty-four million tons by 1910. Just like Amsterdam, London maintained a significant role as an entrepôt for northwest Europe. Among its many docks was the Royal Albert dock, which, upon opening in 1880, was the longest in the world, one and three-quarter miles.[47] London boomed as the age of railways arrived. Between 1850 and 1870, private companies spent £40 million on stations and routes into London, eventually resulting in fourteen mainline termini.[48] In 1863 the world's first underground passenger railway began operation in London – the Metropolitan line between Farrington and Paddington. Then, between 1900 and 1906, the majority of the deep tube lines were burrowed through the London clay in a frenzy of private investments akin to the Internet boom of the late 1990s. The financial investments into London's transportation infrastructure were vast.

The development of London's rail-based suburban transportation systems underlay a fundamental social change that was accompanied by huge economic growth. Over the nineteenth century, London grew from a relatively small (four by six miles), pedestrian-dominated city to a sprawling metropolis with rows and rows of terrace houses fed by urban rail. Separation between workplace and residence became increasingly common and families sought separate accommodations away from the crowded inner city. With a huge input of private capital, aided by favourable tax systems and building regulations, massive suburbanization occurred. As well as huge investments in housing, the change in lifestyle brought increased demand for furniture and other household goods. Changes in the manufacturing and distribution of goods were also accompanied by changes in retail practices, with larger shops and chain stores replacing street sellers. The result was the transformation of the West End into the most affluent mass market in the world.[49]

Throughout its long reign as the Western power centre, but particularly in the late nineteenth century, all of London's financial sectors grew – banking, the stock exchange, insurance, and international finance. Advances in transportation and communications reduced distances and consolidated power in the city. Control of UK banking deposits by London-based firms rose from 35 per cent in 1871 to 65 per cent in 1911.[50] By 1900, forty British-owned overseas banks were clustered within the city's financial district, which became the centre of an international network of over 1000 branches.[51] The value of the 570 domestic firms on the stock exchange was £500 million by 1907.[52] The city's investments overseas were immense. Between 1870 and 1914, an average of 4.3 per cent of British national income was invested abroad, much of it in infrastructure projects in temperate regions. By 1913, overseas assets accounted for 32 per cent of net national wealth and earned British investors £200 million in foreign income.[53] In 1900, about two-thirds of the world's marine insurance business was controlled by London institutions, half through Lloyds.[54] London remains a major financial centre to this day, particularly in banking and foreign exchange, though it was superseded in the twentieth century by New York City.

On 29 October 1929 the New York Stock Exchange collapsed, beginning the Great Depression of the 1930s. A ripple effect was felt around the globe, with stock markets falling sharply. This sequence of events has been interpreted as evidence that the financial epicentre had passed from London to New York, for, had London still been the dominant financial city, it would have propped up the New York exchange, preventing collapse. In any event, by the 1920s, London had lost its status as the sole centre of an economic hegemony bringing order to the world economy; financial dominance was now split between London and New York. Britain had accumulated a large debt from the First World War – a considerable proportion of it from New York banks, and the Bank of England shared the task of running the international monetary system with the New York Federal Reserve. Yet some scholars maintain that New York was not quite ready to step into the role of central world power. In order for Britain and other European countries to repay their financial debts to New York banks, they needed to export industrial goods to the protected American market. This brought the New York banks into direct conflict with American industry, which had a significant presence in the New York economy.[55]

The rise of New York City has some intriguing ties back to Amsterdam and London, the previous two financial centres. The island of Manhattan was first discovered by Europeans when the harbour and river were chartered by the VOC in an expedition captained by Henry Hudson.

The first Dutch settlement on Manhattan was founded in 1624. New Amsterdam was captured by the English in 1664 and renamed New York, but it was then recaptured by the Dutch in 1674. It was returned to the English in November 1674 at the end of the third Anglo-Dutch war, from which the English had essentially withdrawn because of its high costs. New York remained an English possession somewhat as a token gesture; the Dutch were far more concerned with holding on to the more valuable sugar plantations of Suriname. To become the financial centre of the United States, New York had to overcome Philadelphia and other cities, as will be discussed later, but close ties to London also helped. As well as being ideally located for trade with Europe, New York City remained the most British of American cities. The city's commercial ties to London gave it an informational advantage over other American cities; New York newspapers were always first with news from Europe. With good access to British capital, New York emerged as the major American market for industrial securities.[56]

The size and stature of New York grew rapidly around the turn of the nineteenth century. In 1898 New York City merged with Brooklyn, the fourth-largest American city, to become a single city of 3.4 million people over an area of 359 square miles.[57] Close to half of America's millionaires lived in the New York metropolitan area. In 1895 the metropolis had 298 firms with assets of $1 million, with second-ranked Chicago having just 82. Manhattan was home to 69 of America's largest firms. New York's port, which in 1870 had handled 57 per cent of the nation's trade, continued to expand and thrived during the First World War as the embarkation point for over 1.5 million American troops. In 1921 the port was merged with that of New Jersey to create a single Port Authority.

Curiously, New York emerged as the world's hegemon during the Great Depression, a time when 1.6 million of its population of 6.9 million was receiving social relief and one-third of its manufacturing plants had closed. By 1932, when a quarter of the city's population was out of work,[58] New York City had a debt of $1.9 billion, equal to that of all forty-eight American states combined. New York's governor, Franklin D. Roosevelt, was elected president that year, and his administration launched a New Deal that included huge investments in infrastructure throughout the country. New York City alone received $1 billion between 1933 and 1939. Under the mayoralty of Fiorello La Guardia and the direction of 'master builder' Robert Moses, it undertook construction on a massive scale: an extensive public-housing program, three major bridges, sixty miles of intracity expressway, a traffic tunnel for the East River, and additions to the subway lines leading to unification of the transit system. By 1939, La Guardia Airport had opened and fourteen new piers had been added to the port. A whopping $591 million was spent preparing a 1216-acre site for New York's majestic world fair of 1939–40. Significant private-sector buildings were also completed during the 1930s, including the Chrysler Building, the Empire State Building, and the Rockefeller Center. Some of New York's excess labour was put to good use pouring concrete during the Depression.

It was in the late 1940s, following the Second World War, that New York City arguably reached the peak of its power, creating a new world order around itself. It was New York lawyers and bankers who designed the new world institutions that brought security and economic stability to the post-war world.[59] The United Nations was established in New York in 1945. New Yorkers were the principal architects of the North Atlantic Treaty Organization, the General Agreement on Tariffs and Trade, the World Bank (initially housed in New York), and the International Monetary Fund. New York's influence was far greater than that of the American capital, Washington, DC. Indeed, in the 1920s Washington had relied substantially upon J.P. Morgan and Company to administer US foreign economic policy in Europe, China, and Latin America.[60] Moreover, it was the New York policy elites of the 1940s who orchestrated the reorganization of the US government into a national-security state: the creators of the National Security Council, the Department of Defense, and the Central Intelligence Agency were New York investment bankers. The irony of New York's modern, liberal, international philosophy at this time was that it strengthened political, cultural, and economic centres elsewhere, some of which would challenge New York's hegemony in the 1970s and 1980s. Under the New York–created Marshall Plan, New York bankers helped Europe and Japan back to economic prosperity. New York's liberal world view helped cities such as London and Tokyo rise.

In the post-war years, New York continued to grow physically, but also experienced some teething problems. A massive construction boom included the addition of fifty-eight million square feet of office space from 1947 to 1963; this was greater than that in the next twenty-two US cities combined.[61] The growth was driven by rapid suburbanization. In 1955 the city's population of 7.8 million was 52 per cent of that in the metropolitan region. By 1988, the metropolitan region had reached 18 million, while that of the central city had shrunk to just 7.3

million.[62] The city experienced race riots in the 1960s and near bankruptcy in the 1970s. Manufacturing continued to decline and even the number of US Fortune 500 companies headquartered in New York fell from 128 in 1965 to just 48 in 1988. Yet these facts reflected a change in the New York economy, which saw huge growth in financial and business services. New York's role in the US economy was in relative decline, but it remained dominant in matters relating to the international economy.[63]

By the late 1980s, New York's role at the centre of the world's financial hegemony remained intact (although London had become more important for international banking).[64] Forty of the 100 largest multinationals in the United States were still headquartered in the metropolis. Moreover, these forty accounted for $212 billion of the $384 billion in foreign revenues earned by the top 100. By 1985, six of the big eight accounting firms and seven of the top ten management consulting firms were centred in New York. Nineteen of the world's largest advertising agencies were there. With internationalization of the world economy, New York had some 342 overseas bank branches holding assets of $536.5 billion. Moreover, after briefly being eclipsed by Tokyo, at the end of the 1980s, the New York Stock Exchange remained the world's largest capital market, with a total value of near $3 trillion – representing 34 per cent of the world's capital.

Conclusion

Dick Whittington perceived London to be a wealthy city as far back as the fourteenth century, and yet its years of hegemonic financial power did not arrive until the nineteenth, or possibly late eighteenth, century. Venice, Antwerp, Genoa, and Amsterdam came before London, but have since substantially declined in status. New York City arguably remains the dominant financial centre today, although London has perhaps risen again in the new millennium, not as the capital of the British Empire (as previously), but in a new role as the financial hub of an experimental new European super-state. (I shall return to the historical competition between London and New York City – along with Paris – in chapter 4.) Whether New York, or London, will remain as a leading financial centre throughout the current century remains to be seen. Where else might twenty-first-century Dick Whittingtons turn to make their fortunes? Perhaps Shanghai will rise to join or surpass New York City, as did Tokyo briefly in the 1980s, but this will depend to some extent on factors such as culture, technological innovation, and infrastructure.

Hall's work suggests that wealth can have differing impacts on the evolution of culture, technology, and infrastructure in cities. Broadly speaking, cultural revolutions occur in cities with large disparities between rich and poor; technological innovation occurs in less stuffy, out-of-the-way cities lacking old wealth; and new forms of infrastructure have developed in large established wealthy cities at risk of urban breakdown. Reflecting on Braudel's hegemonic cities, however, we can, in some instances, turn this reasoning around. Cultural tolerance and laissez-faire attitudes seem to have been important in the rise of Amsterdam and London as financial centres. The hegemonic financial centres were also technologically innovative; for example, Antwerp for industry, Amsterdam for shipbuilding, and London for subways. These two factors – culture and technological innovation – will appear again in this investigation into the wealth of cities, but I shall not explore them in much depth. This is in part because others, such as Allen J. Scott,[65] have wrestled with them substantially, but also because my particular focus is on urban infrastructure.

Infrastructure, as this book will show, plays a notable role in the wealth of cities. There is a connection between the economies of cities and their infrastructure systems that is so natural, so symbiotic, that it is difficult to discern. Several researchers have identified statistical relationships between infrastructure investment and economic activities in general.[66] These are obvious and beg the question of cause and effect. To look upon a city's infrastructure in its place and function is to see a physical manifestation of the urban economy. Buildings increase in height from suburb to centre, mimicking the urban economists' 'rent curve.'[67] Each motion of a car, truck, and train on a highway or railway line is a small dynamic of the economy at work. Is the frustrated view from a car on a congested highway not a visual clue to some constraint to economic growth? To separate the economy of a city from its infrastructure is like asking how the human body would function in the absence of its skeleton and cardiovascular and nervous systems.

One of the main findings in this book is that the infrastructure of a city influences the consumption of its citizens and hence the city's economy. In chapter 5, when we will pick up on Keynes's observation that a household's propensity to consume is determined by its habitual conditions, it becomes apparent that consumption in cities is dependent on the physical shape of cities. Urban infrastructure, particularly for transportation, has evolved in a way that supports increasingly consumptive lifestyles. As cities changed from being walking cities to radial transit cities and then into sprawling automobile cities, residents became locked in to a commuter lifestyle. The arterial roads and highways of the twentieth-century city not only made residents auto-dependent but also, through low-density land use, allowed house sizes to grow, thereby creating more *space to be filled*. This physical expansion of cities provided employment for many, often in new economic sectors. Accordingly, the physical environment of cities and the consumptive patterns to which it gives rise are as important as increases in industrial productivity in explaining urban economic growth.

Infrastructure has also played a key role in the formation of financial centres, as seen in the review of hegemonic cities in this chapter. All these cities established substantial and often innovative new infrastructure to support their huge volumes of trade. The significance of this will be discussed further in chapter 4.

This brief account of hegemonic cities also highlights just how significant and influential a single city can be in the world at large: Amsterdam controlled Europe's trade, London ran the world's marine insurance, and New York City created a new world order. This alone is a good reason to study the wealth of cities. The ambition of this book, however, is not just to strive for an understanding of hegemonic cities, or financial centres for that matter. True enough, there is much discussion in the following chapters on financial centres, but overall the aim is to understand the growth of urban economies in general – and not just the very rich ones. This is an important point, for it means that the book goes beyond specific historical description to develop a more general theory of how the wealth of cities evolves. In the next chapter, we begin that journey with consideration of a preliminary – but fundamental – issue: How is the wealth of a city best measured?

2 A Theory of Urban Wealth

Hercules built me,
Caesar gave me walls and towers,
and the Saint-King won me,
with García Pérez de Vargas

Inscription on the Gate of Jerez, Seville

In March 1493, when Columbus returned from his first voyage to the Indies, it was fitting that the city of Seville, in the Kingdom of Castile, was his final port of arrival in Spain. The city that had been captured from the Moors by King Fernando III in 1248 was destined to become the unofficial capital of Spain's New World empire. Columbus famously brought with him gifts for King Ferdinand and Queen Isabella: chilli peppers, sweet potatoes, hutias, monkeys, parrots, some gold, and six natives of the Caribbean with ears and nostrils pierced with gold.[1] Following Columbus's monumental lead, many explorers would set off from or return to the port of Seville: Elcano circumnavigating the earth; Cortes returning from the conquest of Mexico; Pizarro from Peru. They would bring back exotic goods such as coffee, chocolate, and tobacco, but above all else they would bring back to Seville hoards of gold and silver.

Situated in a fertile region of Spain on the Guadalquivir River, Seville had been known since Roman times for its olive oil, wine, and wheat.[2] The Moors built great walls around the city, five miles long with about 200 towers and twelve gates. These were crossed by the Carmona aqueduct, which supplied some 300 fountains within the city. With a population of 60,000 by 1520, Seville was the largest city in Castile and was the

1 The Torre del Oro watchtower has guarded the port of Seville since the thirteenth century. The tower has witnessed shiploads of gold and silver sailing up the Guadalquivir River, but, even so, Seville failed to become a major financial centre. (© Photo: Patricia Moore and Steve Ingham)

seat of an archbishop. The most impressive building in Seville was its grand cathedral, completed in 1506 after construction throughout the reign of Ferdinand and Isabella. The cathedral was built on the site of an old mosque; it is 443 feet long, 330 feet wide, and 138 feet high, larger than even St Peter's in Rome. It was here that Holy Roman Emperor Charles V was married to Isabella of Portugal in 1526. Of further significance to the wealth of Seville were her riverside docks, marked by the characteristic Torre del Oro watchtower. In former times the Guadalquivir River had been navigable all the way up to Cordoba, but at the founding of the Spanish Empire ocean-going vessels stopped at Seville.

Following Columbus's relatively modest discoveries, shiploads of gold were to reach Europe through Seville. Columbus is reputed to have discovered natives eating from gold plates on his first journey to the Indies. The royal escort Antonio de Torres returned from Columbus's second journey with twelve ships carrying gold worth 30,000 ducats from La Espanolá.[3] By 1519, with further findings in Puerto Rico and Cuba, the official, conservative, figures showed that nine tons of gold had arrived from the new Spanish colonies.[4] The Spanish pushed onwards into Central America in their quest for gold. In 1521, in one of history's most intriguing encounters, Hernando Cortes and an army of fewer than 1000 men conquered the Mexica's city of Tenochtitlan, though they were disappointed by how little gold they found.[5]

Gold was discovered in large quantities, however, during Francisco Pizarro's astonishing adventure in Peru in 1533.[6] In a tale even more remarkable than that of Cortes, Pizarro and his gang of 160 untrained men were invited into the northern Inca city of Cajamarca. Surrounded by thousands of natives and fearing for their lives, Pizarro's men sprang a trap in the central ceremonial square of the city. Firing a single canon and charging on horseback, they caused the crowd to panic and captured the Inca emperor Atahualpa. The emperor agreed to pay a ransom of gold and other treasures to fill the room in which he was held – 22 feet long by 17 feet wide and 9 feet high. In brutal fashion, Pizarro's men melted down the hoard of ornaments received, destroying 2000 years of Andean craftsmanship. Moreover, Atahualpa was executed. Pizarro returned to Seville with five ships loaded with gold – and this was just the beginning.

Back in Seville, an official in the emperor's treasury wrote in 1534 that 'the quantity of gold that arrives everyday from the Indies and especially from Peru is quite incredible; I think if this torrent of gold lasts even ten years, this city will become the richest in the world.'[7] Indeed, the Inca gold brought much attention to Seville. The city that had always been open to other Europeans – Genoese, Germans, and English – was now flooded by them. Following the news of Inca gold in 1534, the population of Seville tripled in just seventeen years.[8]

Yet the large quantities of gold found by the Spanish were to be overshadowed by their discoveries of silver.[9] The technology for isolating silver improved from 1555 onwards through a process that involved combination with mercury. This was a technology that the Spanish used to great reward. Of particular note were the silver mines of Potosí, high up in the barren mountains of central Peru. With the new technology, silver production at Potosí rose sevenfold between 1572 and 1585. Output from the mine remained above 7.6 million pesos every year from 1580 to 1650. It is estimated that over 70 per cent of the New World's silver came from this mine – at a time when the New World was producing over 80 per cent of the world's silver.

The riches of their new empire were so vast that, from 1562, the Spanish established a system of secured convoys to and from Seville to protect ships from pirate raids, particularly by the English. From 1550 to 1650, the official import register in Seville recorded that over 180 tons of gold and 10,000 tons of silver crossed the Atlantic. A further estimate for the period 1540 to 1700 suggests that the New World produced about 50,000 tons of silver, thereby doubling the existing European stock.[10]

Seville undoubtedly benefited from the convoys of silver sailing up the Guadalquivir, but the wealth of the city did not grow by the extent that locals expected.[11] What happened to all the silver? First of all, there was a simple rule by which one-fifth of all treasure from the Indies went to the crown. The Spanish royals, however, tended to borrow heavily using readily available bills of exchange. Hapsburg emperor Charles V, in particular, borrowed large amounts from Italy, France, Germany, and the Netherlands. At that time there was a ban on exporting specie from Castile, so the international financiers ended up investing their returns in local industry and commerce, as well as buying property in Castile. This was a boom time for Seville. Yet foreigners working out of the great banking houses in Antwerp, Augsburg, and Genoa began to control the Seville economy. The Genoese in particular were financiers for many Atlantic crossings; locals saw them as 'controlling everything' and charging interest at exorbitant rates. After 1555, however, when the ban on exporting specie ended, the foreign masters of Seville's economy withdrew their capital from Spain. Huge amounts of bullion left in the 1560s and 1570s to fund the war in the Netherlands. As one Tomás de Mercado put it: 'In Flanders, in Venice and Rome, there is so much money from Seville that the very roofs could be made with escudos, yet in Spain there is a lack of them. All the millions that come from our Indies, are taken by foreigners to their cities.'[12] By the seventeenth century, it was observed that ships returning across the Atlantic would pause outside the Bay of Cadiz and surreptitiously unload onto foreign vessels 50 per cent or more of the silver they were carrying.[13]

The great influx of gold and silver from the New World was, furthermore, a major factor in the remarkable phenomenon of rising prices that occurred throughout Europe in the sixteenth century.[14] Writing in 1513 with reference to the time of his father, G. Alonso de Herrera noted: 'Today a pound of mutton costs as much as a whole sheep used to, a loaf as much as a fanega of wheat, a pound of wax or oil as much as an arroba.'[15] The inflation of prices is shown by numerous records for a wide range of commodities from wheat to wine, timber to charcoal, salt to honey. On average, prices increased by about a factor of five or six over the century, although the changes were sporadic in nature. Price rises generally occurred quickest in Seville and southern Spain, and spread through Europe, reaching Russia last.[16]

The increase in the stock of silver and gold is recognized as being a significant cause of the inflation. This follows the *quantity theory of money*, which holds that prices are proportional to the money supply, assuming a given volume of trade. There may have been other factors, such as the general growth in the European economy and faster circulation of money. The analysis is complicated somewhat by the change in the price of silver relative to gold, from 1:12 in 1500 to 1:15 by 1650. It is also fair to recognize that the price changes of the sixteenth century were not as large as the inflation experienced during the twentieth century. Nevertheless, aside perhaps from minor inflation in late-fifteenth-century Germany, the rise in prices during the sixteenth century was essentially a new phenomenon for the people of Europe.

The inflation in sixteenth-century Europe was closely associated with the mercantilist economic philosophy that then held sway.[17] From the middle of the fifteenth century, a new merchant class had emerged from the feudal shadows to become in effect the government of the merchant cities of Europe, its interests aligned with those of the emerging national states. Possession or control of gold and silver was central to the policies of governments and merchants alike. In simple terms, treasure was seen as the fundamental basis of wealth. Countries became preoccupied with positive balance of payments and typically encouraged the formation of monopolistic overseas trading companies to increase exports over imports. Accumulation of gold and silver was the primary goal.

The experience of Seville in the mercantilist era demonstrates, however, that there is more to the wealth of a city than just amassing silver and gold. If gains in silver and gold are offset by rising prices, is there any gain in wealth at all? Moreover, if much of the treasure was owned by finance houses in other cities, then to what extent did Seville benefit? To answer such questions requires a clearer understanding of what is meant by wealth, what is its basis, and how it can be quantified for a city.

The purpose of this chapter is to establish a means for quantifying a city's wealth. This is clearly a necessary step before anything can be said about how cities become wealthy. That said, economic history is replete with various explanations for the underlying basis of wealth, such as natural resources, industrial machinery, self-sufficiency, invention, and social capital; and so a review of fundamentals will first be undertaken. In particular, there are three different attributes by which the value of an item can be quantified: embodied labour, utility, and scarcity. Yet all three of these attributes can be seen to apply simultaneously in quantifying urban wealth, when the spatial context of cities is recognized. This is made apparent by the example of a residential home, which takes labour for its construction and maintenance, provides a great deal of utility to its host family, and, moreover, has value based on the scarcity of its location within a city. Consequently, I propose that the simplest way of quantifying a city's wealth is to focus on the value of its citizens' assets, which includes financial assets as well as the value of real estate. This method can be applied to cities at various times in history – not just sixteenth-century Seville but also the great world cities of our own time.

The Nature of Wealth

One of the first to see beyond the mercantilist mentality was the Irishman Richard Cantillon.[18] Born in southwest Ireland in the 1680s, Cantillon came from a family of Catholic landowners who had been dispossessed of their lands by Cromwell. As a young man, Cantillon made his way to Paris, where he established himself as a prominent banker and wine merchant. While in Paris, he became familiar with the monetary schemes of John Law, but, recognizing the flaws in the inflationist practices upon which they were based, Cantillon reputedly made a fortune of some twenty million livres from the Mississippi and South Sea bubbles. From 1721 to his untimely death in 1734, Cantillon was embroiled in legal disputes, was accused of attempted murder, and was twice briefly imprisoned. Having moved to London, he died in mysterious circumstances – allegedly robbed and murdered by his discharged cook, who burned Cantillon's house to the ground in an effort to cover his actions.

Cantillon wrote one remarkable treatise upon which his reputation as the first economic theorist is based. *Essai de la nature du commerce en général* appeared in France around 1732 and was published anonymously in England about twenty years after Cantillon's death. Some of the economic theory in the treatise was evidently developed as part of his legal defence against charges of usury. Cantillon's treatise influenced both the French Physiocrats, through Anne-Robert-Jacques Turgot (1727–81) and Jean-Baptiste Say (1767–1832), and the Austrian school of economists in the late nineteenth century. Although mentioned by Adam Smith in the *Wealth of Nations*, the treatise fell into obscurity in the English-speaking world until it was resurrected and popularized by William Stanley Jevons in the 1880s. It thus influenced both the classical school and the 'marginalist' revolution – a significant development in economic theory that occurred at the end of the nineteenth century.[19] Jevons dubbed Cantillon's treatise the 'Cradle of Political Economy.'[20]

Cantillon's work provides a delightful definition of wealth: 'The land is the source or matter from whence all wealth is produced. The labour of man is the form which produces it and wealth in itself is nothing but the maintenance, conveniences, and superfluities of life.'[21] After Cantillon, other writers either offered variants of this definition or departed from it completely. Alfred Marshall, whom we shall meet again in chapter 6, wrote austerely that 'all wealth consists of desirable things – that is things that satisfy human wants directly or indirectly.' Marshall's simple definition is similar to that of recent writer Peter Jay, who summarizes wealth succinctly as 'material betterment.'[22]

Whether it is satisfaction of human wants, quest for material betterment, or acquisition of the superfluities of life, the struggle to accumulate wealth has been viewed from many different perspectives. American economist Thorstein B. Veblen wrote that 'wealth is now itself intrinsically honourable and confers honour on its possessor.'[23] Karl Marx provided an alternative focus: 'Accumulation of wealth at one pole is, therefore, at the same time accumulation of misery, agony of toil, slavery, ignorance, brutality, mental degradation, at the opposite pole that is, on the side of the class that produces its own product in the form of capitalism.'[24] John Stuart Mill considered the production of wealth to be largely determined by the physical world and human knowledge of that world, but the laws governing the distribution of wealth to be dependent on the design of human institutions.[25]

If asked what a desirable distribution of wealth might be, however, it soon becomes apparent that answers to such questions about wealth are limited by the vagueness of its definition. Joan Robinson wrote that 'economic wealth is not a very precise idea and we must be content with a rough definition of it,' adding: 'Broadly, economic wealth is the command over goods and services that are desired, or consuming power for short.'[26] Her predecessor John Maynard Keynes perhaps had doubts as to whether a theory of wealth accumulation could be developed: 'The whole object of the accumulation of wealth is to produce results, or potential results, at a comparatively distant and sometimes an indefinitely distant, date. Thus, the fact that our knowledge of the future is fluctuating, vague, and uncertain renders wealth a peculiarly unsuitable subject for the methods of classical economic theory.'[27]

Leaving the vague definition of wealth aside for now, there is a further question of what wealth is based on. Here again, the above quote of Cantillon is a useful starting point since it remarkably captures two perspectives: the Physiocrats' emphasis on land and Smith's focus on production. The theories of the eighteenth-century French Physiocrats emerged in contrast to the mercantilist conception that wealth is simply the accumulation of money or precious metals. To them, natural resources, including agriculture, were the basis of wealth. François Quesnay (1694–1774), for example, stated that wealth did not consist of the quantity of money a nation could store up but of the quantity of raw materials available. In the classical school emanating from the work of Adam Smith, labour of all types can contribute to wealth, not just agricultural labour. Smith's *Wealth of Nations* provides the foundation of contemporary capitalism. Smith saw the machinery, tools, and other forms of productive capital in which labour has been embodied as constituting a form of wealth.

There are other conceptions of wealth or explanations for its formation. Austro-German Kameralists in the eighteenth and nineteenth centuries, starting with Johann Heinrich von Justi (1720–71), added an emphasis on self-sufficiency to the mercantilist doctrine; all kinds of produce could contribute to wealth, but only if they were home-produced. John Rae (1786–1873) considered invention to be of primary importance in the creation of new wealth; in some respects, his work is a recognition of the importance of intellectual capital. Similarly, in the work of Friedrich List (1789–1846) and Jean-Baptiste Say, there is understanding of the importance of social or human capital. List recognized that the institutional life of the state – teachers, judges, physicians, and administrators – was essential for the production of wealth. Say considered immaterial products such as physicians' and musicians' services to be a form of wealth in their own right. Finally, the more recent field of ecological economics recognizes that ecosystems and the services they provide to humans, for example, clean air and water, constitute a form of wealth.

A problem encountered by those concerned with social and natural capital is that many so-called goods are actually undesirable. One interpretation of wealth, stemming mainly from the classical school, is to see it as the sum total of all material objects having value in exchange. A problem with this interpretation is that some objects that have value in exchange may be harmful or socially undesirable, such as narcotics, firearms, or wastes. The next chapter shall discuss the city of Hong Kong, whose very creation was a consequence of a trade in opium. To characterize such undesirable goods, John Ruskin coined the term *ilth*.[28] Ruskin argued that wealth is 'the possession of the valuable by the valiant'[29] and, for something to be valuable, it must 'avail towards life.'[30]

Differences between the various ways of defining wealth become particularly difficult to resolve when we turn to the matter of putting a value on wealth, a subject known in economics as value theory. Fundamental problems in value theory go back at least as far as Aristotle. He recognized that a distinction should be made between the value of using an article and its value in exchange. Adam Smith also realized that goods had value both in use and in exchange, but argued that the only objective and measurable value was that in exchange. This, incidentally, is a principle that will be adhered to in this book's theory of urban wealth, once we get value theory worked out.

Value Theory: From Thomas Aquinas to Alfred Marshall

A potential difficulty with developing a precise theory of wealth is that the value of an article may generally depend on three different attributes: (1) the labour required to produce it; (2) the utility of the article; and (3) its scarcity. Value theory has evolved between these three extremes with only a few attempts to harmonize these elements. One of the first thinkers to address the subject – and a leading proponent of the idea that labour was key to value – was the 'Angelic Doctor,' Thomas Aquinas.

Born in Italy in 1225, Aquinas had a prolific career of spiritual writing that took him to several European cities, including Naples, Cologne, and Rome, but it is with Paris – the leading intellectual centre of the twelfth and thirteenth centuries – that he is most commonly associated. The story of Paris's transformation during this era is quite remarkable. The city provides an excellent example of how invention and social capital, discussed above, can contribute to urban wealth. Paris grew from an insignificant town of perhaps 3000 people in 1100 to become one of Europe's most creative and wealthy cities, with a population of 200,000, by 1300. Historian Colin Jones describes this period as the 'greatest quantum leap in the history of Paris, before and since.' He goes on to remark: 'Not much more than a dot on the map even in 1100, by the end of the twelfth century it was the largest city in Christendom and a pre-eminent cultural and intellectual centre.'[31]

The transformation of Paris was attributable to many factors. Military requirements certainly played an important part, particularly during the reign of Philip Augustus, when the addition of fortified walls for the right bank of the Seine (1190–1209) and the left bank (1200–15), in combination with the new fortress of the Louvre, made Paris 'the most heavily defended military stronghold in Western Europe.'[32] Also important was the church. The wealth of religious establishments in Paris, largely derived from agricultural and commercial holdings, helped to fashion an incredibly creative economy.[33] Spending by the church supported large numbers of highly skilled artisans such as architects, sculptors, stained-glass experts, jewellers, goldsmiths, and manuscript illuminators; indeed, Paris was the pre-eminent international centre for many of these high-end crafts. Also owing to patronage from the church, Paris became a centre for learning. Across the river, on the left bank, the University of Paris emerged during the thirteenth century.[34] The university attracted a highly diverse student body, socially and ethnically, from all over Europe. It also supported a substantial service-sector economy of parchment makers, binders, illuminators, copyists, and the like, along with, of course, taverns, inns, bathhouses, and food shops.[35] It was also in Paris, during this era, that the magnificent Gothic style of architecture was created.[36] In some respects, then, twelfth- and thirteenth-century Paris was akin to the creative cities described by contemporary scholar Richard Florida.[37]

Thomas Aquinas first arrived at the University of Paris some time after 1245.[38] Having been schooled in Naples, where he was introduced to the works of Aristotle, Aquinas was dispatched to Paris to work with the great Albertus Magnus. After a brief period in Cologne, he retuned to Paris to complete his bachelor of theology degree. The depth of his faith and the extent of his intellectual abilities were clearly present at this point, for in 1256, at the age of thirty-one, he was appointed to be one of the twelve masters of the Sorbonne, under the title of *magister in sacra pagina* (master of the sacred page). His role was to raise, discuss, and resolve theological issues through study of the Bible. After returning to Italy in 1259, Aquinas began a further period of study in Paris around 1268 or 1269. During this final period in Paris, he is thought to have written the second of the three parts to his most famous work, the *Summa theologiae*. As an integration of faith and Aristotelian reason, the Great Summa was a controversial undertaking. A close reading of the text shows how Aquinas was careful to use Aristotle not to refute the Scriptures, but rather to develop two parallel discussions. It was during this last period in Paris that Aquinas did most of his greatest work on interpreting the work of Aristotle.

Aquinas's writings were extensive and economic theory was just one component of his larger moral philosophy. Similarly to Aristotle, he inevitably had to wrestle with economic questions when considering issues of justice in interactions between man and man. In the *Summa theologiae* he addressed concerns over the just price in a transaction and the appropriateness of interest on loans. Thus, Aquinas was drawn into reflections on value theory in his writings. For him, embodied labour was central in determining the value of an item. He considered the utility of an article to vary widely depending on individual circumstances, and thus it was irrelevant to its value. Instead, on the basis of his moral philosophy, Aquinas believed the just price value for an item to be inseparable from the value of the craftsman's labour used to create it. Hence, the value of the article would in the long run be determined both by the amount of labour required to produce it and by the value of the labour as based on societal norms prevailing at the time.

That is one statement of value theory, and Aquinas put it as well as anyone. It faced few challenges for a long time, until notions of utility attracted more attention in the seventeenth century. From the utility perspective, it is not embodied labour but the ability to satisfy human wants or needs that underlies economic value. As Nicholas Barbon (1640–98) expressed it, 'Things derive their value from their capacity to serve the needs of men's bodies and minds.'[39] Two centuries later, Hermann Gossen (1810–58) took the utility perspective further by proposing that the value of a thing is proportional to its ability to provide enjoyment. Gossen also recognized the law of diminishing marginal utility: the satisfaction provided by each unit decreases with the quantity consumed.

The third element of value – scarcity – came to the fore in the eighteenth century. One of its leading champions was the English economist David Ricardo (1772–1823), who maintained that both scarcity and the quantity of embodied labour influence the value of an object. Subsequently, William Nassau, Sr (1790–1864), went further by suggesting that scarcity was the fundamental aspect of value, whether because of the difficulty in applying labour or because of natural causes, such as with rare metals.

There have been attempts to harmonize the three perspectives on value. Alfred Marshall – and to some extent Leon Walras – is credited with synthesizing the utility and cost-of-production theories of value, the latter of which reflects scarcity and the embodiment of labour. There are basically two parts to the harmonization of the three perspectives. First, there is generally some form of relationship between embodied labour and scarcity, though it is not always straightforward. In some cases, many hours of highly skilled labour can be used to produce something scarce, such as a hand-crafted luxury automobile or a masterpiece painting. In other cases, labour can work against scarcity, such as in the application of mining labour to increase the abundance of a rare metal. Second, there is no absolute or non-arbitrary way of quantifying utility – and arguably the most tractable way of assessing utility is by recognizing that it is constrained by individual or household budgets. Since such budgets are determined by wages, then utility and embodied labour become synthesized through the forces of supply and demand in the market for some good or service. Accordingly, utility and some balance of scarcity and embodied labour are just two sides of the same coin. All three dimensions of wealth must apply simultaneously.

The Value of a Home: More than Bricks and Mortar

Labour, utility, and scarcity are all important dimensions of value, then, but there is another ingredient that also needs to be considered – one that is critical to understanding the wealth of cities. That ingredient is spatial context. Appreciating its role, especially with respect to the location of residential homes, underlines the point made above – namely, that the different dimensions of value can occur simultaneously.

Although space is a distinguishing feature of the contemporary fields of urban economics and economic geography, it was typically ignored by classical economists before Johann Heinrich von Thünen (1783–1850). Thünen was a German landowner from the Mecklenberg area who, through careful study of his farm accounts, made fundamental theoretical contributions to economics.[40] In 1810 von Thünen bought a rural Tellow estate from his brother-in-law. Lying twenty-three miles from the city of Rostock and five miles from the small market town of Teterow, on a featureless landscape, and in an era before railways, the property lay at the heart of von Thünen's classic work, *The Isolated State*, published in 1826. Over a period of ten years, von Thünen made laborious empirical investigations of the costs and returns of farming various products on his estate. From his analysis he established a model of concentric rings around a central city depicting the profit-maximizing locations for different types of agriculture. First came horticulture and market gardens, followed by pasture, arable lands, forestry, and, lastly, hunting lands. Through his work, von Thünen not only provided a foundational model for urban economics; his application of differential calculus to provide a mathematical basis for marginal productivity was a significant development in economic analysis. Fernand Braudel considered von Thünen to be the greatest economist of the nineteenth century, alongside Marx.

A city is, of course, a spatial entity. All cities have well-defined boundaries in a political sense, separating one municipality from another. In an economic sense, however, cities are better defined in terms of 'commutersheds' – the areas in which people travel to work on a day-to-day basis. Such urban areas are often larger than politically defined cities and their borders may be more difficult to define precisely. In economic terms, however, commutersheds are important because they define both labour and real estate markets. There is also spatial context *within* a city, which is clearly important for the utility and scarcity dimensions of urban wealth. The value of housing, for example, will vary throughout a city depending on proximity to desirable locations, often the city centre, where land is scarce.

As shall be further discussed later, homes typically constitute the largest component of the wealth of most cities. They clearly provide a great deal of utility – shelter, warmth, safety. Indeed, homes provide much of what people desire according to the higher categories of Abraham Maslow's hierarchy of needs: water, comfort, and safety;[41] only oxygen, which is free, and food and physical health, which generally require movement, are not explicitly provided by homes. From a utility perspective, it is therefore hardly surprising that nothing else typically contributes more to urban wealth than residential homes.

There is also embodied labour in a home. Work is required not only to construct a home but also to produce its materials and fittings. The value of a house, however, is usually much more than the value of the labour and labour-embodied materials required to produce it. First, the value of a property includes both the structure and the land. Some theories consider land to be a value-producing factor on a par with labour. Yet, as recognized by John Locke (1632–1704), land is valueless without the application of labour. Infrastructure, such as roads, rails, water supply, and, in a modern context, energy supply and sewerage are required in order for land within a city to have any value. Consequently, it is the embodiment of labour in infrastructure that gives value to land. In wilderness areas far away from infrastructure, land has little value at all, unless under special circumstances, where it contains scarce natural resources. Agricultural land is of some value, though typically much lower than urban land, but it also receives labour to clear it, fence it, and maintain it. So the value of land upon which a house stands reflects an embodiment of labour in infrastructure, just as the structure of the house is an embodiment of labour.

The value of homes in cities is higher, often substantially higher, than in rural towns or villages. For example, in 2005 a typical three-bedroom detached home in a respectable Toronto neighbourhood cost close to $500,000. Drive for two hours out into rural Ontario, outside the commutershed, and a similar house would cost under $200,000. The difference in price, which at least for now may be considered a reflection of value, can only partially be explained by the embodiment of labour in infrastructure. It may be argued that the immediate infrastructure in the vicinity of the house in a rural town may be as good as that servicing a similar house in a large city. Towns and villages in rural Ontario do have energy and water supply! Broadening the spatial context, however, it is apparent that homes in cities are served by a far greater amount of infrastructure than homes in rural towns. Not only are houses in cities served by a larger transportation infrastructure offering more places to travel, but cities also have far better cultural, educational, and health infrastructure. Access to concert halls, sports stadia, libraries, colleges, universities, and specialized hospitals adds to the value of houses in cities.

The general rise in house prices from the edge of cities has also been explained in terms of utility. A basic tenet of urban economic theory is that households locate so as to maximize their utility, balancing the increased utility from owning large plots of land against the costs of daily transportation. A further explanation for the higher value of homes in a city is that they are in a location of high income-generating activity. This matter will be returned to in subsequent chapters, but the scarcity dimension is significant here. Scarcity enters into the value of things in many ways. For example, the costs of labour and materials are to some extent reflective of their scarcity. Shortage of housing itself, relative to demand, can cause a rise in prices in a city. In urban economies, however, it is scarcity of central location or other desirable locations that perhaps most influences the value of houses. With the possible exception of a few peculiar American cities, the centres of cities are generally the most attractive places for travel. As centres for financial, commercial, and cultural activity, they are where much of the value-added activities in cities occur. Space is limited in city centres; hence the value of houses in or near to city centres is typically higher than elsewhere in cities.

In brief, then, it can be seen that all three dimensions of value – along with the spatial context in which they operate – are encapsulated in residential homes, and so in the wealth of cities. That leads to the next question: How is the wealth of a city best measured?

Measuring the Wealth of a City

Now that I have clarified how the three dimensions of value simultaneously apply in a city, a simple rule can be proposed: *The wealth of a city is equal to the sum of the net assets of the citizens of the city.* This rule implies that, if the assets of each citizen are added up – their homes, furnishings, motor vehicles, investments, money and treasure, subtracting any debts – then the total represents the wealth of the city.

At first glance, this might seem like an overly simplistic rule that perhaps ignores many complexities of cities, so some effort will be spent here to test and defend my proposition. In particular, it must be conceded that there are many other assets in cities, such as non-residential buildings, municipal infrastructure, and other facilities. Should the value of these assets not be included in the wealth of a city?

Take, for example, city halls. Most cities have relatively expensive city halls, perhaps a solid and imposing older stone building, or a shiny new one in glass and steel. These buildings are expensive to build, perhaps one thousand or more times the price of a residential home. If the market resale value a of city hall is $500 million, say, should this amount not be included in the wealth of the city? As an extreme case, consider Philadelphia's colossal city hall.[42] With 695 rooms, 630,000 square feet of floor space, and a footprint occupying four city blocks, this city hall is the largest municipal building in the United States. It is even larger than the Capitol building in Washington, DC. For a city known for its simple Quaker heritage, Philadelphia's city hall is grandiose to say the least. Inspired by the Palais des Tuileries and the new Louvre, the architect, John McArthur, Jr, chose an elaborate Victorian style known as French Second Empire. Elegant motifs adorn the turreted courtyard stair towers; dormer windows project from the massive slate-mansard roof; the north and south portals house grand staircases; and over 250 sculptures depict historical, allegorical, and mythological people and animals.

The most famous statue of those that adorn the building is the 53,348-lb. bronze statue of William Penn, which stands atop the northside tower. The observation deck below Penn's feet is forty storeys high. The north tower also contains twenty-six-foot-diameter clocks on all four sides. When construction of the city hall first began in 1871, McArthur's aim was to build the tallest structure in the world. By the time of completion, thirty years later, however, the brim of Penn's hat stood short of the Eiffel Tower and the Washington monument. Nevertheless, the city hall was the tallest occupied building in the world until 1909, and it remains the largest and tallest masonry building in the world.

The materials used in constructing the city hall are impressive. The exterior has 98,000 square feet of granite and 730,000 square feet of marble. The structure includes a further 50,000 square feet of dressed sandstone, 88 million handmade hard bricks, 300,000 pressed and enamelled bricks, and 80,000 square feet of slate. Metals include 27,000 tons of wrought and cast iron, 371,346 pounds of bronze, and thirty miles of copper wire to supply the 10,400 lights.

It may come as no surprise to learn that the Philadelphia city hall is the most expensive municipal building ever constructed in the United States. It cost $24.3 million, of which the marble alone was $4.5 million. And these costs are in 1891 dollars! One estimate suggests that it would have cost $6.375 billion to construct the city hall in the mid-1990s. The

2 Philadelphia's colossal city hall is the most expensive municipal building ever constructed in the United States. (Photo courtesy of Temple University Libraries)

building remains a functioning home for city and county offices and courts. Upkeep of the building is expensive, though. In 2000 an eight-year project to renovate the outside walls was begun, at a cost of $347 million.

An intriguing aspect of the city hall's location is that it featured in William Penn's grand, but impractical, plans for Philadelphia in the 1680s.[43] When Penn acquired the 1200-acre site between the Delaware River and Schuylkill Creek, he envisaged the creation of a 'green country towne' chiefly inhabited by wealthy landowners. In his earliest plans he aimed to develop a settlement of gentlemen's estates with houses at least 800 feet apart and surrounded by gardens, orchards, and fields. In some respects he envisaged the American dream of sprawling estates of detached houses centuries before it came to fruition. Around 1683, the Quakers' lands were actually sold in half- or full-acre lots – still very substantial today. The lots were laid out on wide streets in a gridiron pattern, possibly influenced by unfulfilled plans for London following the fire of 1666. At the centre of Penn's Philadelphia plan, at the intersection of High (now Market) and Broad streets, Penn designed a central square. This ten-acre site was to be bordered by civic buildings such as the Quaker meeting house, the state house, a schoolhouse, and a market. It is precisely in this central square that Philadelphia's grand city hall now stands.

The subsequent development of Philadelphia counter to Penn's vision is an interesting aside, which hints at some natural rules behind the distribution of wealth in cities.[44] By 1700, only the lots on the Delaware side of the town had been developed. Most people lived no more than four blocks from the river, where the dock had become the focal point of the town. Efforts to develop the Schuylkill side and the central area had failed. The large Friends meeting house built next to the central square in 1685 was even dismantled in 1702. Furthermore, by 1703, the original 43 plots on Front Street near the Delaware River had been subdivided into 102 smaller properties, some less than 20 feet wide. It proved quite easy to cut a narrow alleyway lengthwise along the edge of a 102-by-396-ft property, thereby providing access to a row of 20-feet-wide tenement houses for workmen. It did not take long for Penn's vision of a 'green country towne' to be obliterated as narrow lots and alleyways turned early Philadelphia into a dense, congested, portside settlement. The notion that Philadelphia could have developed as a community of gentlemen's estates was ridiculous, especially given the need for settlements in the colonies to be highly self-sufficient.

Returning to the main question at hand: Should the value of this elegant city hall that now dominates the central square of Penn's city be included in a calculation of the city's wealth? The answer is no. The utility that the building provides to the people of the city by housing municipal administration is already accounted for in the value of residential property in the city. If the city hall did not exist and the provision of city services were to slide into a state of disarray, this would soon enough be reflected in a fall in housing prices.

What about office buildings and other commercial buildings? Each city has a market for such buildings and so the total market value could easily be estimated. Why should this total not be included in our calculations of a city's wealth? The first issue here is one of ownership. If a company whose shareholders are predominantly non-citizens owns a building in a city, then such an asset should be included in the wealth of other cities. The value of the asset should be proportionally assigned to the cities where the shareholders live. Of course, if the owners of a commercial building are citizens of the city, then the value of the asset has already been accounted for by including the equity of citizens in calculations of the city's wealth. The central issue here is obvious. All companies, from the smallest 'mom and pop stores' to the largest multinationals, are owned by people. Although big businesses are often portrayed as being inhuman, their assets are owned by people – the shareholders. So to count the assets of companies as well as the equities held by shareholders, wherever they might be, is clearly double counting.

Does this mean that cities should deter foreign companies from buying property, since they do not contribute to the wealth of a city? Certainly not. Even if a company is wholly owned by citizens of other cities, it will bring investment, jobs, and income to a city. So, just like Philadelphia's city hall and municipal infrastructure in general, the presence of foreign companies operating in a city and contributing to its economy will be reflected in the wealth of its residents – specifically, in the value of their residential real estate. There may be cases, as with sixteenth-century Seville perhaps, where foreigners can own too many of the assets in a city. This may be detrimental to those cities – especially if large profits go elsewhere. Nonetheless, foreign ownership of assets will generally contribute to the wealth of a city.

There is a further test, however. Though residential real estate is a major component of the wealth of a city, not all citizens are homeowners. How does the ownership by private real estate companies or the state affect our quantification of wealth? The first case is straightforward. Apartment buildings or houses owned by private landlords will be accounted for in the value of these landlords' assets and will contribute to the wealth of the cities where they live. The case of state-owned housing is more tricky. In some cities, particularly in continental Europe, for example, many citizens live in state-owned accommodation. If, say, 50 per cent of households rent their homes from the municipal government, but no government assets are included in the calculation of wealth, would the wealth of such cities be seriously underestimated?

This question is possibly the most challenging to the rule for defining the wealth of cities, but there may be a solution. An insight derived from microeconomic theory, based on solving supply-and-demand curves, suggests that when governments interfere with housing markets, such as supplying houses below market prices, the consequence is an increase in the value of privately owned accommodation.[45] What this suggests is that, if 50 per cent of households live in state-owned accommodation, then the value of the other 50 per cent of privately owned homes might be inflated to such an extent that the total value of private homes is the same as if all homes were privately owned.

There have not been many empirical studies to support this proposition, but experience from Los Angeles in the late 1970s is pertinent.[46] In 1978 the city of Los Angeles introduced differential rent controls. The maximum allowable increase in rent was restricted to 7 per cent per year, but newly constructed units and those with voluntary tenant movement were exempted. After two years, controlled rents rose by 13.7 per cent on average, while uncontrolled rents rose by an average of 46.2 per cent. Moreover, a model based on vacancy rates predicted that an increase in rents of 23.9 per cent would have occurred in the absence of the rent controls. So any apparent reductions in the wealth of a city owing to government interference in property markets may be offset by increased value of private property.

If the net assets of citizens are accepted as the correct measure of urban wealth, then just how wealthy are cities? Well, for my city, Toronto, or to be technically correct, for the Toronto Census Metropolitan Area (CMA), the answer in 1999 was about $400 billion (Cdn). The 4.5 million residents of the Toronto CMA had assets totalling $486 billion and debts of $88.5 billion. The major items were real estate ($294b.), financial assets ($150b.), equity in business ($41.5b.), and motor vehicles ($15.5b.).[47] The major category of debt was mortgages, at $69 billion. After subtracting mortgage debt, net real estate assets, at $209 billion, were the largest component (52 per cent), and financial assets were also large (38 per cent).

The type of assets owned, however, do vary considerably among rich, average, and poor households. Data for the United States from the Federal Reserve's *Survey of Consumer Finances* are pertinent. In 2001 the *median* American household held 66 per cent of its net worth in single-family residential housing.[48] The net worth of primary residences, however, was just 27.2 per cent of total household wealth. The difference occurs because the richest Americans own a disproportionately large percentage of the financial assets and business equity. Average household wealth was $433,000, of which average overall financial assets were $188,000, and average business equity was $76,500. The value of residential housing assets also varies considerably across the United States. Housing is far more expensive in New York than in New Mexico.

Indeed, in 2001, according to a study reported in *The Economist*, the average price of a centrally located two-bedroom apartment was higher in New York City than in any other city in the world.[49] It was a close contest, though; the average prices in New York, Tokyo, and London were all near $800,000. A small change in exchange rate could elevate either of New York's challengers to the position of the city with the most expensive real estate. Following this trio were Milan, with an average price of a two-bedroom apartment at close to $600,000, and Paris, at around $400,000. Then came a string of cities – Sydney, Dublin, Madrid, Frankfurt, Amsterdam, and Toronto – where prices for central two-bedroom apartments were between $400,000 and $200,000. Based on this simple measure – the price of two-bedroom apartments – it seems that the per capita wealth of citizens in New York, Tokyo, and London, in 2001, was typically more than double that of citizens in the second-tier world cities. Moreover, if data on financial assets and high-end residential property were included, it is likely that the citizens of New York, Tokyo, and London would be several times wealthier in per capita terms.

Conclusion

There may be some subtle differences between various ways of defining wealth, but essentially wealth is control over the goods and services that people need or desire. This definition is not flawless; there are still issues with understanding changes to wealth over time; and wealth can still include socially undesirable objects, that is, Ruskin's *ilth*. The key point to emphasize is that wealth is synonymous with power over, or ownership of, assets – and this leads to a practical way of quantifying the wealth of cities: through the assets of citizens.

Seeing ownership as a key attribute of a city's wealth helps to explain, I believe, why sixteenth-century Seville did not become 'the richest city in the world.' It was a prosperous city, no doubt; there were shiploads of silver and gold sailing up the Guadalquivir River. Its streets were metaphorically paved with silver and gold, only the paving stones were owned by the citizens of Genoa, Antwerp, Augsburg, and other European cities. With foreigners flocking to Seville to join in the exploitation of the New World's treasures, the value of property in the city must surely have risen. The citizens of Seville must also have had opportunities to make good incomes from the city's maritime activities – whether as sailors, dockside workers, or suppliers. However, whether for cultural or perhaps for religious reasons, it would seem that the people of Seville as a whole were not entrepreneurial enough to convert their income into long-term wealth, either by financing further journeys to the Indies or by accumulating capital through domestic investments back home. Consequently, Seville failed to become a significant European financial centre, or even a particularly wealthy city in its own right – its wealth was owned by others.

By way of counter-example, then, the case of Seville makes plain that the wealth of cities can be best quantified in terms of the assets of their citizens. The residential housing, financial assets, and business equity owned by citizens constitute the main components of urban wealth. Housing is a particularly special type of asset. The value of residential property incorporates all three attributes of value theory – utility, scarcity, and embodied labour. Moreover, the total value of real estate in a city is typically the largest component of its wealth. Perhaps this is not surprising given the comfort, safety, and shelter provided to those fortunate to have a home.

There are other assets in cities that are not owned by individual citizens. These include tangible infrastructure such as municipal buildings, water pipes, roads, and schools, as well as intangible assets such as green space and public know-how. Such things are difficult to value directly. Several techniques have been proposed for valuing infrastructure, including the cost of building anew, the 'book value' incorporating depreciation, or an evaluation based on some form of benefit-cost analysis. I argue, however, that the appropriate way to value such infrastructure is through its contribution to the wealth of citizens. The same holds for so-called intangible assets. Such assets do contribute to the wealth of cities, but they are already reflected in the value of residential properties. Take away water supply, a school, or a local park from a neighbourhood and house prices will soon fall. So even Philadelphia's $6.4-billion city hall does not get added into the calculation of urban wealth.

In counting the assets of citizens, it becomes apparent that all of the wealth of cities is reflected somehow by markets – which is convenient for the purposes of this book. The primary asset of many families is their residence – the value of which is determined by real estate markets. Then for many households there are one or more automobiles, which can be sold in second-hand car markets to determine their value. Of course, there are countless other pieces of equipment, furniture, and the like. These can all be valued through the price they can fetch on a second-hand market. Indeed, these days one can get a quick sense of the market value for any household asset through a quick visit to the websites of e-Bay or craigslist. Citizens also own financial assets – such as bonds and shares in various forms, which are clearly valued through financial markets.

The simple conclusion of this chapter is that the wealth of a city can be measured by the sum of such market-based assets owned by citizens. So, towards this book's objective of understanding what underlies the wealth of cities, the next chapter turns to uncovering just how these markets work.

3 Markets

... a barren island with hardly a house on it ... it seems obvious that Hong Kong will not be a Mart of Trade.

Lord Palmerston, 1841

The words of the British foreign secretary, Lord Palmerston, while firing his talented superintendent of trade in Hong Kong, Charles Elliot, could not have been more wrong. The barren island won by the British in an unlikely confrontation with China in the 1830s was a colonial backwater for decades, but later grew dramatically in population, and by the 1970s had become one of the world's greatest trading cities. With limited space, the city spiralled upward, fuelled by an impressively dynamic and wealthy real estate market.

The founding of Hong Kong has its roots in a bizarre trade dispute between Britain and China, much of it centred around the city of Canton.[1] In many respects it was a clash between two cultures – a capitalist, industrial, progressive country trying to force a Confucian, agriculturalist, and stagnant one into a trading relationship.[2] From Britain's perspective, the small group of British merchants in Canton had been frustrated in their efforts to trade with the Chinese by some peculiar restrictions, including the prohibition of foreign women in the city. The British were, of course, arrogant, as well as unruly. The waning and termination of the East India Company's trade monopoly in 1833 did not help matters; the remaining free-enterprise British merchants were largely out of control. The 'barbarians,' as the Chinese viewed them, frequently broke local rules and regulations, and the appointment of a series of short-lived superintendents of trade sent by London to maintain order only made things worse by implying that there was a separate rule of law for the British. Yet, despite these frustrations and misunderstandings, a relatively regular trade was maintained, with tea, silk, and rhubarb exchanged for woollens, cotton, and a few Western wares. Beyond the official trade, moreover, was a much larger and well-recognized trade in opium, which was illegal by Chinese rules but continued nonetheless. The opium trade grew rapidly in the 1830s, from 20,000 chests per year in 1834 to 40,000 in 1838.[3] Both British and Chinese traders profited handsomely, but the addiction of the Chinese people was clearly a problem. Furthermore, the drug was paid for through the illegal export of bullion, which caused a strain on China's reserves.

In 1839, after much deliberation, the Chinese took stiff action against the drug trade, in a manner that sparked the Opium War. The emperor's envoy, Lin Tse-hsü, arrived in Canton, arrested many of the Chinese opium dealers, and confined all British and other foreigners to their factories. Lin demanded the surrender of all opium in the port and river, written agreements from merchants to quit the opium trade, and the surrender of prominent British merchant Lancelot Dent.[4] The British superintendent, Charles Elliot, could not possibly assist with the last demand, but he reluctantly supported Lin on the first and encouraged all foreign merchants to surrender their opium. In one of the largest drug hauls in history, a staggering one thousand tons of opium were delivered and subsequently burnt by Lin.[5]

The British were outraged by the holding of their countrymen as hostages and also faced the difficult issue of compensating their merchants for £2 million of burnt merchandise – even if it was opium. As a show of power, the British navy blockaded several Chinese cities and then, on 7 January 1841, captured the forts guarding the Bogue channel into Canton. The ease with which the British won the battle was an embarrassment to the Chinese, who soon looked to settle. Acting independently of London, which was an ocean journey of four months away, Elliot negotiated terms with the Chinese. These included 'the cession of the island and harbour of Hong Kong to the British crown' and a payment of £6 million.[6] Upon learning of the settlement, Lord Palmerston was irate. Why had Elliott negotiated so little and what was the purpose of occupying the barren island of Hong Kong? Why not Formosa or another larger island? Elliott, though, had been a naval officer and saw things differently. He recognized that Hong Kong had an excellent and defensible harbour for ships of any size. In a report of 25 January 1842, he noted that Hong Kong had 'the advantages of a large and safe harbour, abundance of fresh water, ease of protection by Maritime ascendancy, and no more extent of Territory or Population than may be necessary for our convenience.'[7]

The population of Hong Kong was, of course, destined to grow considerably.[8] In the first census of 1841, there were 4350 inhabitants recorded, not including 2000 or so transient fishermen. The British wasted little time in constructing a road and selling off lots. Docks, batteries, and a hospital were all established early – and by 1842 the island had a newspaper and a temporary theatre. By 1895, the population had reached 248,500 and over the first half of the twentieth century it increased almost tenfold, reaching 2.36 million in 1950. With pressure from an influx of refugees in 1956, Hong Kong recognized its limited supply of land and relaxed height restrictions on buildings. Into the 1960s, Hong Kong remained somewhat of a colonial backwater; there was still a cricket pitch at the city centre. This was all to change, however. The population grew by another million in the 1960s and accelerated to over five million by the turn of the century.

The second half of the twentieth century also proved to be a period of remarkable economic success for Hong Kong, which by 1996 saw its per capita GDP become the fourth highest in the world.[9] A number of factors contributed to Hong Kong's rise. The 1960s were a decade of free-market enterprise with a limited role for government. Lacking any form of democratic pressures, Sir John Cowperthwaite, the financial secretary from 1961 to 1971, pursued a non-interventionist strategy, close to textbook economic ideology.[10] While Western countries still adhered to the model of the Keynesian welfare state, Hong Kong became a Gladstonian paradise with a single-minded dedication to money making. Real wages rose 50 per cent over the decade, but social conditions were appalling for many, especially with respect to housing. Cowperthwaite encouraged the limiting of spending on health and education, rewarding managers who underspent their budgets.[11]

Under Governor Murray Maclehose, however, the 1970s were a golden age of social spending.[12] Government expenditures increased by 50 per cent from 1970 to 1972 and steadily rose thereafter. Water, power supply, education, health care, and above all housing were the highest priorities. Large projects included the University of Science and Technology and the underground mass-transit railway. A network of new satellite towns began to stretch along the coast, providing housing for some 2.5 million people by 1995. As with other great cities in their golden years, the pace of infrastructure development was phenomenal.

3 Hong Kong grew from a colonial backwater to become a great trading city, with one of the wealthiest real estate markets in the world. (© Photo: Moon Lee)

'The planning effort involved was huge, perhaps without parallel, involving as it did the reconstruction of a transport system, rehousing half the population, and providing acceptable levels of education and health care, all in short order.'[13]

An intriguing and important factor in Hong Kong's remarkable economic growth was the multifaceted role of China. Among the many Chinese who flooded to the city during the 1949 communist revolution were the energetic Shanghainese, who rebuilt their fortunes to become the financial elite of the island. These and other Chinese challenged the established colonial order, creating businesses in shipping and lightweight manufacturing, and were later prominent as the island grew to become a financial- and commercial-services centre for southeast Asia.[14] Meanwhile, in spite of, or perhaps because of, ideological differences, Hong Kong and China both benefited during their estranged relationship. By the 1970s, China had a significant and favourable trade balance with Hong Kong, supplying most of the island's food and substantial quantities of water.[15] Hong Kong also served as an exporting centre for China's goods and a convenient place for trade contacts and access to

Western technology. China's open-door policy of 1979 strengthened its economic ties with Hong Kong, accelerating the island's transformation into an international financial centre. By the 1980s, China was using Hong Kong to service up to 80 per cent of its capital needs. Then in 1997, after 156 years as a British colony or semi-autonomous city state, Hong Kong ceded its sovereignty to China.

With such rapid growth in population and prosperity, the development of real estate in Hong Kong was prolific. From 1983 to 1992, real estate accounted for 61 per cent of capital investment in Hong Kong and averaged close to 25 per cent of GDP.[16] In the mid-1990s, the real estate and construction share of total market capitalization was conservatively estimated at 48 per cent. This compares with under 5 per cent for US markets and under 10 per cent for the United Kingdom.[17] The total housing stock grew from 1.06 million units in 1983 to 1.74 million units in 1995. Just under half was public housing.[18] The subsidization of housing is perhaps an exception to the free-market philosophy of the island; the Hong Kong government receives about one-third of its revenues from real estate. The government also controls a key component of the real estate market – the supply of land.

Land is scarce in Hong Kong, indicating that Charles Elliot had been wrong on that point at least. Of the territory's 405 square miles, 80 per cent is mountainous and thus difficult to develop.[19] The remaining land has been intensively developed, with population densities unparalleled in major Western cities. Land is so scarce that it typically represents 60 to 70 per cent of total real estate values in Hong Kong, that is, the structure is only 30 to 40 per cent of the building's value. The government can make good money from the sale of new land, which prior to 1984 it released at a rate of about 247 acres per year.[20] Some of the new land stems from the rehabilitation of former industrial lands. There has also been significant creation of land through infill of the harbour. The main response to the scarcity of land, however, has been the construction of high-rise buildings.

The necessity of constructing tall buildings and the high pressures of the Hong Kong market led to the formation of highly efficient construction processes controlled by large, vertically integrated corporations. To purchase expensive land and develop scale- intensive residential complexes requires access to large capital resources and high liquidity. As a result, the Hong Kong development market is dominated by a few major companies. In 1992 the top five developers had 60 to 70 per cent of market share.[21] In 1996 the top four development corporations – Sun

Hung Kai Properties, Cheung Kong Holdings, Henderson Land Development, and New World Development – had a combined market capitalization of (US)$62 billion,[22] making them as large as multinational manufacturing corporations.

During the fifteen years preceding Hong Kong's return to China, real estate prices boomed. From a recession in the early 1980s to a peak in 1997, prices for residential property increased by a factor of five in real terms.[23] The period from 1990 to mid-1994 was particularly spectacular, with the price of residential real estate rising at 30 per cent per year.[24] A 1984 British-Chinese agreement limiting the release of new land for residential development to just 123 acres per year[25] may have been a factor in the price rises. Perhaps more important, however, was Hong Kong's foreign-exchange policy.

Central to Hong Kong's macroeconomic policy was a fixed exchange rate at around (HK)$7.8 to one US dollar. While providing stability for Hong Kong businesses, the fixed exchange rate meant that interest rates in Hong Kong were effectively determined by US interest rates, even when they were inappropriate for the local economy. As US interest rates dropped between 1990 and 1994, the best lending rate in Hong Kong was lower than the local rate of inflation.[26] This made it attractive for overseas investors to bring their capital to Hong Kong, leveraging it with low-interest loans. Masses of capital poured into Hong Kong for investment in real estate assets. In 1991 and 1992, an estimated (HK)$15 billion entered the Hong Kong real estate market from China alone. Residential real estate prices rose so much that, by the height of the peak in 1997, a 500-square-foot entry-level flat was selling at (HK)$2.25 million.[27]

The Hong Kong real estate bubble inevitably had to burst, and what a spectacular burst it was as a financial crisis spread throughout Southeast Asia in 1997. From the third quarter of 1997 to the fourth quarter in 1998, residential real estate prices in Hong Kong dropped by an average of 42 per cent.[28] The crisis began in Thailand and spread rapidly, as investors lost confidence in Southeast Asian markets. As capital flowed out of the region, currencies devalued, banks closed, unemployment rose, and income fell.[29] Many pointed to weak, antiquated financial systems, yet real estate markets had played a significant role in destabilizing financial markets. Global movement of capital had been accelerating, and much of it had been invested in building projects in cities of Southeast Asia. The major cities of the region – Bangkok, Jakarta, Kuala Lumpur, Singapore, Taipei, Hong Kong, Shanghai, Beijing, Seoul – had become centres of grand, innovative, new building design. Real estate markets, though, are notorious for overshooting, with prices exceeding true market value. There was an oversupply of buildings with heavy reliance on foreign capital. In the aftermath of the crisis, defaults on bank loans were higher in real estate than in any other sector. Hong Kong fared better than the other cities in this regard, since the Hong Kong monetary authority had appropriate controls on real estate lending.[30] Nevertheless, the wealth of the city, as reflected by real estate assets, plummeted.

The story of the rise and fall of Hong Kong markets poses some additional challenges to understanding the wealth of cities. While the assets of citizens may determine urban wealth, the example of Hong Kong demonstrates that these assets are customarily spread between two types of interrelated markets, real estate and finance. To grasp what lies behind the wealth of cities, then, it is necessary to investigate the forces influencing supply and demand in several markets. Real estate accounts for more than 50 per cent of wealth in many cities, but, as the Southeast Asia financial crisis showed, its value is tied to capital flows and foreign-exchange markets. These are bigger in scale and scope than cities, and so the wealth of cities can depend very much on how well its citizens understand, participate in, influence, or even control them.

Studying the behaviour of various markets and the interactions between them illuminates their role in the accumulation of wealth, urban and otherwise. It also yields a remarkable finding: despite the ups and downs of markets, wealth is extraordinarily steadfast. Some markets can seemingly rise and fall on a whim; the incredible history of the Mississippi and South Sea bubbles will be recounted below as examples. When financial markets are considered in combination with other markets, however, a different picture emerges. Some cities can gain or lose relative to others, but, because of their size and diversity, cities are generally more resilient to market bubbles than individuals.

This chapter explores the relationship between urban wealth – in the form of citizens' assets – and markets. It is a relationship that, as we shall see, has more than its share of complications.

Supply and Demand

Before we embark on an explanation of how various markets behave, a cautionary note on the theory of supply and demand is necessary. There can be little doubt that this theory (often conveniently presented in texts as the theory of the firm and consumer behaviour) is one of the most central in economics. The theory is undoubtedly an excellent one, consistently aiding in the explanation of many economic phenomena. Nevertheless, there are many practical challenges in applying the theory of supply and demand which need to be explained in order to understand how markets really work.

Flicking through the pages of any microeconomics text, one sees many x-y graphs of quantity versus price, showing the theoretical supply-and-demand curves for some good or service. This beautiful exposition of the theory in graphical form is generally accredited to the French mathematician Antoine Augustin Couront (1801–77). The demand curve is downward sloping, with the demand for the good rising as its price falls. The supply curve is often shown as upward sloping, although this is not always necessarily the case; it depends on how suppliers' costs vary with the quantity of good supplied. Where the two curves intersect is the market equilibrium – the price at which supply and demand are equal.

The first practical problem is lack of knowledge about real demand curves. A close look at the demand curves in textbooks reveals that these curves are rarely, if ever, based on real data. It is incredibly difficult to conduct a survey or experiment in a real market from which one can plot the points of a demand curve. At best, economists typically get merely an estimate of the elasticity of the curve at one point.[31] So, in practice, there is only some approximate knowledge of the slope of the demand curve at any given time.

Supply curves are generally easier to determine, though again the task is not without challenges. The supply curve for a single company is the same as its cost function. It shows how the company's cost of production changes with the quantity of good supplied. Unless the company is a monopolist, the industry supply curve is given by some combination of the companies' supply curves. Herein lies a potential problem, though. Companies that are in competition may not really want to inform each other about their production costs. Each will likely have a sense of the overall industry supply curve, but once more there is uncertainty.

There is one point on the price-quantity graph that often can be established. Assuming that somebody records data on the market, then at any given time the price and quantity at which a market transacts can be determined. At a later period, the observed market price and quantity of transaction may have moved to another point on the graph. This sounds promising: with two points there is more information. Collect data for a third period and perhaps a curve can the traced; but which curve? The problem here is that price and/or the quantity is changing in time. In theory, this means that either the supply curve or the demand curve, or both, has shifted. So in essence there are really two theoretical curves, neither of which we can be very certain about, now shifting around over time. This makes things even more difficult to grasp.

Further complexity arises when one considers that markets rarely exist in isolation but are interconnected with each other. When the supply or demand curves theoretically shift, it may be due to a change in the market for a complementary or competitive good or service. The linking of markets in the context of real estate shall be discussed shortly. For now, it may simply be remarked that the analysis of linked markets is clearly more difficult than the analysis of one market alone.

In summary, a great deal of skill and substantial experience is required by economists in order to understand specific markets. There may be cases where a small amount of data and some educated guessing are used in applying the theory of supply and demand. More often, however, the theory is used to provide *conceptual* understanding of how markets behave. There is clearly a lot of uncertainty in predicting which ways markets are going. Are they too high or too low? Bursting bubbles are inevitable.

Real Estate Markets

The real estate market is not a single market per se, but is best understood as the interaction of several markets, of which two types, markets for *space* and markets for *capital assets*, are most central.[32] Markets for space include those for office, commercial, and residential activities, both rented and owner-occupied. It is residential real estate that is of most concern here, given that, as discussed in chapter 2, it is such a major component of urban wealth.[33] There are also a variety of markets for building assets, but again our focus is on the residential sector. An important distinction is between new and existing buildings. All capital assets depreciate and so there has to be some construction of new buildings just to maintain the current stock. Where there is excess demand at market prices, the supply of real estate can expand. It is the total market value of this real estate capital that contributes to the measure of the wealth of cities, but to understand how this comes about we first need to understand the market for space.

With a given building stock, the demand for space will determine the rental value of the space. The key factor in this process is the vacancy rate.[34] As demand rises, the vacancy rate falls; hence, rental prices rise.[35] Conversely, as demand falls, the vacancy rate increases and rental prices fall. The next pertinent question, then, is what determines the demand for space. A first simple answer is ability to pay. As household earnings go up, so does the demand for space. This is reflected by *the income elasticity of demand for housing*, which describes the percentage change in demand for space relative to the percentage change in household income. The income elasticity of demand for housing is typically about 0.3 to 0.7 in the United States, but can be higher in other countries; for example, in Japan it is 1.4.[36] If the income elasticity of demand in a city is, say, 0.5, this means that, for a 1 per cent increase in household income, the demand for housing space goes up by 0.5 per cent. If the space is not immediately supplied, then rental prices rise.

Another factor that will raise demand is increasing population, or, to be more precise, an increasing number of households. With growing global population and greater urbanization, it is clear that populations are increasing in most cities. Furthermore, the average household size is decreasing, particularly in the developed world, for a variety of reasons, including longer lifespans and higher divorce rates. This means that the growth in households is even higher than the growth of population in many cities. Obviously, the more households there are, the greater demand for houses.

Both of these factors – increasing income and households – were of significance in the dramatic rise in rental prices in Hong Kong discussed above. From 1980 to 1995, the population of Hong Kong grew by 1.3 per cent per year, but, because of shrinking household size, the growth rate of household formation was 4.8 per cent. Meanwhile, from 1975 to 1995, real per capita GDP had tripled. Moreover, the income elasticity of demand for housing was estimated to be as high as 2.4.[37] With such a high rate of household formation, high income growth, and high income elasticity of demand, Hong Kong rental prices shot up. By 1996, private rental space was around (US)$3000 to $4000 per month for a 753-square-foot unit.[38]

Now, turning to the capital market, it is clear that rental prices have a substantial impact on the value of capital assets.[39] For private rental properties, which are owned solely for investment, the rational value of the asset is the discounted value of the stream of future incomes that would accrue to the owner. As such, the value depends on the rental price, discussed above, with adjustments for maintenance. In order to determine the present value of the future income, however, also means that the net rents have to be discounted at an appropriate rate of return. This expected rate of return is very much dependent on local interest rates, with adjustments for the risk of investment and taxes.[40]

The arrival at interest rates at this point in our examination of the wealth of cities represents a shift in scale. As just noted, the rental price of property is determined by the level of household income and growth in the number of households – both of which are characteristics of the city. Interest rates, however, are typically determined at the national or global scale, by central banks, and in many respects by international economic drivers. This is a first glimpse of urban wealth being decided by outside forces.

Returning to the case of Hong Kong, it has been found that the user cost of housing capital, that is, mortgage rate minus the rate of housing appreciation, is very effective in explaining house prices.[41] Indeed, from 1991 to 1994, when Hong Kong's interest rate was less than the rate of inflation, the user cost of housing was strongly negative, which explains the phenomenal growth in house prices. Of course, if the value of houses goes up, a natural market reaction is to produce more houses; thus, the supply side of the real estate capital market is turned to next.[42] In an unconstrained real estate market, the construction of new space occurs when the expected sales price is greater than the cost of development.[43] If the market were at equilibrium, the quantity of new space developed would be such that its cost would equate to the prevalent market price. It takes significant time, however, for new construction projects to get under way. Hence, the supply of new real estate will often lag behind demand – and then overshoot when demand drops. Real estate markets are seldom at long-term equilibrium.

The Hong Kong market is actually somewhat of an exception to overshooting. Because of the scarcity of land, the real estate market there is constrained and so does not suffer much from overbuilding. The high cost of land, at 60 to 70 per cent of development cost, means that developers face very high fixed costs. This has forced the industry to become efficient, lowering its variable costs of construction.

A further consideration in the supply of real estate is that the existing stock is continually aging.[44] As buildings get older, become run down, or just go out of style, they depreciate in value. Thus, even in a city where there was no increase in income or the number of households, there would still be demand for new real estate just to replace aging stock.

To summarize briefly, at least seven factors influence the value of real estate. Growth in income and the number of households drives rents. Asset values depend on the expected rate of return from such rents – a function of interest rates and expectations about asset appreciations. The ability of the market to meet demand depends on the supply of land, the efficiency of construction, and depreciation of the existing stock. Most of these factors are at work in the city, except, notably, interest rates and to some extent expectations about asset appreciation. This latter factor provides a link to the next component of urban wealth. In some respects it is not the expectations about asset appreciation that matter, but expectations relative to other opportunities – and those opportunities often lie in financial markets.

Financial Markets

The other major component of urban wealth, along with real estate, is financial assets. There is a diverse range of financial markets. People, firms, and institutions buy and sell: stocks, shares, commodities, equities, bonds (debentures), mutual funds (unit trusts), bills, commercial paper, foreign currencies, Euro currencies, derivatives … the list is confusing because the terms have different meanings in different English-speaking countries. Business equity can also be added to this list, which is private ownership of business assets as opposed to ownership acquired through public stock exchanges. The valuation of equity is essentially the same whether it is privately or publicly held. It is theoretically the present expected value of a future stream of profits stemming from ownership of assets. In some respects, there is similarity here with valuation of real estate; expected value is subject to confidence in markets, as well as interest rates, and so the value of financial assets rises and falls with markets.

The total value of the world's financial assets is staggering. Back in 1993, an estimate based on eighteen of the wealthiest countries put the total at (US)$42.6 trillion.[45] Most of this, $28.9 trillion, was directly held by individuals, whether self-managed or externally managed, through mutual fund managers. The remaining $13.7 trillion was owned by public and private pension funds, charities, and insurance companies. Such assets, however, ultimately represent the wealth of individuals: pension plans pay current and future incomes; insurance assets provide for current and future claims; charities typically provide consumable goods and services to those in need.

The world's financial assets of $42.6 trillion in 1993 were held in various forms.[46] The largest portion, $13.8 trillion, was held as cash. This does not literally mean as coins and banknotes, rather just holdings in a highly liquid, or easily accessible, form. Equities accounted for $10.3 trillion, of which $8.51 trillion were domestic holdings. A further $8.9 trillion were held as bonds, and $9.6 trillion were in various other categories. In 2006 the market value of the world's stock markets reached $50.6 trillion, with domestic and international bonds valued at $67.9 trillion.

Of all the financial markets, the bond market is particularly important since it provides a basis for all the other markets. A bond or debenture is an acknowledgment of debt made by a government, company, or institution typically for a specified period of time and usually carrying a fixed rate of interest. Bonds are thought to have originated in the Italian city states about eight hundred years ago.[47] They provide a means for money to be borrowed from a broader range of institutions than just banks. Since governments tend to borrow substantially on the bond markets, it is this market that determines the interest rate for the wider economy. The head of a leading bond fund company notes: 'Bond markets have power because they're the fundamental base for all markets. The cost of credit, the interest rate, ultimately determines the value of stocks, homes, all asset classes.'[48] Financial historian Niall Ferguson considers the invention of the bond market to be the second great revolution in the history of finance, after the creation of credit by banks.[49]

The next great leap forward in financial history, according to Ferguson, was the formation of joint-stock companies. The novelty of the joint-stock company is that its capital is jointly owned by multiple investors, but each only has limited liability for the company's transactions since the company is treated as a separate legal entity. Ferguson recognizes the Vereenigde Oost-Indishe Compagnie, discussed in chapter 1, to be the first joint-stock company.[50] Of course, with the advent of companies such as the VOC came the need to establish stock markets to trade their shares.

The procedures by which financial markets function differ between cities and have evolved significantly over time; changes in the way that equities have been transacted on the London Stock Exchange serve as an example.[51] Prior to 1986, an investor wishing to purchase or sell shares would approach a stockbroker, who acted as a middleman between the investor and a stockjobber. The stockjobber was a wholesaler, buying and selling shares and profiting from the margin between the buying and selling prices. The stockbroker would give advice and transact shares on the investor's behalf, with an obligation to get the best price possible; the broker received a fixed commission in return. Reforms that began in 1986, known as the 'Big Bang,' removed the minimum commission asked by brokers and also permitted firms to act with dual capacity, that is, there was removal of the distinction between principal and agent. Many UK and foreign banks acquired stakes in former broking and jobbing firms; thus, large financial firms were now dealing directly in the market. The role of the stockjobber was essentially replaced by computers that displayed all bid and offer prices and, after October 1997, began to execute the transactions automatically. Acting through a retail-service provider (a member of the exchange), small investors could now buy and sell shares using a remote personal computer.

There are established methods of valuing financial assets that may be used by those who make long-term investments in financial markets. The value of any asset is essentially the sum of future net cash flows accruing on that asset discounted at the appropriate rate of return.[52] The discount rate reflects the investor's desired rate of return, but also incorporates a risk premium. Investors generally require higher average rates of return on more risky investments.

When valuing stocks, in particular, investors generally expect to receive two types of cash flow: dividends during the period of holding the stock and a price for the stock upon its sale.[53] Technically, however, the value of the stock at the end of the holding period would just be the discounted future value of dividends that would accrue after the sale, that is, to the next owner(s) of the stock. Thus, the value of a share is simply the sum to perpetuity of the expected dividends per share discounted at the required rate of return.

Of course, not all investors are interested in the long-term value of stocks. The markets actually function more effectively because of the speculators who are looking to buy at low prices and sell at high.

The Rise and Fall of Markets

Speculating is a risky business, though, since financial markets are well known for rising and crashing. Some of yesteryear's asset price bubbles were so extreme that they have gone down in the folklore of the financial world. In the Dutch tulip-bulb bubble of 1636, the price of an everyday bulb increased by several hundred per cent.[54] The year 1720 was a financial rollercoaster, witnessing first the Mississippi bubble and then the South Sea bubble. During 1928 and the first eight months of 1929, stocks on the New York exchange rose over 70 per cent in value[55] before crashing 89 per cent between Black Thursday (24 October 1929) and July 1932. In more recent memory, during the Internet boom of the late 1990s, the average value of stocks trading on the NASDAQ increased by over 100 per cent during the year up to the peak of 10 March 2000; the subsequent crash will be well remembered by those who witnessed – and experienced – it. Then, of course, the collapse of equity markets in 2008, along with the collapse in the US housing market with which, as we shall see, the world of finance was closely associated, heralded the beginning of the steepest economic downturn since the Great Depression of the 1930s. In short, every generation has seen its fair share of turmoil in financial markets.

Of all the market bubbles in history, however, the South Sea and Mississippi bubbles of 1720 were perhaps the most extraordinary in terms of imaginative financial tricks, political corruption, and economic impact. Although the names suggest otherwise, each of these two manias was centred on the great rival cities of London and Paris respectively. Their genesis was tied to the changing European political landscape after the War of the Spanish Succession (1701–14),[56] which saw a shift in power away from Louis XIV's French Empire towards England, Holland, Austria, and the German states.

The origins of the South Sea bubble lie with the emergence of the Sword Blade Bank as a challenger to the Whig-supported Bank of England in the early 1700s. The name sounds like a spoof today, but the company had indeed been incorporated in 1691 to manufacture hollow sword blades. Because of its charter privileges both to hold land and to issue stock, the Sword Blade Company was later transformed for political purposes into a de facto bank.[57]

Upon its conception in 1694, the Bank of England was a private enterprise run by a syndicate of wealthy businessmen in the city of London. It essentially made loans to the government in return for a charter to act as a national bank. In some respects it was an immediate success, providing the financing for British continental wars and sharing in the Duke of Marlborough's glory by receiving the sole right to incorporate as a joint-stock bank in the whole of England.[58] The government had borrowed heavily, however, to finance the duke's battles, and so in 1710 there was a change in political tide. Robert Harley replaced Francis Godolphin as the chancellor of the Exchequer, carried on a wave of Tory country gentleman concerned about, among other things, mismanagement of the country's finances. Harley was faced with the tough task of fixing the nation's finances without recourse to the Bank of England, which had been aligned with Marlborough, Godolphin, and the Whigs. To do so he called upon the assistance of John Blunt and others from the Sword Blade syndicate.

On 2 May 1711 Harley presented to Parliament a bill to transform the government's entire unsecured public debt of £9 million into compulsory shares in a newly chartered South Sea Company.[59] The company was to conduct trade and traffic in the lands of America reputed to belong to the crown of Spain. The bill was a 'marvelous synthesis of finance, commerce and foreign policy' and rapidly passed through Parliament, with the Sword Blade Company organizing the transformation and holding controlling shares in the new enterprise. The formation of the South Sea Company pre-empted the 1713 Treaty of Utrecht by which England, after having already won the decisive battles, made peace with France and Spain. The company was given contracts to carry slaves and to establish seven trading ports in South America, although one-quarter of the profits was still reserved for the king of Spain.

Enthusiasm for the company should have waned as it made losses on the slave trade and mismanaged its trade in goods, yet such failures hardly seemed to matter. The English went through a succession crisis, with the last of the Stuarts replaced by the Hanoverian King George I. The new king was keen on the South Sea Company and eagerly acquired his own holdings. The new Prince of Wales became governor of the company before the king took the role himself. In spite of its limited trading success, the royal patronage boosted interest in the company and by May 1715 its stock reached par value of 100 for the first time since the day of issue.[60] Yet, by 1718, Britain and Spain were again at war; the company's assets were seized by Spain and it was reduced to a naked financial corporation.

Meanwhile, in Paris, the death of King Louis XIV, in September 1715, had created an opportunity for one of the most creative financiers of all time, the Scotsman John Law. A sagacious, daring, and imposing man, Law was born of a wealthy family and, through his own extensive financial skills, had acquired a fortune of 1.5 million livres (£107,000) by age forty.[61] He travelled throughout Europe, where he was well known, having effectively been banished from his home country for killing another man in a duel. Law was convinced he had the know-how to increase the world's wealth beyond the shadows of men's minds, but had seen his ambitious plans turned down in several European cities. Upon the death of the Sun King, however, France was in economic chaos, with a debt of over 700 million livres and an insecure regent, Philippe of Orleans, ruling alongside the new boy king.[62] Law, who was living in Paris at the time, proposed a financial solution to restore France's fortunes – and step by step the regent ceded to the Scotsman's plans.

John Law's Mississippi scheme unfolded as follows.[63] In April 1716 he opened a new note-issuing bank, the Banque Générale, for which he was the sole director and dominant shareholder. Then, in August 1717, he purchased controlling interest in the Mississippi Company, a struggling trading company that had been formed in 1712 for the purpose of conducting trade with Louisiana and other French possessions in the Mississippi watershed. Shares in the Mississippi Company were refloated under the name Company of the West, although the former name stuck. With help from his bank, Law took solid steps to reinvigorate the company, expanded trade with French North America, and widely promoted interest in the venture with French aristocracy.

In 1718, under threat from a rival syndicate, Law moved into a higher gear. In the autumn, he convinced the regent to allow the Banque Générale to be transformed into the Banque Royale – a French national bank completely under his control! The following year, he devilishly created a bull market for the Company of the West stock by offering to buy company shares at prices close to double current market rates for delivery three months hence. He had essentially invented a derivative. Given Law's immense reputation, investors were convinced that he was acting on inside knowledge and the price of shares in the company boomed just as the great man had wished.

Building upon this success, Law built a paper empire. By May 1719, his company had consumed all of Frances's other trading monopolies: the companies of the East Indies, China, and Senegal. He crushed the rival syndicate, secured a national monopoly on coining money, and then proceeded to capitalize the whole national debt of France into shares in his new conglomerate, the Company of the Indies. He created, at least on paper, the largest capitalist enterprise the world had ever seen. As Law's enterprise grew, shares were issued in successive waves, each at ever-rising prices. By August 1719, shares that had started at a low of about 150 livres were trading at a price of 2250 livres.[64] In the early part of the following year, prices rose to over 10,000 livres! Paris, indeed the whole of Europe, was carried away by financial euphoria. Money and people flocked to Paris to get rich quick in Law's expanding system.

There was more to the incredible rise in market prices than just financial euphoria. Law introduced monthly instalment plans for those wishing to buy shares, that is, the shares could be purchased on credit. He also made it necessary to participate in each share release if investors wished to buy in the next release; in other words, his plan worked like a pyramid scheme. The most crucial ingredient for Law's project to work, however, was a supply of money. All this time, his Banque Royale had been issuing a flood of banknotes into Paris. For example, on 25 July 1719, just two days before an issue of 50,000 shares, the Banque Royale released some 220 million livres in banknotes.[65] By May 1720, a total of some 2.1 billion livres had been released by Law's bank.[66] It was all one huge inflationary bubble.

Back in London, the government looked on with anxiety as British capital took flight to Paris. Indeed, some 30,000 foreigners from all over Europe had flooded into Paris to speculate in person on shares in the great new trading company. Some called for John Law to be invited home. Others called for the British to mount a scheme to capitalize its debt before France ruined Britain's trade.

The time was ripe for John Blunt and others of the Sword Blade Syndicate to raise the fortunes of the South Sea Company once more. A plan was hatched to capitalize again the British government's debt, which stood at £31 million.[67] The London-based syndicate did not have the power that John Law held in Paris. Nevertheless, it had other means of pulling off the plan. First, the other directors of the South Sea Company were persuaded, then the finance minister, John Aislabie, and then a few prominent members of Parliament. In total, bogus payments in South Sea stock worth £574,500 were made to various politicians to push the plan through Parliament.[68] The company's old rival, the Bank of England, made a competing offer, but the company sweetened the pot, offering the government an additional £7.5 million in cash, and it carried the House.

Through the first half of 1720, the South Sea Company released a series of shares, which a feverish market gobbled up at increasing prices. After the recapitalization plan was approved, the price of the company's stock stood at £160. By 19 March, after the first subscription had been sold, the stock price had climbed to £218. News then broke from Paris that Law was having difficulty containing inflation, spurring a jump in the price of South Sea stock to £320 in just three days.[69] London was consumed by stock-market mania, just as Paris had been. There was a rising whirlwind of speculation in a range of bizarre and out-landish companies trading in everything from ostrich feathers to heat-resistant paint.[70] Then, incredibly enough, the government passed the Bubble Act to eliminate the mushrooming, spurious promotions. The result was further strengthening of the 'dependable' South Sea stock; its price rose to £400 after a second round of subscriptions on 30 April. Back in Paris, Law was drastically devaluing his currency, but no such inflationary pressures were felt in London, for the Bubble Act had focused investment into the South Sea stock. The exception was in the price of land and luxury real estate around London, which climbed as the fortunate South Sea stockholders exercised their new-found wealth. News of a third stock release sent the market into ecstasy, with the stock price jumping from £610 to £870 over the first two days of June 1720.[71] Anybody who was a 'somebody' bought stock in the third subscription; the list of subscribers reads like a Who's Who of Britain. By midsummer, South Sea stock had jumped to over £1000, and London was awash with luxury spending.

The value of the South Sea stock was a tad exaggerated, however. By September it was apparent that the company did not have the profits to pay its promised dividends. As the stock value plunged, John Blunt went from being the most courted man in London to the most hated and despised in a matter of just two weeks.[72] An exasperated speculator tried to shoot him in the street. There might have been more attempts on his life if Londoners had known that his Sword Blade syndicate had siphoned off £1.16 million in cash to a new, protected company.

The bursting bubble sent waves through the English economy, with banks failing as many burnt speculators defaulted on their loans. The distress spread from London, where sales of luxury goods collapsed, to the countryside. The Duke of Portland, previously one of the richest men in England, was virtually bankrupt. Meanwhile, in Paris, John Law had been ousted from control of the banking system; the French abandoned paper money, returning to the use of trusted gold and silver coins.

As the price of South Sea Company stock plummeted in October, a small group of politicians that included Sir Robert Walpole encouraged the Bank of England to step in and buy out the company at a share price of £400. The bank delayed, for it was itself subject to a run and was in danger of closing down. It pulled out of the proposed deal, sending

South Sea stock down to £135.[73] The price of the company's stock had risen and fallen by close to 1000 per cent in less than a year. Eventually, the South Sea Company closed its doors, unable to make cash payments to its creditors.

What lessons do the Mississippi and South Sea bubbles contribute to understanding the wealth of cities? In chapter 2 it was asserted that the value of financial assets, such as company shares, are a significant component of personal wealth and hence the wealth of cities. Yet the psychology of humankind is such that the value of such shares can take on a life of its own, rising and falling without regard to the true profits of companies. Is much of urban wealth based merely on market expectations?

Although the bubbles of 1720 were particularly spectacular, it should be recognized that such financial crises are not rare. Economic historian Charles Kindleberger has documented forty-six financial crises between 1618 and 1998.[74] Does wealth just rise and fall on the whims of the stock market? The answer is that, for individuals, such as the unfortunate Duke of Portland, it certainly does; but, for cities, there is a little more to be said. To help see through the craze of the market, let us turn to some research conducted in the city of Basel.

Conservation of Wealth

The city of Basel is a quirky place. Located on the banks of the Rhine River in northwest Switzerland, the city is close to the intersection of the Swiss, French, and German borders. Basel is known for its chemical industry, modern art museums, and an ancient medieval core housing a decorative town hall and Romanesque cathedral. It is also home to one of Switzerland's most famous carnivals, the Basler Fasnacht, in which the city folk dress up in creative, scary, and often pagan-looking costumes. Of interest to the question at hand, however, is Basel's housing of the Bank of International Settlements (BIS). A relic of the pre–Second World War League of Nations, the BIS serves as a bank for central banks. As the world's oldest international financial organization, it acts as an agent for international financial operations, provides a forum for discussion and policy analysis, and is a centre for economic and monetary research.

Among the research conducted at the Bank of International Settlements has been a study of the peaks in equity prices and housing prices. Data from thirteen industrial countries from 1970 to 1999 show that housing-price peaks routinely follow equity-market peaks, typically with a lag of around two years.[75] In the United States, for example, there were equity-market peaks in the fourth quarter (Q4) of 1972, Q3 of 1987, and Q3 of 2000. These were followed by housing price peaks in Q4 of 1973 and Q4 of 1989. A further peak around 2002 might have been expected, but it did not occur until 2007–8. There are some similarities in the trends between countries, but not all peaks occur at the same time. The United Kingdom, for comparison, had equity-market peaks in Q1 of 1972, Q2 of 1979, Q3 of 1987, and Q2 of 1999; and housing market peaks in Q3 of 1973, Q3 of 1980, and Q3 of 1989. Of course, what the BIS's study implies, but does not state, is that equity-price peaks also follow housing-price peaks, but with a somewhat longer time delay. In brief, the two main components of urban wealth – real estate and financial assets – run on cycles that are out of phase with each other. This suggests that urban wealth may not be such a flimsy, psychologically driven quantity after all – and it may perhaps be conserved in some fashion, or at least change in a less sporadic manner than financial markets.

Conservation of wealth makes sense at the transaction level too. Consider the unfortunate holder of shares for some stock traded on the New York Stock Exchange at the end of the day on Black Tuesday (29 October 1929).[76] He may well have seen the value of his holdings drop by 25 per cent over the previous two days. The week before, however, some more fortunate investor may have sold her shares at the peak of the market, having seen them climb by 35 per cent over the past eight months. Also, do not forget the market dealers, who, in the midst of a crisis, stand to make a pretty penny given the high volume of transactions at such times. Moreover, if the fortunate investor and market dealer know their markets well, they will invest their surplus cash in real estate until the stock market picks up again. The point is that, when financial markets rise and collapse, wealth gets redistributed, not necessarily reduced.[77]

Returning to the South Sea bubble of 1720, it should be noted that some individuals came away from the fiasco very wealthy. Beyond the crooked directors of the Sword Blade syndicate, their friends in Parliament, and seemingly the king,[78] some did make legitimate fortunes. Having held South Sea Stock since 1711, Thomas Guy sold his holdings in six instalments between April and June 1720; his healthy reward of £234,000 later helped with the founding of Guy's Hospital in London.[79] Sir Isaac Newton successfully sold his £7,000 stock in

April, making a neat profit of 100 per cent, but he was then tempted back into the market again, losing an ugly £20,000.[80] Richard Cantillon made back-to-back gains in the Mississippi and South Sea bubbles; he was among the top twenty-five Mississippi millionaires, making a fortune of twenty million livres. This was not all from pure stock-market speculation; indeed, he sold out well short of the peak in Mississippi share prices. Cantillon also made gains from exchange-rate hedging and options dealing.[81] This mention of exchange rates is significant, for, as described above, the growth of London's South Sea bubble occurred just as Paris's Mississippi bubble was bursting. Cantillon had the uncanny knack of locating himself in the right city at the start of a boom.[82] He bought South Sea stock early in boom and again sold out well before the peak. He then amazingly showed up in Amsterdam and invested there in a bubble that started just as the South Sea stock began to nosedive.

Generally speaking, the wealth of cities should be less prone to bubbles in domestic financial markets but may gain or lose in international transactions. Assuming that cities contain roughly equivalent numbers of winners and losers in the market roulette, then the overall wealth of citizens may remain relatively constant. There may be exceptions to this in an international context. It could well have been the case that Law's financial wizardly transferred net wealth from unlucky Londoners to lucky Parisians. Another fascinating example is that of the canton of Berne, which had a large holding in South Sea stock with pre-bubble value of some £200,000; Berne is rumoured to have sold the stock at the peak of the market around July 1720 for about £2 million.[83] Now that is one way for a city, or canton, to get rich quick!

With the notion of conservation of wealth in mind, consider again, this time from a broader perspective, the collapse of the Hong Kong real estate market during the Southeast Asia financial crisis of 1997. In particular, it is worth recalling what was going on in the United States in these years, especially in the technology sector.

On 11 January 1994 a summit on the Information Superhighway was held on the campus of the University of California at Los Angeles (UCLA). Among the members of business, government, and academia who had come to discuss the future of the Internet was Al Gore. The U.S. vice-president was a champion of the information-technology (IT) revolution. Back in 1991, he had pushed a bill through Congress known as the High Performance Computing and Communication Act. Gore's bill helped with creation of faster, higher-capacity Internet infrastructure and led by 1993 to the development of the graphical Mosaic web browser at the National Centre for Supercomputing. At the UCLA summit in 1994, it was clear that a new era of information technology lay ahead, but no one was really sure where the technology was headed. Investors soon began to catch on, though, and three years later the dot-com boom had begun.

Many of the companies synonymous with the IT revolution emerged or substantially grew in or around 1997. Online bookseller Amazon.com began service in July 1995 and had its initial public offering on the NASDAQ on 15 May 1997. After hiring its first employee in 1996, a small company called AuctionWeb changed its name to eBay in September 1997 and went public the following year. Use of the World Wide Web grew rapidly around this time, with 90 per cent of surfers using the Netscape software after the company's initial public offering in August 1995. Internet service provider America Online expanded dramatically from mid-1996, when it moved to new headquarters and switched from hourly rates to a monthly service fee of $19.99. Hotmail was launched in 1996, offering one of the first free webmail services, and was acquired by Microsoft in 1997. The established hardware giant Cisco grew throughout this period, becoming in March 2000 the most valuable company in the world with a market capitalization over $500 billion, before the dot-com bubble burst.[84]

So, blaming antiquated financial systems or overheated real estate markets for the Southeast Asia financial crisis of 1997 only gets at part of the picture. The capital flowed out of Hong Kong and other cities of the region because there were judged to be more attractive investment opportunities in the U.S. technology sector. Then, once the dot-com bubble had burst, most of the wealth was captured by the rising housing markets in American cities.

Flight to Gold

Something unusual happened to the real estate markets in U.S. cities after the turn of the millennium. Based on the pattern identified by the Bank of International Settlements, housing prices should have peaked around about 2002. They continued to rise, however, throughout most of the decade. Then, starting around 2007, the U.S. real estate market collapsed, with prices falling about 20 per cent. Moreover, the collapse brought the stock market down with it, triggering a global financial crisis. While there may have been other contributing factors, the securitization of U.S. subprime mortgage debts was widely considered to be the cause of the financial meltdown. The property markets and financial markets had become tied together through the complex bundling of mortgage debt sold as collateral by banks in New York and London. As American homebuyers defaulted on their mortgages, there was a chain-reaction that caused securities backed by declining real estate assets to fall simultaneously.

If the real estate and financial markets can – and did – both collapse together, what happened to the conservation of wealth? Is it possible to have near simultaneous bubbles in the property and equity markets that burst in tandem, with the value of assets essentially vaporizing? Perhaps it seems this way to an individual investor, but it cannot happen collectively. The answer, at least for the 2008 financial crisis, was that investors did what they historically have done when faced with a situation of severe uncertainty – they bought gold.

Uncertainty first crept into the equity markets in the fall of 2007. At that time the price of gold was below $700 US/oz., while the Dow Jones Industrial index was peaking at over 14,000 points. Over the next nine months or so, the Dow fell gradually to just over 11,000, while the price of gold rose to over $900 US/oz. Real crisis hit the equity markets in September 2008, with the Dow rapidly falling down to almost 8,000. The gold market itself had a spasm at this point, but it recovered, reaching close to $1,000 US/oz. in February 2009. Meanwhile, the Dow sank below 7,000 – a 50 per cent drop in just over a year. As unemployment rose through much of 2009, governments around the world pumped billions into infrastructure projects and stock markets slowly started to recover. Investors remained cautious, however, and the high demand for gold continued, pushing its price over $1200 US/oz. in late 2009.

Although the property and financial markets collapsed, not all cities suffered during the 2008 crisis. Indeed, one city in particular seemed to prosper quite well: Dubai, home to one of the world's largest gold markets. The Dubai Gold Souk, situated in the heart of the eastern business district, is a fascinating place. The Souk is a traditional market, bordered in fact by Dubai's fruit and vegetable market. There are over 200 retailers and more than 100 wholesalers situated either in the Souk or nearby.[85] The primary trade is in gold jewellery – a dazzling selection of rings, necklaces, bracelets, earrings, chains, and charms – as well as solid gold bars. Some estimates reckon that as much as ten tons of gold are present in the Souk on any day. The flow-through is quite impressive, though; the Souk has a reputation for low profit margins and high volumes. In a typical year, Dubai imports around 300 tons of gold, with Switzerland being the largest supplier of gold ingots.[86] Much of the gold jewellery is exported, some 25 per cent of it to India. In 2003 the value of Dubai's gold trade was $5.8 billion. No wonder it is called the 'City of Gold.'

Dubai has a long history as a port of trade. The region had a fishing and pearl- diving industry for hundreds of years that helped establish it on the trade route between Europe and China.[87] The British East India Company established a base in Bur Dubai. Then, in the late nineteenth century, Dubai became a British protectorate and tax-free haven for all foreign traders. By 1900, Dubai had established itself as the main entrepôt for the Persian Gulf, with commerce, in particular the re-export business, being the main source of revenue.[88] Although the pearl industry collapsed in the 1920s, Dubai prospered following the discovery of oil in 1966. Substantial port infrastructure was built from the 1960s, allowing the gold re-export business to flourish.

In the first decade of the twenty-first century, Dubai attracted many foreign businesses, created a tourist Mecca, and symbolically built the tallest building in the world, the Burj Khalifa. This 2,717-foot-tall structure, costing $1.5 billion, is without doubt impressive. The colossal bundled tube tower of shimmering glass trounced the previous record-holding building, the Taipei-101, by some 1,046 feet. One might wonder, however, what the addition of five million square feet of floor space, all in one building, might have done to Dubai's property market; it almost certainly contributed to Dubai's troublesome government debt. In any event, the most notable indication of the city's new-found global status is not the Burj Khalifa but the Dubai Gold and Commodities Exchange (DGCX). Opened in November 2005, with the trading of gold futures contracts, the DGCX is the first commodities derivative exchange in the Middle East.[89] As other products, such as silver, oil, and Indian rupee futures, have been added, the volume of trade on the Dubai's exchange has exploded. From 2006 to 2009, the value of contracts rose from (US)$15.5 billion to (US)$79 billion – a 500 per cent increase in just three years. It would seem that the DGCX is achieving its goal of being the market of choice for the Middle East.

4 The 2717-ft-tall Burj Khalifa shattered the record for the world's tallest building, but the opening of the Dubai Gold and Commodities Exchange is perhaps
a more important indication of the city's new global status. (© Photo: Anton
Foleros)

Conclusion

There are many types of assets that are traded on markets. Economic historian Charles Kindleberger lists a few of the things that investors have speculated in: 'commodity exports, commodity imports, agricultural land at home and abroad, urban building sites, railroads, new banks, discount houses, stocks, bonds (both foreign and domestic), glamour stocks, conglomerates, condominiums, shopping centres and office buildings.'[90] Many of these items of value fall under the categories of urban real estate or financial assets – the two main components of urban wealth. Also included among the commodities traded is gold, which proved to be the critical form of wealth during the 2008 financial crisis. There are other items of wealth too. For example, on 4 May 2004 Sotheby's in New York auctioned Pablo Picasso's *Garçon à la Pipe* for $104.2 million. This was the first time a piece of art had sold for over $100 million; the record was superseded by three private sales in 2006, all between $135 and $140 million.[91] The turnover reported by Christie's in 1997 was $2.02 billion, a little more than its close rival Sotheby's.[92] Nevertheless, this is small relative to the total value of the world's financial assets, which was estimated to be $42.6 trillion in 1993.

This chapter has explained how the two main components of the wealth of cities – real estate and financial assets – are, in theory, determined. Real estate may be valued as the expected return of a future stream of rents, thus being linked to the citizens' incomes, interest rates, markets expectations, and supply-side factors. In the case of Hong Kong, exemplifying microeconomic theory, growing income, limited supply of land, and efficient construction processes produced a city of magnificent towers that includes some of the world's most valuable real estate. The value of financial assets depends on the type. It is straightforward in the case of cash. For equities, the theoretical value is the present value of expected future payments. Of course, not all investors have the same expected rate of return, nor do they necessarily take a long-term view in valuing assets. Hence, the market prices of such assets are subject to the whims of speculation.

It has been argued, however, that total wealth is much more steadfast. It is conserved, or moves relatively steadily, as capital transfers between real estate, financial markets, gold, or other forms. Such transfers generally provide stability to the wealth of cities, although there are still cases where the value of assets in a city can change significantly. I have argued that the slump in Hong Kong's real estate values during the Asian financial crisis of 1997 was inherently tied to the beginning of America's dot-com boom. Further historical evidence of conservation of wealth was the transition from the 1720s Mississippi bubble in Paris to the South Sea bubble in London to a third bubble in Amsterdam. The expression *conservation of wealth* needs some care, though; total wealth is not literally fixed at some universal constant; rather, it may expected to grow at some relatively steady rate, in a non-sporadic fashion. The studies of peaks in housing and equity markets conducted at the Bank of International Settlements in Basel have also shown that housing prices typically rise from trough to peak by 40 per cent but fall from peak to trough by only 20 per cent.[93] In other words, there is a long-term upwards trend. Of course, learning from the flawed genius of John Law, we must be careful to distinguish between real growth of wealth and inflationary growth. Simply printing more banknotes does not produce an increase in wealth.

A more telling sign of increasing wealth is the opening of a new financial market, because, as I shall argue next chapter, cities that host and operate financial markets are destined to be wealthy. The opening of the Dubai Gold and Commodities Exchange is therefore a significant event, clear evidence that Dubai is competing strongly with other cities in the region. It is this topic – the competition between great cities' financial markets, and the factors that determine which ones emerge triumphant – that we turn to next.

4 Competitive Financial Centres

The Bank of the United States ... was a monster, a hydra-headed monster, ... equipped with horns, hoofs, and tail and so dangerous that it impaired the morals of our people, corrupted our statesmen, and threatened our liberty.

President Andrew Jackson[1]

In the early nineteenth century, a fierce competition between cities for the supremacy of their financial centres took place in the United States. As everyone knows, New York's Wall Street became the financial centre of the country, but for several decades it trailed behind Chestnut Street in Philadelphia.[2] It took a bold canal investment and some high-stakes politics to turn the tide New York's way.

A number of factors gave Chestnut Street an early lead over Wall Street in providing financial services to the fledgling nation.[3] Philadelphia had been the capital of the United States prior to the move to Washington, DC, in 1801. It was close to Chestnut Street that the genius of Alexander Hamilton designed the contemporary financial system of the United States – currency, banking, taxes, markets, and related institutions.[4] As such, Chestnut Street was home to the first central bank in the United States. In fact, it was home to the first *two* central banks; the first Bank of the United States was closed in 1811, only for the Second Bank of the United States to be opened five years later.[5] Although Philadelphia's position upstream in the narrow Delaware River made it inferior as a port to New York, Boston, and other cities, in the 1790s it nonetheless accounted for 20 per cent of US imports, by value, and was somewhat of a commercial capital in the sense that it had replaced London as the country's source for mercantile information. Philadelphia was also home to the most innovative financiers in the United States. Because of men like Clement Biddle, Stephen Girard, Michael Hillegas, Robert Morris, and Thomas Willing, Philadelphia was the first US city to provide marine, fire, and life insurance; commercial, savings, and investment banks; building and loan societies; and securities markets.[6] Wall Street followed closely and opened up similar services within a few years. Even so, Philadelphia was arguably America's financial centre until 1830.

The first key event that shifted financial power towards New York was the opening of the Erie Canal in 1825. It was an ambitious project connecting the Hudson River to Buffalo on Lake Erie by a channel that was 363 miles long, 40 feet wide, and 4 feet deep. Construction had symbolically begun on 4 July 1817. Many New York City politicians were at first opposed to the idea, fearing they would face great costs but receive little benefit. President James Madison vetoed federal funding for the scheme on his last day of office, perhaps not wishing to boost the New York economy in relation to his native Virginia's.[7] Nevertheless, New York Governor DeWitt Clinton championed the canal and produced funding for the project. The Canal Fund created in 1817 included a loan from the state, to be repaid by toll revenues; sale of land donated by speculators, who expected to profit from rising land prices; a levy on goods sold at auctions; lottery proceeds; and taxes on a variety of items including salt, steamboat travel, and land.[8] The total debt on the construction exceeded $7 million.[9] Critics at first called the canal 'Clinton's Folly' or 'Clinton's Ditch,' but it proved to be a financial success. The loan on the original canal construction was repaid by 1837 and a program to widen and deepen the canal was begun in 1834. Towns such as Buffalo, Detroit, Rochester, and Syracuse benefited economically, as did, of course, New York City.

The canal gave New York City a considerable geographical advantage over Philadelphia. The canal connected the port of New York to the Great Lakes system and the US interior, placing it at the head of a vast inland waterway. Philadelphia, by contrast, was on a relatively small watershed separated from the interior by the Appalachians. The geography is such that many parts of Pennsylvania are more naturally connected to the ports of Baltimore, the Great Lakes, and even New Orleans than to Philadelphia.[10] Philadelphia tried to catch up to New York with canal schemes and later railway investments of its own. Much of the effort came in the 1830s, but by this time most of the city's most innovative financiers were no longer alive and the next generation did not have the vision to overcome the geographical advantage that now favoured New York.

New York's growth as a trading centre, strengthened by its canal investments, accelerated. Americans increasingly had to make or receive payments in Manhattan rather than Philadelphia, for that is where the merchant activity was. The subsequent impact is well described by Robert E. Wright:

> In short, New York bootstrapped itself into a virtuous cycle. Wall Street financed the creation of a very long but strategically located ditch. It also lent to the merchants who transformed that ditch into the nation's most important interior commercial artery. In return, Wall Street was entrusted with a big chunk of the nation's cash, which it used to make its stock exchange yet more attractive for investors. Wall Street's financiers then turned those investments into additional projects, including extensions of the canal system, railroads, steamships lines, and the cotton and cotton goods trades. All that trade brought yet more deposits to Wall Street's banks, giving the positive feedback cycle yet another spin.[11]

In spite of the growing power of Wall Street, Philadelphia still had the country's central bank, but that institution was destined to fall in a political struggle that culminated in the Bank War of the 1830s. Although it had a troubled start, being blamed for prolonging a recession after the 1819 financial crisis, the Second Bank of the United States, under the leadership of Nicholas Biddle, gained the trust of Americans.[12] With Second Bank branches in at least two dozen cities throughout the United States, Americans still perceived Philadelphia to be the financial centre of the country throughout the prosperous years of the late 1820s and early 1830s.

The bank's charter, however, automatically ceased in 1836, and its renewal was opposed by the formidable political team of President Andrew Jackson and the 'sly fox' Martin Van Buren.[13] Jackson was a fearsome war hero who had won great battles against the British and the Indians in which he survived gunshot wounds to his chest; later, as president, he also survived an assassination attempt. Van Buren was a crafty, turncoat politician who founded one of America's first political parties – the Albany Regency. He had formed a coalition with Jackson which helped the general to gain the presidency in 1828, the same year as Van Buren became governor of New York. The two were then running mates for the crucial election of 1832 upon which the future of the Second Bank hung.

Jackson, who had twice been nearly bankrupt, apparently had an intense hatred of banks – and in particular the 'monstrous' Second Bank. He entered the 1832 election with the intention of vetoing the renewal of the bank's charter at the end of his term of office. Indeed, Jackson made the bank an election issue, going so far as to accuse it of being a 'tool of evil aristocrats and leechlike financiers.'[14] Being immensely popular with the electorate, Jackson won the presidency again and subsequently began to move government funds away from the Second Bank in preparation for ending its charter by his veto four years later.[15] Van Buren, in the meantime, had restructured New York's banking rules so as to create a safety fund for the banks.[16] The scheme was ultimately flawed, but at the time it was perceived as a suitable back-up to the financial system, replacing the central bank's role as lender of last resort. Jackson was wary of the New York banks too, but these were where much of the government holdings migrated to.

The Second Bank was not going to close down without a fight, though.[17] Biddle began to protect the bank by restricting loans, throwing the national economy into a recession. By 1837, the nation's banking system was in a state of crisis, with many banks suspending payment of specie. Rather than see the Second Bank wind down, Biddle had it successfully rechartered as the United States Bank of Pennsylvania. Then, in a desperate counter-attack, Biddle attempted to manipulate a run on the Wall Street banks. The attempt failed and the former Second Bank was ruined in the effort, eventually closing down in February 1841. The Bank War was over; Philadelphia would prosper as an industrial centre for another century or so, but New York City was now in uncontested control of the US financial system.

The demise of Philadelphia and rise of New York City during the 1830s Bank War illustrates the relative scarcity of financial centres. Why could the two not have continued together as financial centres for the young republic? After all, Chicago and later San Francisco did become substantial regional financial centres in addition to New York. Perhaps Nicholas Biddle's aggressive tactics put an end to Philadelphia's future as anything but a minor regional financial centre, or was Philly just too close to New York City?

This chapter first considers what it takes for a city to become a significant financial centre, relying on a four-phase process identified by Norman Gras that appears to work quite well in the European context in explaining how the growth of three sectors (commerce, industry, and transportation), one after the other, can enable a city – if other circumstances are favourable – to achieve power in the world of finance. This leads to a second question: How is it that only two cities – London and New York – have become the pre-eminent global financial centre in the last two centuries, with London holding the distinction in the nineteenth century, then yielding to New York in the twentieth? Exploring this question will lead to an investigation of the historic rivalry between London and New York City, with side glances at Paris. Our review of this history will take us down many highways and byways, from the French Revolution to the Franco-Prussian War, the First World War to the Great Depression of the 1930s, the Second World War to the advent of Margaret Thatcher, and at the end we will reach a broad conclusion: national economies matter, but wealthy cities can maintain their power for decades after nation-states decline.

Theories of Financial-Centre Formation

Beyond the ownership of financial assets by citizens, really wealthy cities go a step further by hosting and operating financial markets. Employment in financial markets is lucrative, bringing substantial income to the cities that host them. For example, in 2006, it was estimated that more than 4000 workers in the city of London took home year-end bonuses in excess of £1 million, with the total bonus pot for the city estimated to be £8.8 billion.[18] Moreover, the knowledge and skills associated with running markets arguably give the citizenry of such financial cities an edge in making their own investments. There is a snowball effect here; not only do financial centres make great income, they know how to invest it and hence make even more income. Not every city, however, is home to a stock market, operates a currency exchange market, or hosts a string of merchant banks or insurance companies. This is why the opening of Dubai's new Gold and Commodities Exchange was so significant. Whether it is by chance, competition, or design, cities that operate financial markets are destined to be wealthy.

So what does it take for a city to become a financial centre? Several authors have noted that neither international trade theory – that is, the factor-endowment approach of Eli Heckscher and Bertil Ohlin – nor von Thünen's distance-from-centre approach is particularly useful for explaining the location of financial centres.[19] A study conducted for the (modern-day) Bank of England identified several key factors for the existence of a financial centre.[20] These included: rights of establishment; supply of skilled personnel, premises, equipment, and machinery; and a supply of funds at costs that are reasonably competitive owing to suitable regulation and efficient payment/settlement systems. The study recognized, however, that large past ('sunk') costs, external economies of scale, and economies of agglomeration are most important for sustaining financial centres. The large sunk costs, particularly in terms of building relationships with clients and other firms, make it less desirable for established firms to relocate. Economies of scale and agglomeration will be discussed further in the next chapter; the key point is that a high concentration of financial firms in one place improves information flows, provides greater levels of liquidity (i.e., available capital), and achieves greater market efficiency. The country in which a city is located can also affect that city's potential to become a financial centre. The country should have a stable currency system with constant and substantial supply of money; a well-managed balance of payments; a history of non-confiscatory policy; political stability; and favourable regulation.[21]

Another noteworthy study of metropolitan development was done by University of California professor Allan Pred in the 1970s. Pred went beyond analysis of cities in isolation and attempted to identify the processes by which systems of interdependent cities grow in advanced economies.[22] He presented substantial empirical data on the relationships between cities, including hierarchies, particularly in the United States. Pred also advanced a conceptual model of the development of city-systems, but concluded at that time that the state of knowledge of metropolitan development was still primitive.[23]

A further theory of metropolitan development attributable to economic historian Norman Gras suggests that financial centres should be scarce.[24] The theory is that a metropolis grows through four phases, as a centre for (1) commerce, (2) industry, (3) transport, and (4) finance. There is increasing concentration towards the highest phase, and thus only a few cities reach the status of financial centre. Gras's theory of metropolitan development is largely historically based. The four phases are not necessarily clearly defined; there may be times when a city moves from one phase to another and many elements of an earlier phase will persist. Moreover, for a city to reach the next phase of development, it must substantially engage in the activity of that phase. Having a Main Street bank does not make a town a financial metropolitan centre!

The first phase, the organization of commercial markets, involves development of institutions and practices to supply large agglomerations of people.[25] Small towns can, of course, have markets where goods are bought and sold. It is the development of wholesalers, rather than retailers, that Gras sees as distinguishing the first phase of metropolitan development from ordinary town activities. Organization of wholesale markets requires firms that specialize in trading goods in or out of cities, others that handle the arrival of goods, and still others that undertake storage or simply carry goods. A metropolitan centre is more efficient at organizing wholesale trade than a group of towns of equivalent population; it makes more efficient use of capital, transport, and labour and can offer more goods of a greater variety.

At the heart of cities in the first phase of metropolitan development are dedicated locations for wholesale exchange. Other than perhaps Babylon and Alexandria in ancient times, and a few minor exchanges in small towns, Antwerp is recognized as the first city to have developed a substantial metropolitan exchange. Antwerp's bourse, founded in 1460, is thought to have derived its name from the wealthy Van der Burse family of Bruges; the home of Van der Burse was where merchants gathered to do business.[26] Antwerp also became an international centre for wholesale buying and selling of goods, rather than nearby Bruges because of the silting up of the latter's harbour. Other cities, such as Lyon, Amsterdam, Hamburg, London, and Frankfurt, soon followed Antwerp's lead. Sir Thomas Gresham modelled London's first Royal Exchange after the Antwerp exchange in which he had often conducted business. The first Royal Exchange had a square surrounded by colonnades in which merchants assembled; there were also shops above for retailers and cellars below for storage. The Royal Exchange in colonial Boston was patterned in a similar fashion. Such exchanges were a distinguishing feature of the first phase of metropolitan development.

The second phase of metropolitan development is characterized by growth in manufacturing activities.[27] Again, industry does not have to be located in cities; but, having developed the organizational capacity to feed and otherwise provide for large numbers of people, cities are attractive locations for manufactures since that is where the demand is. Moreover, as Jane Jacobs would argue, many industries are first established in cities because of the latter's role as centres of innovation. Of course, an industry that is set up in cities may eventually move out to the countryside where production costs are cheaper. The ability of industry to move away from cities and send its goods back there is tied to the development of transport – Gras's third phase of metropolitan development.

'All roads lead to Rome.' The old saying neatly summarizes the third stage of development. Of course, in England, all roads lead to London; and in France, they lead to Paris. Whether it is roads, rails, canals, or steamship lines, phase 3 sees the metropolis develop as the hub of a transportation network.[28] The network provides access to a wide variety of goods, but in other respects it is a way of exerting power and influence over a city's hinterland. The development of the Erie Canal, expanding the reach of New York City into the US interior, is a prime example, as discussed earlier in this chapter.

Thus comes the fourth stage of development – that of financial centre – with which this chapter is most concerned.[29] Gras is quick to argue why the development of financial skills is distinct from the other three phases. By financial organization he means more than just the private banking that occurred in Venice, Genoa, and Amsterdam, and more than the primitive banking performed by the goldsmiths of London. He also means more than the simple banking activities performed by county banks, for the metropolis mobilizes the capital of its hinterland, storing it and directing its excess. The fourth phase is one in which capitalists and money middlemen have begun to direct an increasingly large share of business.

Part of this increase in power is related to the development of advanced, efficient stock exchanges. The term 'stock exchange' needs to be used carefully here, though. The storage of stock – that is, agricultural goods and merchandise – can be performed by a city in phase 1. Cities in phase 4 are concerned with the storage and control of financial capital rather than merchandise. According to Gras, the first city to reach this fourth phase of metropolitan development was London in about 1890. This followed its phases of commercial development (1550–1750), industrial development (1750–1830), and growth of a railway transportation network (1830–90). London's stock exchange building had been built as early as 1773, but the activities of brokers and jobbers were for a long time considered disreputable. In 1698 speculation in securities was considered so obnoxious that the merchants of the Royal Exchange expelled the brokers and jobbers, leaving them to operate in the streets around Change Alley. It was not until the late nineteenth century that London's financial sector came to be so powerful.

The power held by the financial sector during a city's fourth phase of development was particularly apparent in New York City in the early twentieth century.[30] A handful of companies headed by J.P. Morgan and including private banks, joint-stock banks, trust companies, life-insurance companies, and a few others in manufacturing and transportation formed a tightly knit group which controlled about $23 billion of the economy. The Pujo Committee report of 1913[31] found that companies outside the elite group often found it difficult to raise large loans, especially when they were in direct competition with those companies on the inside.

Gras provides a further example, contrasting the development of northwest England with London.[32] He argues that the Liverpool and Manchester region reached only the third phase of metropolitan development. It achieved commercial independence from London, having its own hinterland in northwest England and Wales. The region certainly developed its own substantial industry, particularly in textiles. Liverpool became a shipping hub through which the region had its own trade links with North America and Asia, while Manchester became the centre of the regional rail network. Other than Liverpool's insurance companies and, formerly, a handful of local banks, however, the region remained largely financially dependent on London.

There is a hierarchy among financial centres. At the top are the global financial centres – New York, London, and Tokyo – with a huge concentration of banking and other financial activities. These are followed by international and regional financial centres of different levels. The lesser centres are able to compete with the higher centres only if they possess information advantages, for example, niche markets or timezone discrepancies, or cultural advantages, such as language.[33] The hierarchy has shifted over time, as shown by Howard Reed's study of seventy-six financial centres from forty countries over the period from 1900 to 1980.[34]

Contemporary urban scholars would possibly argue that the world's greatest cities have entered a fifth phase beyond the four described by Gras.[35] John Friedmann's world-city hypothesis describes a new role for major cities within the 'spatial organization of the new international division of labour.'[36] He describes three functions for global cities within the world economy, as headquarters, financial centres, and key gateways between national/regional economies and the global economy. These three functions are perhaps already encapsulated within Gras's theory. What has changed, however, is that with new telecommunications and information technology, and massive growth in air travel, the scope and magnitude of transnational inter-city relations are of a historically unprecedented scale. This higher degree of interaction between cities means that global cities serve an increasingly sophisticated *control function*, which has seen expansion in their economic activities related to management, finance, corporate services, and the media.

Saskia Sassen takes the argument further by describing how today's world cities are more than 'command centres'; they are 'global service centres.'[37] She argues that modern world cities are distinctly different from the banking and trading centres of yesteryear. The need for cities to act as *command points* in the global economy has produced a demand for finance and business services in cities. To meet this demand, cities have also become the locations at which new innovative products and services are created for these leading economic sectors. Thus, there is a 'virtual economic cycle' whereby world cities produce and consume new services within the global economy.[38] In terms of Gras's theory, this new form of global service activity can perhaps be considered as a fifth phase largely catering to the financial function of a city (phase 4), which itself resulted from traditional commercial and industrial activities (phases 1 and 2). Meanwhile, the role of cities as transportation centres (phase 3) remains of importance as cities become increasingly connected within a world-city network.

Taken together, the theories reviewed here provide a fuller picture of how financial centres are formed. The most critical element is Gras's theory, which explains the four-stage process through which financial centres evolve. Pred correctly points out that there is a hierarchy among cities and that, to make it to the status of financial centre, cities must triumph over other challengers. Once a city has become a financial centre, it has large sunk costs plus economies of scale and agglomeration that act to maintain its status, as the Bank of England study identified. There is perhaps a further stage beyond that of financial centre, Friedmann's command centre or Sassen's global service centre – a possible extension of Gras's theory.

The Emergence of European Financial Centres

How well does Gras's theory explain the transformation of particular cities into financial centres? The answer is partially provided by Charles Kindleberger's study of the emergence of financial centres, with a particular focus on banking from the eighteenth century onward. Kindleberger specifically studies five European countries plus Canada and the United States. New York's toppling of Philadelphia has already been discussed and the unusual case of Montreal versus Toronto will be studied in the Conclusion. So for now we shall briefly recount the formation of banking centres in England, France, Germany, Italy, and Switzerland.[39]

London's emergence as the principal banking centre for England is relatively straightforward. As the largest city, capital, port, ancient commercial centre, and eventually hub of the national rail network, London was the inevitable location of the country's financial core. This is not to say that banking did not occur elsewhere in England. From the 1750s onward, there was a surge in the number of smaller independent county banks throughout the country; indeed, with the main exception of the NatWest bank, most of today's larger English banks have their roots in provincial banking. However, with the growth of the rail network from the 1830s, and later the telegraph, London became rapidly accessible from the rest of the country. It was the obvious place for large banks to locate their headquarters as the industry consolidated.

The story in France was quite different, though it has a similar ending. Paris was well established as the financial centre of France during the era of Louis XIV. During the turmoil of the French Revolution, most of the banks left for Geneva, Germany, or elsewhere, but returned to Paris when peace was achieved. The Banque de France, created by Napoleon, established subsidiaries in Lyon, Dijon, Rouen, Nantes, Bordeaux, Le Havre, Lille, and Marseille. These later became semi-autonomous regional banks with limited activities, but were still very much subservient to the Banque de France. During the financial crisis of 1840, the national bank allowed the regional banks to fail in order to take over the issuing of notes. The 1850s and 1860s saw the formation of the Crédit Mobilier and new large credit banks to fund large-scale infrastructure development throughout the country. France's second-largest city, Lyon, perhaps had a chance to establish itself as an independent financial centre, given its key position for trade with the south of the country as well as Italy and Switzerland. The Crédit Lyonnais became one of the largest French banks, with a substantial network of branches, but these really drew funds to Paris rather than Lyon. Although its head office was eventually moved to Paris in 1882, by some accounts the Crédit Lyonnais was the world's largest bank at the turn of the century.[40] Nonetheless, Paris remains the unquestionable financial centre of France to this day.

Germany did not unify as one nation until the 1870s and so before then had many financial centres, notably Cologne, Frankfurt, Darmstadt, Berlin, Dresden, Leipzig, and Hamburg. Afterwards, Berlin emerged as the country's chief financial centre, largely because of Prussia's key role in unifying Germany and its victory in the Franco-Prussian War of 1871. Most of the banking activity consolidated in Berlin, although Hamburg, with close ties to London, remained the main centre for financing Germany's foreign trade. After the Second World War, with Berlin isolated, the United States tried to establish a decentralized banking system, with each of the ten Länder having its own financial centre. The experiment was futile and consolidation gradually occurred. The Deutsche Bank, for example, went from ten independent banks in 1945 to three regional ones (in Frankfurt, Düsseldorf, and Hamburg) in 1952 and a single bank headquartered in Frankfurt by 1957. With its large international airport and, for a while, substantial American government presence, Frankfurt attracted most American multinationals in the post-war era and thus became West Germany's financial centre.

Several cities had the potential to be Italy's financial centre. Venice, Florence, Genoa, and Naples were all ancient banking centres. However, from 1860 to 1890, Kindleberger suggests, Turin was the leading financial centre of Italy. This was in spite of efforts to move the financial headquarters to Florence and then Rome. The latter, which became capital in 1870, was located in an unproductive part of Italy with poor transport connections. Turin was likely the leading financial centre because of its close proximity and good connections to France. Relations between France and Italy weakened, however, in the late nineteenth century, and financial ties with Germany became more important. Kindleberger notes the importance of the opening of the Gotthard tunnel in Switzerland, which provided access between Lombardy and southern Germany. Completion of the Gotthard tunnel in 1882, and later the Simplon tunnel, gave Milan a key advantage over Turin and enabled it to become Italy's financial centre.

The opening of the Gotthard tunnel was also significant in establishing Zurich as the financial centre of Switzerland. Before 1850, Zurich was far less important than Geneva or Basel as a banking centre. Indeed, the city of Winterthur, in the same canton as Zurich, was just as active in banking. In 1873 Winterthur was devising a scheme that would have seen it become the key link in the Swiss railway system. Zurich responded by establishing itself as a focal location on the railroad – and prominent Zurich banker Alfred Escher cemented Zurich's dominance by promoting the Gotthard tunnel. Zurich's population increased elevenfold between 1850 and 1910. Basel, Berne, and Geneva still house significant banking activities today, but Zurich is undoubtedly the financial capital of Switzerland and a major international money and capital market.

To conclude, Kindleberger's study does not cover all phases of Gras's theory – it misses phases 1 and 2 – but the importance of becoming a transportation hub (phase 3) before a city can attain the status of financial centre is clear. London and Paris are the hubs of national rail networks – as well as other transportation modes. Construction of a key piece of infrastructure – the Gotthard tunnel – established Zurich and Milan as transportation centres. The case of Germany is more complicated, but, after political attempts to decentralize banking activities (working against natural hierarchy), Frankfurt's eventual emergence as Germany's financial centre was perhaps due in part to its international airport.

Achieving Global Supremacy

Gras's theory provides a reasonable explanation of how a city may become a financial centre, but what does it takes to become *the* leading financial centre? This is a difficult question to answer. Several measures come into the judgment: the amount of capital; the size of banking institutions; the presence of foreign banks; the presence of merchants, insurance companies, and other firms; the size of complementary markets; and the strength of the national currency.[41] To help navigate through so many measures, and interpret the changing roles of London, Paris, and New York as international financial centres in the past two hundred years, this section draws extensively upon Youssef Cassis's *Capitals of Capital*. With the addition of insights from a few other sources, we can describe how the competition for financial supremacy played out over the past two centuries.

By the beginning of the nineteenth century, London had surpassed Amsterdam as Europe's and – by extension – the world's financial centre. It had been a long-drawn-out process, which is hardly surprising; once a city has amassed a great amount of wealth it is very hard for another to overtake it. By 1790, the English had surpassed the Dutch both in trade and in warfare, but Cassis suggests that the big Amsterdam banking houses still had more capital than their London rivals.[42] These included Hope and Company, founded by a Scottish family that had emigrated to Amsterdam in 1734, which, with a capital of ten million florins, was possibly the largest bank in Europe as of 1780.[43] In financing international trade and issuing foreign loans, however, Amsterdam fell behind London and Paris. In 1794, for example, the Austrian government took out a loan of fifty-eight million florins in London, an amount that was said to greatly exceed Dutch resources.[44] Perhaps it was during this last decade of the eighteenth century that Amsterdam was eclipsed by London. Amsterdam's relative position would deteriorate further during the Napoleonic Wars and never fully recover.

Paris, too, was hard hit by France's defeat in the Napoleonic Wars, following as they did the turbulence of the French Revolution. Paris had been a significant financial centre in the eighteenth century. In 1721, shortly after the Mississippi bubble, it had fifty-one banking houses, and this would rise to over seventy by 1780.[45] One Frenchman claimed: 'Paris has an incredibly wide-ranging sphere of banking activities; it could be said that there is no city in the universe that is superior to it in this respect.'[46] After the Revolution, however, many of the banks had fled to other cities. With closure of the bourse, liquidation of the Caisse d'escompte, dissolution of joint-stock companies, and seizure of currencies by the Jacobins, Paris's role as a financial centre was seriously undermined.[47] Napoleon Bonaparte brought some stability with the establishment of the Banque de France in 1800, with a capital of thirty million francs. France, however, was in desperate need of funds, which led it to sell Louisiana to the United States in 1803. It is noteworthy that such a significant transaction was financed by the Barings Brothers of London in partnership with Hope and Company of Amsterdam; the two banks accepted $11.25 million in US treasury bonds yielding 6 per cent per annum in return for paying an equivalent in gold to the French.[48] By 1815, Barings had become the largest bank in Europe, having bought out Hope and Company. Following Napoleon's defeat at the Battle of Waterloo, it was again Barings of London that provided banking services to France. The war indemnity of 700 million francs inflicted upon France was largely financed through loans from Barings. The financing of France's war debt was a clear sign of London's ascendance as the leading financial centre.

London's pre-eminence as a financial centre continued throughout the first half of the century. It became the world centre for the issuing of foreign loans. Countries such as Prussia, Austria, Russia, Belgium, Spain, Brazil, and Argentina took out loans in the British capital. Between 1822 and 1825, over twenty foreign loans totalling £40 million were issued by London banks.[49] Many of these were financed by N.M.

Rothschild, which had grown to overshadow Barings as London's leading merchant bank. Furthermore, starting with a loan to Prussia in 1818, these loans were typically issues in pounds sterling with interest payable in sterling. The British currency, which returned to gold convertibility in 1821, became the world's currency for international transactions.

It did not take long for Paris to revive its role as an important financial centre. A number of foreign immigrants moved to Paris to establish banks under the Restoration; these included James de Rothschild, the youngest of five brothers from the great banking family. In 1817 he founded his own bank, de Rothschild Frères, which soon came to dominate the Parisian clique of banks known as the *haute banque*.[50] Paris became an important European financial centre once more, because, among other reasons, France was one of the few European countries to have a positive trade balance with Britain and the United States. Paris was where the British and Americans sought bills of exchange to pay for some of their imports. Paris was also a centre for European merchants to pay off their debts to the Anglo-Saxon nations.[51] Thus, the French franc became a significant international currency and capital began to accumulate in Paris once more. The group of twenty or so banking houses, led by de Rothschild Frères, made Paris an alternative to London for financing trade and obtaining foreign loans.

Several key factors, however, kept London ahead of Paris as a financial centre at mid-century.[52] In 1850 the United Kingdom supplied over 20 per cent of the world's trade; by 1860, the figure had risen to 25 per cent. France had half that amount: 11.4 per cent in 1850 and 13 per cent in 1860. Moreover, whereas Paris is situated far from the coast, the city of London was immediately next to the port of London – the largest in the world. The port of London was very significant in maintaining London's entrepôt status; it brought in the merchants who still generated much of the financial activity. Echoing Gras's theory, the *Financial News* noted: 'Banks exist in Lombard Street because the merchants of old created a demand for them. Shipping companies flourished ... because of the freights with which the merchants provided them. Lloyd's is but a necessity of these mercantile freights and bottoms. And the stock exchange lives light-heartedly on the patronage of the banker whom the merchant brought into being. So it is not too much to say that it is the merchant who has made the City of London.'[53]

Cognizant of their inferior geographical location, Parisian strategists took remarkable steps to compete with London. The Second Empire, starting in 1852, was a great period of infrastructure investment in France. The era saw the emergence of large French banks. These notably included the Crédit Mobilier, founded in 1852, which specialized in industrial development, transportation, and public utilities.[54] The development of the French national railway system reduced travel time between Paris and the key ports of Marseille and Le Havre. While Baron Haussmann was famously rebuilding the city of Paris, the French ports were also being modernized and plans developed to form large warehouse districts around the railway terminals in Paris. The 1869 opening of the Suez Canal, funded by French capital, significantly increased the importance of Marseille as a port. Such infrastructure could potentially have helped Paris to catch up with London as a centre for trade.

During this era, Paris did surpass London as a centre for exporting capital. The House of Rothschild in Paris grew to be larger than that in London. In the early 1850s and 1860s, France exported more than twice the capital Britain did.[55] Paris was the main source of capital for continental Europe, while London remained dominant in loans to the rest of the world. The value of securities on the London Stock Exchange, however, was still close to double that on the Paris bourse and the pound sterling was still the world's first-choice currency.

Yet even the dominance of the pound sterling came under attack with a French proposal, in December 1866, to create a new universal currency based on the franc. The British were naturally cool towards the idea; it would have boosted Paris's role relative to London. The United States and several European countries participated quite actively in discussions held at the Quai d'Orsay in Paris from 17 June to 6 July 1867.[56] The plans for a universal currency for the Western nations failed, however, because of opposition from Britain and the German states.

Moreover, within four more years, military conflict with the Germans would effectively end Paris's challenge to London's financial supremacy. As France engaged in war with Prussia, the French franc was removed from convertibility with the gold standard, leaving the pound sterling unrivalled as the international currency and London as the only world market for precious metals. The subsequent Prussian victory saw France pay a massive war indemnity of five billion francs.[57] France was able to make the payment by drawing upon its large national savings, but this left little opportunity for Paris to export capital. From this point onward, London was dominant. If Paris had eclipsed London for a decade or two, their fortunes seemed to have been reversed by the Franco-Prussian War, which 'destroyed whatever chance of rivalry might be left; so that by 1875 London was supreme in cosmopolitan and domestic money markets alike.'[58]

The following forty years or so, until 1914, were a classic period for the city of London, which stood unchallenged as the world's financial centre. The political environment during the 'Age of Empire' was conducive to the rapid growth of all international financial centres. The export of capital reached new heights and the Western financial centres became more closely integrated owing to the increasing speed of communication. The collapse in the value of silver starting from 1870 encouraged many of the world's leading nations to join Britain in the gold standard, thereby strengthening the pound sterling yet further. There were some changes in London's financial sector over the forty-year period: joint-stock banks replaced the private banks in importance; many foreign banks opened in London; and insurance companies and investment trust companies blossomed, as did professional-service firms such as those of accountants and lawyers. The nominal value of stocks on the London Stock Exchange rose from £2.3 billion in 1873 to £11.3 billion in 1913.[59] British capital investments abroad approximately quadrupled over the same period. By 1913, 42 per cent of world's $44 billion stock of foreign investment was British.[60]

New York City, however, was a rising star during London's golden age. At the beginning of the 1860s, New York was already ranked the third-wealthiest city in the world, after London and Paris.[61] Moreover, the size of the US economy surpassed that of Britain in 1870. New York City was not a global financial centre, but it was important because of its position at the centre of the dynamic US economy, which was attracting large amounts of foreign investment. The US investment banks also grew substantially from 1870 on, participating in the financing of railways and, from 1890, large manufacturing companies. These included the United States Steel Corporation, which, upon its formation in 1901, was the largest enterprise created to that date, with share value exceeding $1 billion.[62]

August of 1900 had also witnessed the significant event of a £10-million foreign loan made to Britain to assist with financing of the Boer War.[63] The loan was financed by John Pierpont Morgan, who was to emerge as the world's leading banker of the early twentieth century. New York banks would subsequently make as many as 250 smallish foreign loans, totalling a nominal $1 billion between 1900 and 1913.[64] The loan to Britain of August 1900 was particularly symbolic, though, and caused the British finance minister to receive considerable criticism from the city of London, which was concerned about future competition from New York.

New York City, however, was still immature as a financial centre, and the limitations of the American banking system meant that it remained quite dependent upon London. There was massive export of capital from London to New York, and much of the financing for US foreign trade was still handled by bills drawn from London. Moreover, the American banking system struggled to provide liquidity to US companies because of seasonal fluctuations in the main US exports, which were still agricultural goods.[65] The fragility of the US banking system was particularly apparent during the crisis of 1907. A run on the Knickerbocker Trust Company in August of that year severely stretched the gold reserves of the New York banks. Even though the intervention of J.P. Morgan helped ease the panic, it was still necessary for New York to borrow a large quantity of gold from London. Over $100 million was borrowed during November and December that year.[66] (To meet such a demand, the Bank of England had to raise its interest rates and borrow £3 million in gold from the Banque de France.)[67] Moreover, as of 1913, the value of securities on the London Stock Exchange was £11.3 billion. This was almost as much as the value in Paris (£6.2 billion) and New York (£5.3 billion) combined.[68]

The outbreak of the First World War proved a significant turning point for New York City, particularly because of the skills of Treasury Secretary William McAdoo, who guided the United States through the ensuing financial crisis.[69] As the war prompted European nations to withdraw gold from America, McAdoo took a number of bold actions to protect the integrity of the US dollar: closing Wall Street for four and a half months; shoring up US gold supplies; persuading J.P. Morgan to bail out the city of New York from its European debts; and jump-starting the US Federal Reserve banking system. Through such actions, the US dollar was able to stay true to the gold standard, thereby establishing it as an international currency of integrity. Sterling, by contrast, had been suspended from the gold standard, as was usual for nations at war. Thus, the dollar was well on the way to rivalling sterling as the premier international currency.

New York City and London emerged from the First World War in competition for top spot. The United States finished the war with net private assets of $4.5 billion, having had a net liability of over $3 billion in 1913.[70] Britain, by contrast, experienced a reduction of $3 billion in its holdings of foreign assets, primarily through the sale of American stocks. New York and London were neck and neck in the financing of foreign trade, with London perhaps having the upper hand. The abundance of US savings, however, pushed New York ahead in the export of capital; in the second half of the 1920s, foreign issues in New York City exceeded those in London by 80 per cent. J.P. Morgan and Company had probably become the largest private banking house in the world; with assets of $680 million, it was four times the size of the largest merchant banks in London.[71] In the United Kingdom, a series of mergers had led to the formation of the 'big five' domestic banks, which were unmatched by retail banks in New York City. These were, moreover, beginning to act as multinational banks; Barclays, in particular, had established some 506 overseas branches.[72] Still, with strong industrial growth, the 1920s witnessed a boom in issues of American stocks, and New York was much more successful than London in attracting funds for domestic investment. The London Stock Exchange largely lost the international role that it had before the war. Yet London still ranked number one in the world in terms of its stock of capital invested abroad.

In assessing the relative fortunes of New York and London at this point, it is also pertinent to go beyond Cassis and look in more detail at where the capital of the two cities was invested, in particular with regard to railway stocks. British investors had a long history of investment in railways, which were considered as reliable as government securities. It was said that 'American Railroads' in particular was the largest department of the London Stock Exchange.[73] In 1913 some 41 per cent of British capital was invested in railways, compared to just 9.6 per cent in industrial stocks.[74] By comparison, the value of the 76 railroad stocks on the New York Stock Exchange was $5.5 billion in 1913, while the value of the 252 industrial companies was $6.8 billion.[75] These represented 21 per cent and 26 per cent of the total market capital respectively.[76] The key point is that railroad stocks must surely have lost a substantial amount of their value over the twentieth century, as railways were superseded by automobiles and air travel. Railroads in the United States covered 300,000 miles in 1929, but thereafter the total trackage dwindled and about one-third of the railways were decommissioned. The UK rail network, similarly, reached its maximum size of 20,412 miles in 1928 and had shrunk to half that size before the end of the century.[77] With New York investors more diversified into industrial stocks, they may well have weathered the decline in railroad stocks far better than London investors.

The Wall Street crash of 1929 brought the Roaring Twenties to a close and led into the Great Depression, which ultimately broke any remaining claims London had to be the leading financial centre. Some signs of the 1930s depression had been evident in 1928, particularly declining industrial production. After New York's raging bull market crashed in October 1929, the whole world plunged into a recession of almost mythic proportions. By 1932, global industrial output had dropped by 30 per cent and world trade by 48 per cent in value.[78] Germany and the United States were the most affected countries in terms of unemployment. The breakdown in international trade reduced the value of bills of exchange on London's discount market from £365 million in 1929 to £134 million in 1933.[79] The city's greatest crisis, however, involved the pound sterling. Overvalued since Britain returned to the gold standard in 1925, and vulnerable to a shortage of British currency reserves and a worrisome budget deficit (not to mention German industry defaulting on loans from British banks), the pound suffered a fatal blow on 21 September 1931, when its convertibility to gold was suspended. As Cassis notes: 'The abandonment of the gold standard marked a decisive turning point in the history of London as a financial centre. Confidence in "impregnable" sterling was shaken for good.'[80] Interestingly, some French writers saw London's fall as an opportunity for Paris to rise, but Paris and New York were both soon plunged into turmoil. Many banks in France and the United States collapsed as the Great Depression deepened – and eventually the franc and the dollar had to be devalued.[81]

New York City emerged from the Second World War as the world's main financial centre and continued to grow in subsequent decades. It was the command centre of a country that produced 50 per cent of the world's industrial output in 1946. With such a level of industry, supported by huge gold reserves, the dollar was king. In September 1953, the New York Stock Exchange reached its previous peak of August 1929. A new wave of US multinational companies spent $5.4 billion in direct capital investment between 1950 and 1954.[82] Among these were the likes of General Electric, Standard Oil, and IBM, all based in New York. In 1954 the New York commercial banks held total resources of $32.3 billion, compared to $19.8 billion in London.[83] Moreover, the US retail banks were growing rapidly; the Bank of America, First National City Bank, and Chase Manhattan Bank had all passed London's Barclays Bank in total assets by 1960. In this new economic era of state intervention and rebuilding of domestic economies, international capital flows were much smaller than before 1930. Nonetheless, New York City also led the way in foreign loans, issuing $4.17 billion between 1955 and 1962, compared to just $1.06 billion by London.[84]

Nevertheless, in the late 1950s, after two world wars and decades of slow British economic growth, a new international role for London emerged.[85] This was as a centre for the Eurodollar market. Technically, the term Eurodollar can be misleading: a Eurocurrency means any currency borrowed and lent outside the country that uses that currency; that is, it is not restricted to dollars nor to Europe.[86] It so happened that around 1957 a few European banks, particularly in London and Switzerland, began to deal in US dollars.[87] A number of factors led to the emergence and growth of the Eurodollar market: a large-scale entrance of US companies into Western Europe; banking regulations in the United States, including reserve requirements and exchange controls, which made it financially attractive for American banks to work from branches in Europe; the convenience of trading in dollars in Europe during regular working hours; and a desire of Eastern European governments to hold dollars in non-American banks, where they were less vulnerable to political changes.[88] The language, law, and business culture of London, as well as light regulation by the Bank of England, made the city an ideal home for the Eurocurrency markets.

During the 1960s and into the 1970s, two distinct cultures developed in London.[89] With the breakdown of the Bretton Woods international monetary system and the oil-price shocks of the 1970s, the growth in Eurocurrency trading was enormous. London's reputation for political neutrality made it a competitive choice for the deposit and investment of petrodollar surpluses from Arab countries. Thus, the international culture of the city, with many foreign banks and security houses, allowed it to participate in the lucrative, dynamic, and competitive Eurocurrency markets. Meanwhile, the domestic half of the city based on the Stock Exchange, domestic banks, and other financial institutions remained organized in self-regulating, often cartel-like clubs, which were typically as inefficient as the UK economy.

The election of the Margaret Thatcher government in 1979 blew apart the cultural divide between the domestic and international parts of the city.[90] The Tory government removed exchange controls and opened up the domestic financial system to international competition – another major feature of the 'Big Bang' reforms that began in 1986. The international debt crisis of 1982 saw growth in the markets for Eurobonds, yet another unregulated international market centred on London. By the 1990s, London had become the world's largest market for foreign-currency exchange. Bonetti and Cobham summarize the city's new status as follows: 'Its new role was more that of an entrepot financial centre, borrowing from the residents of one country to lend to those of another. It had several "first mover" advantages: in Eurocurrencies; abolition of exchange controls; and first European nation undertaking radical stock market reform. Other financial centers, such as Paris and Frankfurt, challenged, but were behind.'[91]

Overall, though, New York City remained at the top of the world's financial hierarchy at the start of the twenty-first century, with London and Tokyo playing significant second-tier roles. The top six investment banks in 2001 were all American (or joint American-Swiss in the case of Credit Suisse First Boston).[92] Moreover, in 2001, the market capitalization of the New York Stock Exchange was $11,000 billion (not to mention $2,900 billion for the NASDAQ), compared to $2,300 billion in Tokyo and $2,100 billion in London.[93] Tokyo's market capitalization had eclipsed that of New York in the spring of 1987, but the Japanese economy struggled during the 1990s. Tokyo's status as the leading Asian centre was increasingly challenged by Hong Kong, Singapore, and Shanghai. Similarly, with Frankfurt chosen as headquarters for the new European Central Bank, some thought that it might rival London as Europe's financial centre. Yet, with a regional population of just 1.6 million, Frankfurt was not big enough, not cosmopolitan enough, and not English-speaking enough to displace London.[94] By 2004, 311,000 people were employed in London's financial sector, just behind New York with 314,000, but well ahead of Tokyo (172,000) and Frankfurt (90,000).[95]

If a broad conclusion can be drawn from this review of the top financial centres over the past two hundred years, during which only two cities – London and New York – occupied the top spot on the international stage, it is that the nation with the dominant national economy eventually produces the leading financial centre. The commercial and industrial activities of the nation, which feature only in the first two phases of Gras's theory, do in the long run influence which financial centre dominates. The passing of the mantle from Amsterdam to London to New York City, with Paris not quite making it, is consistent with this conclusion.

There is, however, significant delay in the change in dominant financial centre, relative to the change in dominant national economy. It was almost sixty years after the American economy outgrew the British that New York had clearly surpassed London as the leading financial centre. This makes sense because the leading financial centre has an entrenched position from which it has greater power to invest in the industry of the rising contender. Military conflicts were significant in the transition from one centre to the next; losses in the Napoleonic and Franco-Prussian wars were important in curtailing Paris's ambitions. One reason why wars trigger the coming of a new financial hegemon may simply be that they involve destruction of large amounts of capital. Beyond this, though, it might also be noted that wars tend to spur, or coincide with, technological change; part of being the dominant financial centre is the necessity of staying up to date with the latest wave of technology. To maintain their wealth, cities must own assets of technologies that are growing in value, rather than yesterday's steam engines.

Conclusion

New York City beat out Philadelphia in the Bank War of the 1830s, but this was not the only contest in New York's campaign to become the financial centre of the United States. It also had to fend off Boston, Baltimore, New Orleans, and Chicago, although these battles were perhaps not as high profile. The prize of such contests – control of financial markets – makes a city powerful and hence wealthy. No wonder, then, that London and Paris have been trading blows for a few centuries.

The emergence of financial centres is well described by Norman Gras's historically based theory, which, as we have seen, claims that a metropolis grows through three phases, as a centre for commerce, industry, and transport, before becoming, in the fourth phase, a financial centre. (Contemporary scholars might add a fifth phase, that of global service centre.) Many cities can reach the first two phases, but competition to reach the fourth phase is fierce. In testifying to the Pujo Committee in 1912–13, somewhat in defence of his syndicate, J.P. Morgan suggested that there were 'economic laws which in every country create some one city as the great financial centre.'[96] Our review of the formation of financial centres in Europe revealed several failed political attempts to create financial centres, in Italy and Germany in particular. What was often missing was the crucial third phase of transportation infrastructure by which a metropolis exerts power over its surrounding region. In the success stories, New York's Erie Canal, the Gotthard tunnel linking Zurich and Milan, and perhaps Frankfurt's airport were all significant in helping to establish these financial centres.

The title of pre-eminent centre is manifested in several ways, for example, by the size of banks and the strength of national currency. Perhaps the capitalization value of a centre's stock market, though, is the ultimate measure of power, and in this respect New York still holds the top position. The total value of assets listed on a financial city's stock exchange is no doubt far greater than the value of equities held by its citizens, but such a measure fits nicely with our asset-based approach to expressing the wealth of cities.

It is striking, however, that the wealth and power of cities, as reflected in their assets, can exist only if there is an expectation that the value of such assets will generally increase over the long term. Investment in stock markets is quite an unattractive proposition if, on average, investors stand to lose. So we arrive at the question of how assets, and thus urban wealth, grow in value. This look at the formation of financial centres has already touched upon one mechanism in the growth of cities – the virtuous cycle. Investment in the Erie Canal began a circular process that saw an ever-increasing amount of capital in the hands of New York bankers. Such cyclical phenomena, or snowball effects, are essential to any growth process. In biological terms, they are somewhat akin to the Krebs cycle, by which chemical energy is created and transported during metabolism. But what is it that controls the rate at which such virtuous cycles operate in cities, or causes them to come to an end? The following chapters will seek to gain a fuller understanding of the economic growth of cities, moving beyond markets and competition between financial centres to consider other factors that need to be added to the mix. The first step in this endeavour will be to examine, in the next chapter, the role of production and consumption in cities, exposing in particular how urban physical form – a consequence of infrastructure planning – influences consumptive patterns.

5 Economic Growth, Production, and Consumption

Soon London will be all England.
King James I[1]

The fire started early in the morning of Sunday, 2 September 1666, at the house of Thomas Farriner in Pudding Lane.[2] While such fires were common in this age, this one was troublesome in that it occurred in a particularly dense area of the city where wooden pitched houses nestled along narrow streets and alleyways. Moreover, there had been a long summer drought and a strong easterly gale now blew across the city. Most of the neighbours were able to escape with their most valued possessions, but by 3 a.m. the fire could be seen by one of Samuel Pepys's servants over a quarter of a mile away. It spread rapidly through the Thames Street area where the tradesmen stored 'tarr, pitch, hemp, rosen and flax.'

The heat of the fire made it difficult for firefighters to get close to it, and the blaze unfortunately destroyed Pieter Morice's water engine near the northern end of London Bridge. The fire advanced quickly, but, being a Sunday morning, the people, including the unfortunate Mayor Thomas Bludworth, were slow to act. By the end of Sunday, it had burned about half a mile along the riverfront. The king ordered the lord mayor to pull down houses, not sparing any property, in an effort to make firebreaks, but burning debris spread by the wind thwarted this last remaining strategy. Even the wider streets such as Cornhill and Cheapside were jumped by the flames.

As the fire burned on from Sunday to Monday, a sense of desperation rose. Many small boats laden with belongings took to the river and the price of carts in the city rocketed. The king replaced the ineffectual Bludworth with the Duke of York as the official in charge of bringing the fire under control. This perhaps helped to maintain law and order, but the duke was unable to stop the flames from spreading. He watched helplessly as a great windblown firebrand set Dorset House alight. Many other great buildings were also lost, especially on the Tuesday. These included the grand Royal Exchange in Cornhill, Whittington's Guildhall, numerous churches, and the cathedral of St Paul. When at last the wind died on Wednesday, some 85 per cent of the area within the city walls was destroyed, including one-fifth of all houses in the metropolis of London.

The Great Fire of London could not have happened at a more troublesome time for the English. The previous year had seen many killed by the plague – an estimated 69,000 in London alone.[3] The country was engaged in a second war against the superior Dutch, who were joined by the French. The war and the plague severely disrupted trade, which only added to England's economic troubles. For the financial year of 1666–7, government income fell to £686,000, compared to a value of £893,000 just two years earlier.[4] The national debt rose to £2.5 million. On top of all that, the damage caused by the Great Fire was estimated at between £7.4 million and £10.8 million.[5]

Yet London was rapidly rebuilt – in a much grander fashion than before and with remarkable economic effects. By 1671, over 85 per cent of the houses had been rebuilt, including many business establishments.[6] Moreover, these were typically larger than before and were now faced in brick or stone, fitted with proper downspouts for drainage and conforming in height and shape to new uniformity guidelines. The street pattern remained remarkably similar to before, to the dismay of the likes of Christopher Wren, but many streets were widened, straightened, and paved. Admittedly, it took Wren about two decades to finish most of the fifty-one new churches and the rebuilding of St Paul's was not completed until 1710. Nevertheless, aside from the religious buildings, the city had largely recovered within five years of the fire.

The economic growth of London and England in the years following the restoration of the monarchy (1660) and the Great Fire was quite remarkable. Economic historian D.W. Roberts saw the period as a watershed in the economic history of England: 'The year 1660 marked for England the beginning of a series of changes which have completely transformed almost every aspect of national life.'[7] London's trading community proved particularly resilient: 'The damage caused by the

Great Fire of London in 1666 ... was rapidly made good.'[8] Indeed, two of London's great trading companies – the Hudson's Bay Company (1670) and the Royal Africa Company (1672) – were formed not long after the fire, while others such as the East India Company and the Muscovy Company increased their trade.[9] Economic historian Roger Backhouse notes: 'London was magnificently rebuilt after the Great Fire of 1666, and the city's prosperity attracted comment from critics and admirers.'[10] How is it, though, that London's economy could grow so rapidly after such a huge fire?

One of those to inquire into the growth of London was Sir William Petty (1623–87) – a man whose rise to riches is itself a remarkable tale.[11] The son of a poor clothier from Romsey in Hampshire, Petty had impressive practical skills and intellect, learning Latin, Greek, mathematics, and navigation as a boy. At age fourteen, he had the misfortune to break a leg while serving as a cabin boy for an English merchant and was promptly left abandoned near Caen on the French coast. Taken in by Jesuit fathers, he continued his education. Upon return to England, he joined the Royal Navy for a while, but left for the Netherlands as the English Civil War blazed. There he studied medicine at Utrecht, Leyden, and Amsterdam before making his way to Paris, where he made the acquaintance of Thomas Hobbes and other displaced scholars. By 1648, Petty had moved to Oxford, via London, where he became professor of anatomy two years later. He subsequently became physician to Cromwell's invading army in Ireland, a position that he held for seven years to his great benefit. While in Ireland, Petty conducted a land survey and came to be sole executive in the task of distributing forfeited property to officers and soldiers – a process that resulted in him becoming a rich landowner himself. He continued to travel frequently between London and Ireland, fighting lawsuits, keeping good face with the changing political powers, and continuing his interests in a wide range of matters, including natural philosophy, economics, and ship design. He was a prominent man of influence in Restoration London and was a charter member of the Royal Society upon its incorporation in 1662.

Among his writings, Petty made several inquires and calculations pertaining to the growth of London. Consistent with the spirit of the Royal Society, he took a scientific approach, expressing himself in 'numbers, weights and measures,' although, by his own admission, some of his numbers were rough estimates. In *Verbum Sapienti* (1664) he estimated the wealth of London to be £16.66 million.[12] This was one-fifteenth of his total for the whole of England, comprising estimated values for lands, houses, personal estates, shipping, cattle, money, and goods. Twelve years later, in *Political Arithmetick* (1676), Petty claimed that the value of housing in London had doubled over the past forty years and that the city itself had doubled in size.[13] He also remarked that tradesmen working on buildings alone had earned some £4 million in the four years subsequent to the Great Fire, without any diminution of any other sort of work or economic activity.[14] In his later essay on the *Growth of the City of London* (1682), Petty presented calculations (possibly provided by the early demographer John Gaunt) based on burials and christenings to support his claim that London had doubled in size and reached a population of approximately 670,000.[15]

Petty also made limited attempts to explain the cause of the growth of London.[16] He noted that, from 1642 to 1650, many people moved into the city from the countryside seeking shelter from the Civil War; that, from 1650 to 1660, the Royalist political party relocated there as well; and that, with the Restoration in 1660, the royal household itself came to London, with no doubt a sizeable entourage. Petty, however, did not seem to think that these happenings were sufficient to explain London's increasing population. He wrote: 'I had rather quit even what I have above-said to the cause of London's Increase from 1642 to 1682, and put the whole upon some Natural and Spontaneous Benefits and Advantages that Men find by Living in great more than small Societies.' Later in the same essay he recognized the benefits of division of labour that occur in large cities, although he made no further connection between this and the growth of the city.[17]

A fitting, concluding comment by Petty on the growth of London after the Great Fire occurs in *Observations upon the Cities of London and Rome* (1687). The following comparison with both Paris and Rome attests to how great and powerful London had become. Petty writes: 'Since the great Fire of London, Anno 1666 about 7 parts of 15 of the present vast City hath been new built, and is with its People increased near one half, and become equal to Paris and Rome put together, the one being the Seat of the great French Monarchy, and the other of the Papacy.'[18]

With the hindsight of over three hundred years of economic thought, more can be said about London's growth after the Great Fire. Some clues to the process are perhaps apparent from the manner in which the rebuilding was financed. The kingdom was in great debt because of plague and war. So, to finance the rebuilding of churches and other public buildings, a tax on sea coal was introduced at one shilling per ton. This mechanism was meant to last ten years only, but the tax was soon raised to three shillings per ton and remained in place for over two hundred years. It was the investment in private buildings, however, that likely underlay much of the economic growth. The landlords were largely left to finance the rebuilding of homes, although assisted by their tenants in some cases. But where did they get the funding? One potential source might have been the goldsmiths – the bankers of the day – who were thought to have saved most of their riches before their premises were taken by fire. Indeed, money and goods worth about £1.2 million managed to be stored in the Tower of London for safekeeping from the fire. Yet it was also apparently common for citizens to hoard much of their wealth in money bags and chests, which they no doubt carried with them when fleeing the flames. For example, at their death, tradesmen in late Stuart London (1660–1714) left an average of £255 in cash, and merchants £671. So, in the time of a crisis, there were plenty of funds available for rebuilding. By investing their hoarded treasure in new buildings, Londoners recharged the economy while at the same time making use of wealth that was otherwise idle.

It is also clear that the rebuilding of London after 1666 provided an immense boost to economic growth, which in turn, in classic circular fashion, acted as a further stimulus to growth in the late seventeenth century and beyond. The Rebuilding Act of 1667 – largely the work of two men, the scientist Robert Hooke and the architect Christopher Wren, who were both friends and colleagues in the Royal Society – required that buildings be faced in brick and stone, established main streets that were wide enough to act as firebreaks, and removed some restrictive practices in the building trades. The act was also pioneering in its approach to infrastructure planning, including a provision to appoint a commissioner for sewers and paving.[19] The result of all this was an expansion in the construction, materials, and transportation sectors of London's economy. There is also an indication that commercial activities flourished because the new larger houses also served as shops, warehouses, and workhouses:

> The City was rebuilt according to new standards of construction and design. Never before had there been such wide-ranging control of building activity. The standardisation of house-building, with precise specification of ceiling heights, wall thicknesses, and materials, although it was a codification of accepted practice, was another of the City's pioneering of new

town planning techniques. It resulted in a City which was orderly and regular, but which was visually varied and never monotonous. Purged by the Fire of the remaining vestiges of the once numerous medieval town mansions of the aristocracy and gentry, the new London was also and above all a commercial City. The houses of its merchants and craftsmen were not just houses but shops and warehouse and workshops as well. The City's purpose built trading facilities were of an unprecedented scale and standard. Its inns, taverns and coffee houses served commercial functions as well as hospitable ones, and in many cases the entertainment became merely a convenient adjunct to business.[20]

A further aspect of the Great Fire was that it accelerated the breakdown of restricted trading practices. This was no doubt challenging in the short term, but long-term benefits may have resulted from increased competition. Although their power was waning, guilds, which maintained medieval oligopolistic trading practices, still largely controlled commerce in London and other cities. With the disaster of 1666, however, the need for change was unavoidable. While the fire was still burning, the king lifted the restrictions by which English boroughs could limit trading to their own freemen, thus enabling those who had been burnt out by the fire to practise their trades elsewhere. The removal of trading restrictions on non-Londoners was also necessary to help the city get back on its feet. The result of the king's decree was a significant decrease in the power of the guilds; indeed, at least four of the forty-four livery company halls destroyed in the fire were not rebuilt. The fire, then, destroyed not only the physical structure of the city but also its intricate web of business relationships, replacing the latter with something better suited to economic growth.

The response of London to the Great Fire helps to illuminate how its urban economy grew. Clearly, London's rising from the ashes of 1666 owed much to the strength of the national economy, but in particular the extent of the assets held by citizens and the resources of London's markets. Important too were the actions of the state, both in implementing far-sighted changes in the city's physical shape and in recognizing the value of competition to economic health. All of this is significant, to be sure, but how can the growth of cities be explained in a more comprehensive manner? How is it that the real income of citizens can continually increase year after year? In the previous two chapters, we focused on the growth of financial centres. Though the points made there concerning the role of markets are certainly key, they are not the whole picture. The process we are studying is a complicated, multi-faceted one driven by a variety of forces. The purpose of this chapter, therefore, is to add another dimension to the story by moving beyond financial centres to consider the factors that drive growth in all cities. Using a more macroeconomic approach than the microeconomic one followed in chapters 3 and 4, this chapter will first review existing theories of how economies in general, and cities in particular, grow. These will prove, however, to be lacking. It will be argued that even great works by the likes of Adam Smith and Jane Jacobs are insufficient to explain urban economic growth, because they focus on the production side of the economy. Hence, the discussion introduces the notion that urban form – that is, the physical shape of cities – can influence economic growth through its impact on citizens' consumption. When taken together with the role of markets, this element deepens our understanding of how cities grow.

The Productivity of Cities

Inquiries as to how urban prosperity can be fostered have a long history. One of the earliest, as we saw in chapter 1, was by the Greek Xenophon (c. 430–354 BC), author of *Oikonomics* (which translates as 'household or estate management') as well as a short article entitled 'On the Means of Improving the Revenues of the State of Athens.' In the latter work, Xenophon first attributes the prosperity of Athens to the excellence of the region's agriculture, boasting: 'For such as will not even grow in many countries bear fruit in perfection in Attica.'[21] Then he proceeds to suggest that prosperity can be enhanced in several ways. One is by being open and hospitable to foreigners. Particularly keen to attract and grant privileges to merchants and shipowners, he writes: 'It would be for our advantage and credit also, that such merchants and shipowners as are found to benefit the state by bringing to it vessels and merchandise of great account should be honoured with seats of distinction on public occasions, and sometimes invited for entertainments; for, being treated with such respect, they would hasten to return to us, as to friends, for the sake, not merely of gain, but of honour.'[22] In his discussion of the importance of catering to such merchants, Xenophon alludes to the central role of infrastructure: a fine and safe harbour, lodging houses for seamen, public houses of entertainment, and houses and shops for retail dealers. He also suggests that as much labour as can be spared should be employed in the nearby silver mine.

Lastly, he sees the avoidance of war as central to prosperity: 'For those states, assuredly, are most prosperous, which have remained at peace for the longest period.'[23]

If such strategies were followed, Xenophon was confident, the revenue of Athens would increase:

> Who, indeed, if the city were on the enjoyment of peace, would not be eager to resort to it, and shipowners and merchants most of all? Would not those who have plenty of corn, and ordinary wine, and wine of the sweetest kind, and olive oil, and cattle, flock to us, as well as those who can make profit from their ingenuity and by money-lending? Where would artificers, too, and sophists, and philosophers, and poets, and such as study their works, and such that desire to witness sacrifices, or religious ceremonies worthy of being seen and heard, and such as desire to make a quick sale or purchase of many commodities, obtain their objects better than at Athens?[24]

In modern times, rather than use the term revenue, economists have measured the gross domestic product (GDP) of cities, alternatively termed the gross metropolitan product (GMP). A city's GDP is the market value of the final goods and services that it produces. It is essentially the same as the total income of its residents with the addition of an allowance for deterioration of capital assets. Whether measured as the production of goods and services or as approximately equal to the income of citizens, GMP is an essential determinant of urban wealth.

Growth in urban wealth – that is, citizens' assets – and growth in income – or metropolitan product – are not the same thing, but they are interrelated. The wealth of a city increases when the net value of property and financial assets held by its citizens goes up. For the value of real estate to increase, either more buildings must be constructed or citizens must be able to afford higher rents. In either case this comes about only if the overall income of city residents increases. Similarly, for the value of citizens' holdings of stocks and shares to rise, there has to be an overall market expectation that economic growth will occur – increases in production come hand-in-hand with increases in consumption, which occurs when incomes rise. Thus, increases in urban wealth are inherently tied to economic growth.

To make a comparison between cities of different sizes, it is useful to study the per capita GDP of cities, which is also termed urban productivity. Of course, a more fundamental form of growth is measured by population, but for economic growth economists use per capita GDP. Measuring economic growth with GDP is not without problems. In some respects, it is really a measure of recorded economic activity, gauging income from activities whether they are desirable or not.[25] Moreover, it captures only paid activities, missing important things like household work. Some might ask whether increases in GDP really represent growth or merely represent an increased recording of activity, for example, because of increased female participation in the workforce. Nevertheless, given that since 1780 productivity has increased in real terms (i.e., allowing for inflation) by a factor of twelve in Western countries, there is clearly something significant to such growth.[26]

An interesting finding with respect to cities is that, in a given country, urban productivity tends to increase with city size. One study in the mid-1970s found that manufacturing industries in the New York region were 50 per cent more productive than those in a typical small region with a population of 50,000.[27] Some later studies questioned whether the size effect was so large and wrestled with the impact of industry size versus city-population size. Nevertheless, the overall finding from many studies is that urban productivity increases with city size.[28]

One concept that contributes to explaining the scale effect of urban productivity is agglomeration. In simple terms, firms located in close proximity to one another, as in cities, can save costs by sharing factors that are external to each firm. Consider a pizzeria serving lunches to employees from a mix of companies located in a bustling quarter of a city. Because of the sheer number of clients, the pizzeria can exploit economies of scale and serve well-priced lunches at a satisfactory profit. The provision of cheap lunches to employees does not in itself save their companies money. Consider, however, if just one of the companies moved to an isolated remote area. Unless the firm is very large, the pizzeria would find it unprofitable to set up next to the remote company and so it would be necessary for the company to provide cafeteria services to its employees, perhaps subsidizing them at its expense.

There are other examples of more substantial cost savings achieved through agglomeration. Companies located close together can reduce the costs of business services such as accounting, advertising, legal advice, management consulting, and computer expertise.[29] Companies within the same industry may reduce the costs of raw materials and other inputs to their businesses such as the cost of training labour.

Another important agglomeration effect is knowledge sharing. Go back to the employees from various companies sitting around the table at our pizzeria. Those from similar industries share knowledge of new technologies, good business practices, even inevitably their own inventions. Good ideas from one company are combined with those of others, making the overall local industry stronger. Imagine a group of 'techies' exchanging ideas on how to set up some new-fangled computer software as they feast on pizza over lunch. Perhaps such an agglomeration effect was what William Petty had in mind when he wrote on the natural and spontaneous advantages of men living in cities!

Another theory – known as the city-hierarchy theory – can also explain the higher productivity of large cities.[30] This theory also bears some relation to agglomeration, but the aspect to consider now is that, by virtue of their size, larger settlements have more specialists earning higher salaries. Take medical services as an example. Every settlement from a small town to a large city requires doctors. Not every small town has a hospital, though; these are typically in larger towns that provide hospital services to nearby smaller settlements. Further up the hierarchy, small cities may have larger hospitals offering more specialized services. Only when we arrive at mid-sized cities are medical schools likely to be found, attached to universities, which provide training for doctors. At the upper end of the city hierarchy there are also other establishments which serve the broader region around them, for example, international airports, state or provincial courts, large concert halls, and other entertainment venues. The key point is that people undertaking more specialized or responsible work at such establishments deserve and receive higher incomes. High court judges, university presidents, brain surgeons, airport directors, and so on do not live in small towns (unless they are within commuting distance of a city). Moreover, the headquarters of large companies are also in cities, so that is often where the presidents, CEOs, and vice-presidents live. Now this entails seriously large salaries. Overall, large cities at the top of the hierarchy will have larger proportion of citizens having high salaries. Thus, the urban productivity – income per capita – will be higher.

A third theory of urban productivity with roots in thermodynamics can also be entertained. Consider a vessel of any gas at some given temperature and pressure. As the molecules move around colliding with one another in the vessel, there are many ways in which they can be arranged. Thermodynamicists quantify the degree of disorder using *entropy*. Now, if double the quantity of the gas is placed in a vessel that is twice as large, at the same temperature and pressure, then it turns out that the entropy of the systems is more than double. What has this

got to do with the productivity of cities? Recall that GDP is in a simplistic sense a measure of paid activity. Large cities are more complex
than smaller ones, with more people, more locations to go to, and more
transportation routes between them. Therefore, just like a large vessel
of gas, large cities can be expected to have more activities per person
than smaller cities, that is, they have higher per capita GDP as a result
of their entropy.

It is tempting to ask which of these three theories of urban productivity is correct, but perhaps that is an inappropriate line of inquiry. The
three theories are not necessarily in competition; they do not contradict
one another. If it is accepted that cities are complex places, then perhaps
all three theories hold to some degree. Nevertheless, they are only explanations for why income per capita is higher in larger cities; they do
not fully explain how cities grow.

On this note, it is appropriate to mention the macroeconomic principle of the *circular flow of money*. It provides some basis for understanding the growth of cities and will also help demonstrate later how
many theories of economic growth are partial, that is, how we lack a
comprehensive theory of urban growth. At the heart of macroeconomic
theory are exchanges between two groups in an economy – households
and firms. Households provide labour to firms in return for wages.
Meanwhile, households also consume goods produced in return for
payments to firms. Thus, there are two circular flows – money flows
in one direction, and goods, services, and labour flow in the opposite
direction.

There is also a third agent – government – typically shown at the
centre of diagrams of the circular flow. This position is appropriate in
a national context. Governments play a major role in the circular flow
– taking in taxes on income and consumption, then spending on infrastructure, government services, and household benefits. The role of
government is equally significant in an urban context, but, since the
main financial flows are to national or regional governments, then perhaps the position at the centre of the diagram is less appropriate.

There are other flows into and out of the circular flow. On one side,
firms import and export goods and services; they also provide investments into the economy. Households may also receive some income
from outside the urban economy by way of their investments. A significant point in the circular flow is where the financial flows leave households – much of this is as consumption – but households can also save,
which essentially involves a flow into the banking sector. In a closed

economy, these savings would be equal to investments by firms. Urban economies, however, are very much open.

In order for the economy of a city to grow, all the main quantities in the circular flow must increase in per capita terms – output from firms, income to households, and the combination of savings and consumption. The next sections proceed to some theories of how this happens.

Scottish Enlightenment

On 4 July 1776, the eminent philosopher and historian David Hume held a farewell dinner at his home in Edinburgh. Hume was an enlightened liberal thinker who was sympathetic to the American cause of independence. Indeed, it has even been suggested that his terminol-.ogy was drafted into the Declaration of Independence during Benjamin Franklin's editing of Thomas Jefferson.[31] His dinner on 4 July, however, had no relation to American affairs, for it would have taken weeks for news of that day to reach London, let alone Edinburgh. Hume was dying, from what has since been suspected of being chronic ulcerative colitis, and he was throwing a goodbye party for his friends.[32]

Among Hume's guests that night was his close friend Adam Smith, a younger man by twelve years. It is hard to imagine what the conversation would have been about that evening. Smith, however, had just four months earlier seen the publication of his book *An Inquiry into the Nature and the Causes of the Wealth of Nations*. This celebrated book is still regarded as the most influential text on economics, at least in the English language. Given that it had taken twelve years to write and publish,[33] it might well have received some comment at the dinner table.

Economics was also a topic that Hume himself had written on. His philosophical studies of the nature of the human psyche convinced Hume that luxury spending was the most important factor driving the economy. He believed that labour was the basis of wealth, and that people needed luxury spending as an incentive to work. Smith, however, saw things differently. His doctrine put less emphasis on consumption, for he regarded investment in *capital* as key to economic growth. He saw less need for luxury spending to maintain demand, since it merely employed unproductive labour. Saving, and thus investment in capital goods, made use of productive labour, which 'adds to the value of the subject on which it is bestowed.'[34]

In the *Wealth of Nations*, Smith clearly explains the notion of capital, recognizing it as a component of *stock* and categorizing its various forms. In its original sense, a stock is a collection or accumulation of goods that a worker is able to produce from his labour, whether it be farming, manufacturing, or other employment.[35] Such stock can, when necessary, be exchanged for other goods. When a man possesses such a large amount of stock that he can maintain himself for years, he naturally seeks to derive revenue from his excess.[36] The stock can thus be considered to have two components: that which supplies the man's immediate consumption; and the *capital* from which revenues can be generated.

Two ways in which capital can be broadly employed are described in the *Wealth of Nations*.[37] When goods are raised, manufactured, or purchased, and subsequently sold for profit, such goods take on the form of *circulating capital*. Such capital leaves the holder in one form and returns in another, periodically being exchanged as cash. Goods exchanged by merchants and animals exchanged by farmers are of the circulating form of capital. The other form of capital is *fixed*. Such capital, whether it is the instruments of a shoemaker, the looms of a weaver, or the great furnaces and forges of an ironworks, can produce a profit without changing masters.

Fixed capital can further be classified in four categories: first, useful machines and instruments of trade; second, profitable buildings, such as shops, warehouses, workhouses, and farmhouses; third, improvements to land such as clearing, draining, enclosing, and manuring that make the land profitable for agriculture; and, finally, human capital: 'the acquired and useful abilities of all the inhabitants or members of society' achieved through education, study, or apprenticeship.[38]

There were, of course, several other elements to economic growth set out in the *Wealth of Nations*, some of which can be traced back to the French Enlightenment and others to the likes of Aristotle. In particular, Smith recognized the importance of the *division of labour* in economic growth. It is more efficient for labour to specialize and exchange goods than for us each to produce everything for ourselves. Division of labour, however, is limited by the size of the markets.[39] So Smith saw development of transport infrastructure as important for expanding markets.

It is of side interest to note Smith's assessment of the role of government. He is well known for his enthusiasm for the laissez-faire approach of letting the 'invisible hand' of the market operate for the benefit of all. Yet government was important, not only for defence and keeping law and order, but also for maintaining institutions and for public works.[40]

Smith considered transport infrastructure to yield insufficient profit to repay its expense of construction. So, given its enormous benefit to society, it was appropriate for infrastructure such as roads, bridges, and canals to be supplied by government. This does not mean that fees or tolls should not be used – Smith was in favour of these – but the Prince of Capitalism saw no role for private ownership of infrastructure!

Although it is perhaps often overlooked, Smith did also discuss urban economies in his famous book on nations. He observed that wages in cities were typically 20 to 25 per cent higher than those 'a few miles away.'[41] His explanation was that people in thriving cities have 'great stock' to employ and often must compete vigorously for workers, thereby raising wages.[42] This gives another explanation for higher urban productivity in large cities.

Smith also wrote on the natural exchange between cities and the countryside: 'The great commerce of every civilized society is that carried on between the inhabitants of the town and those of the country. It consists in the exchange of rude for manufactured produce, either immediately, or by intervention of money, or of some sort of paper which represents money. The country supplies the town with means of subsistence and the materials of manufacture. The town repays this supply by sending back a part of the manufactured produce to the inhabitants of the country.'[43]

Chapter III of book 3 is wonderfully entitled 'Of the Rise and Progress of Cities and Towns after the Fall of the Roman Empire.'[44] (The title may well have been influenced by Edward Gibbons's classic book on the decline of the Roman Empire, printed by Smith's publisher Strachan – also the publisher of Samuel Johnson's dictionary – just a few weeks before *The Wealth of Nations*.) In this section, Smith describes the gradual increase in city burghers' independence in return for their support of sovereigns in struggles against rival lords and barons. In the post-Roman era, the powerful landowners lived in rural fortified castles, and towns were inhabited by essentially servile tradesmen. A few free traders gained their rights in exchange for taxes to kings. These free city burghers gained in power, began to own land in cities, and, through incorporation, appointed magistrates, established town councils, passed by-laws, built city walls, and raised local militias. In areas such as modern-day Italy and Switzerland, the power of burghers was such that independent city-states emerged. A key economic aspect of these developments was that cities became safer places to accumulate *stock* away from the power of rural lords, or even sovereigns.

Smith's understanding of how capital investment contributes to economic growth has stood the test of time – and yet his classic work can only partially explain the growth of cities. How, for example, would he explain the incredible growth of London after the Great Fire? The breaking down of the guilds' restrictive trading practices might possibly have increased the size of markets, but surely this is insufficient to explain London's extraordinary economic success. One problem is that Smith's economic doctrine is somewhat static – and does not leave much room for innovation. Machines can be made more efficient in Smith's world, but they still produce the same type of goods. The growth of cities is an organic process that involves developing new types of products and services. The person who has arguably understood this best is Jane Jacobs.

Jacobs and New Forms of Production

One of the most original twentieth-century thinkers on the economic growth of cities is undoubtedly Jane Jacobs. In *The Economy of Cities*, Jacobs offers fascinating insights into the ways that urban economies function – at least from a production perspective. Much of the theory that will be developed in the next chapter is consistent with Jacob's view of cities, so it is useful to review her ideas here.

Jacobs's theory is that cities develop and expand through the creation of *new work*. She begins by recognizing that the division of labour is only a means of organizing existing work and that this alone is insufficient for economic growth.[45] Trade is important, but a city must do more than just export goods and services – it must continually grow exporting firms, that is, it must generate new kinds of work. Jacobs argues that it is the smaller, innovative firms rather than the larger ones that create new work.[46] Moreover, she asserts that these innovative firms typically exist only in cities, rather than rural locations, because they are fostered as a result of existing work in cities.[47] She concludes that cities do not grow by *preformation* – enlargement of what already exists – but by *epigenesis* – a process of gradual diversification and differentiation of the economy.[48]

Jacobs goes on to describe the major processes in a growing city's economy, which occur as related reciprocating systems.[49] First, a numerous and diverse collection of local firms supply goods and services to established exporting firms within the city. Second, some of the local supply firms begin to export their own work. With its growing ability to export, the city earns a substantial variety of imports. Third, however, the city begins to replace imported work through its own locally produced goods and services. This causes explosive growth, which, because of multiplier effects, makes room in the economy for entirely new types of goods and services. As a result, the city generates a new, large, and diverse range of exports. Some of these will compensate for older exports that may be lost through obsolescence or to local production in other cities or rural areas. In vibrant, growing cities, this process of generating new exports and replacing imports continues on and on.

An interesting aspect of Jacobs's theory, which perhaps runs counter to much of neoclassical economics, is that successful, growing cities are not efficient.[50] In order to be innovative, it is best for cities to have a diverse mix of firms, typically small in size. This may mean an inefficient dispersion of capital and reduced economies of scale, but, with the creation of more opportunities for trial and error, more firms likely to create new exports will emerge. By way of example, Jacobs offers a comparison of Manchester and Birmingham in the mid-nineteenth century.[51] Manchester was seen as an advanced city at the time because of its large efficient textile mills that dominated the economy. Birmingham, by contrast, was full of small firms doing bits-and-pieces work for other small firms. Yet, into the twentieth century, at least until 1969 when Jacobs was writing, Birmingham fared much the better of the two cities. Manchester suffered with the decline of the textile industry while Birmingham kept adding new work.

Jacobs's perspective on the growth of cities has withstood statistical tests remarkably well. One study of the growth of large industries in 170 US cities found that her theory better explained employment-growth patterns than two other well-established theories,[52] that of MIT/Harvard strategy guru Michael Porter and that based on the works of eminent economists Alfred Marshall, Kenneth Arrow, and Paul Romer. The diversity of geographically proximate industries and the amount of competition, it was concluded, offered a more convincing explanation of growth than specialization by geographically concentrated industries and local monopoly.

Keynes and Consumption

The great works of Adam Smith and Jane Jacobs offer important contributions to understanding the growth of cities, but they capture only half the picture. Consider Smith's classic example in which, through capital investment and division of labour, ten men could produce 48,000 pins per day, thereby replacing the work of at least 2400 men of similar ability.[53] The question to ask, however, is who wants all those pins anyway, and, moreover, what are the 2390 or more redundant pin makers to do now? Similarly, Jacobs might argue that import replacement is key to the growth of cities, but why does the city want the imports in the first place?

The theories of economic growth that we have reviewed so far have essentially focused on firms and their production activities. It has been taken as given that consumers will have increased demands for the greater quantities of goods and services provided by increased productivity or new work. But is this true? To answer that question, we need to return to Hume's dinner table on the night of 4 July 1776, listening this time not to Adam Smith but to the host himself. In contrast to Smith's economic reasoning, David Hume's put far more emphasis on consumption. It was through opulence, the material desire of man, the desire for luxury goods, that people were encouraged to work. Hume's assertion that the *love of gain* drove labour to work had been made by others before him, by Petty for example, but attention to consumption in economic growth largely disappeared in the 150 years after Hume's death. Following Adam Smith, classical economists such as David Ricardo, Jean-Baptiste Say, and John Stuart Mill paid little attention to the fundamental nature of consumption, assuming that *supply created its own demand*. It was not until the work of John Maynard Keynes that a fuller macroeconomic theory of consumption was developed.

Keynes was arguably the most influential economist of the twentieth century.[54] Born in 1883, he attended Eton before enrolling at King's College, Cambridge, in 1902. He then briefly entered the British civil service, with a position in the India Office, before Alfred Marshall encouraged him to return to Cambridge as a lecturer in economics. In 1915, with the First World War under way, Keynes was summoned back to London to work in the Treasury office. It was through his work there on war finances that Keynes first gained notoriety. He became the Treasury's representative at the 1919 Paris Peace Conference and criticized the Treaty of Versailles as unjust and economically counter-productive (it placed a huge financial burden upon Germany, while removing her ability to repay her debt). Keynes went public with his condemnation of the treaty and resigned his public office. In the interwar years, Keynes spent his time between London, where he held several financial directorships, and Cambridge, where he was developing much of his revolutionary work in economics. When the Second World War broke out, Keynes, even though he had suffered a severe heart attack in 1937, once again returned to serve his country. He was one of Churchill's principal economic advisers guiding wartime finances. His economic principles had also begun to influence US presidents. Indeed, in 1944, the now Lord Keynes was the leading British economist at the Bretton Woods conference, which laid the foundations of the post-war international financial system, and in 1946 he was key to the negotiation of a $3.25-billion US loan to Britain.

Keynes's most famous work, *The General Theory of Employment, Interest and Money*, published in 1953 (but first drafted in 1934), was primarily concerned with developing a theory to 'discover what determined volumes of employment.'[55] His brilliant contribution was an interpretation of the macroeconomic circular flow of money by which employment was determined by the equilibrium between aggregate supply and aggregate demand. Aggregate supply describes how the total output of a community varies as a function of employed labour; aggregate demand is the total demand for goods in an economy. Keynes's view of aggregate demand was particularly novel; he argued that companies need to employ labour both to provide for a community's level of consumption and to generate new investment, that is, gross capital formation.[56] Investment, which Keynes argued is usually equal to savings, is required to provide for future consumption. Keynes concluded that 'employment can only increase pari passu with an increase in investment; unless, indeed, there is a change in the propensity to consume.'[57] He goes on to note that consumption is 'the sole end object of economic activity.'[58] This is a key point to consider in developing an understanding of how urban economies grow.

Keynes's theory of how consumption levels are determined was revolutionary. He observed that a community's level of consumption primarily depends on its level of income. He defined 'marginal propensity to consume' to be the rate of change of consumption with respect to a change in the income of a community.[59] Keynes noted several factors that would influence the marginal propensity to consume. These included objective circumstances such as changes in the difference between income and net income, for example, because of taxes,[60] and windfall changes in capital assets (such as the South Sea bubble). He also added that a community's consumption would depend partly on 'the subjective needs and psychological propensities and habits of the individuals composing it and the principles on which income is divided between them.'[61]

In theory, the marginal propensity to consume could be any value between 0 and 100 per cent, but Keynes suggested that a community of the 1950s would consume not much less than 80 per cent of its real income – in other words, savings would be about 20 per cent.[62] He noted, however, that the marginal propensity to consume might not be constant. Poorer communities will consume nearly all of their income. As a community's income increases, Keynes suggested, it will wish to consume a gradually smaller proportion of that income.[63]

Economists working since Keynes typically divide consumption into two components. The first is *autonomous consumption*, which is spending that communities must undertake to meet their basic needs, such as sustenance and shelter. It is consumption that takes place regardless of the community's income; it may entail some individuals borrowing, receiving food stamps, social assistance, and so on. The second component is more concerned with luxury or non-essential consumption. This is financed through some portion of the community's disposable (that is, after-tax) income. The proportionality constant, borrowed from Keynes, is known as the *marginal propensity to consume*. Together, these two components provide the result that communities with higher incomes will save a greater proportion of their income – a result similar to that expected by Keynes.

Consumption and Growth

Having provided some background on economists' understanding of consumption, we can now return to the central question of how economic growth occurs, particularly in the context of cities. The first point to be made is that per capita GMP can increase in cities only if citizens increase their consumption, or savings, or the net of both. Moreover, it is an increase in *autonomous consumption associated with urban form* that largely explains the historical growth in per capita GMP.[64]

The evolution of highly consumptive cities is obviously related to technological change, which is already well recognized as being fundamental to economic growth. The role of technology and capital investment in economic growth is recognized in the twentieth-century works of Joseph Schumpeter, Robert Merton Solow, and Paul Romer. It is clear, however, that the application of technology to achieve higher productivity at the level of the firm is necessary, but not sufficient, to explain economic growth. Firms can use technology as a substitute for labour and thereby increase output per employee, that is, labour productivity. This may be necessary in a competitive industry in which the new technology helps companies to lower costs. Yet, unless the labour that is made redundant by technological substitution finds work elsewhere, the income of the community has not increased overall. The displaced labour must find an alternative means of income. A small part of it might be employed in capital investment (manufacturing the machines that replace other workers), but otherwise the redundant labour will find income only if there is an increase in the community's overall consumption.

A similar argument applies to the application of technology in increasing the size of markets. Among the various technologies that have been linked to economic growth since the Industrial Revolution, those relating to transportation and communications have arguably been the most important. Canals, steam-powered trains, automobiles, and airplanes; telegraphs, telephones, satellites, and the Internet – these technologies have been fundamental to economic growth. As Adam Smith explained (before the invention of most of the above), such infrastructure increases productivity by increasing the size of markets and enabling the division of labour. But again it must be recognized that overall economic growth can then occur only if the resulting redundant labour is employed in building the infrastructure or by providing for an economy's higher demand for consumption.

For a new technology to contribute to economic growth, it must not only increase the competitiveness of firms but also, in doing so, pass on additional costs to consumers such that their overall expenditure increases. Moreover, while some of the increased expenditure may be considered favourably by consumers – for instance, if it is for a desired luxury item – it may more often be the case, or evolve to become the case, that society becomes locked in to the new technology, such that it is indispensable. In other words, the technology evolves to become part of autonomous consumption.

A first example can be provided from the current age of information technology. The Internet has been around since the 1960s, developed by the US military as a means of electronic communication. Computers have been around even longer, although these were rather large and cumbersome at first. The development of the personal computer (PC) in the 1980s, however, heralded a fundamental technological revolution. Not everyone saw it coming. A famous statement, today passed around on the Internet, is that of Ken Olsen, president, chairman, and founder of Digital Equipment Corporation (a computer manufacturer), remarked in 1977 that 'there is no reason anyone would want a computer in their home.' Digital missed out on the PC market and shortly went out of business. Even Bill Gates, the founder of the highly successful Microsoft Corporation, is rumoured to have said something to the effect that '64 K is more than enough memory for anyone's needs'! He had yet to catch on to the idea, invented by Microsoft's competitor Apple, that software to create 'graphical user interfaces' (which allow users to interact with electronic devices with images rather than keyboard commands) would turn out to be key to society's mass adoption of the personal computer.

Let us not be too hard on Olsen or Gates, though. At the time of their remarks, they were actually right! There really was no need for anyone to have a personal computer in 1977. Olsen just lacked foresight. Roll on to the mid-1990s, with increasing computer power and the development of HTML and the Mosaic browser, and suddenly Internet and PC technologies had combined to create the World Wide Web. Sitting in front of personal computers, we were able to access and exchange information with millions of websites around the globe. The IT revolution was upon us.

It did not take long for business to recognize the power of this technological revolution. Banks, for example, began to provide Internet banking services. It was cost- effective for them; they laid off staff and closed down branches. Many other companies, too, found ways to save costs and become more productive by use of the Internet. They all, of course, relied on the fact that almost everyone now had a PC – it was an indispensable item of household expenditure. E-mail, which had been in use since the 1960s, had become completely pervasive. Movies, books, games, and videos were now accessible over the Internet, exploiting ever-increasing computer power. The combination of Internet and PCs created substantial new industries, with jobs from chip manufacturing to software programming and computer technical support. Meanwhile, the PC had surreptitiously become part of households' autonomous consumption.

As new and exciting as the Internet revolution may have been, its effects were arguably no more significant than some previous technological revolutions. The ability to participate in a video conference on the other side of the Atlantic is quite impressive, but the breakthroughs achieved by the Atlantic telegraph cable and the jet airplane were just as substantial; the former reduced the communication time between New York and London from a few days to a few seconds, while the latter reduced transatlantic travel time to three or four hours by Concorde passenger jet. Then again, perhaps like Ken Olsen, we are guilty of a lack of foresight and the Internet's greatest impact has yet to be realized.

In terms of cities, however, the technology that has had an enormous impact is clearly the automobile. As Henry Ford bluntly put it, 'The automobile, which may have been a luxury when first put out, is now one of the absolute necessities of our latter day civilization.'[65] In short, the use of the automobile is so pervasive in most Western cities that it has become part of autonomous consumption – and thereby has increased the GMP of cities. To add substance to this argument, the next section provides a comparative example.

Freiburg and Chula Vista

The cities of Freiburg, Germany, and Chula Vista, California, are both relatively affluent, but when it comes to transportation planning they are poles apart. The medieval city on the edge of the Black Forest and the growing fringe city in San Diego County both have populations of close to 200,000. Over the past thirty years, the two cities have pursued drastically different urban design practices, leading to remarkably different levels of automobile use.

Freiburg, which means 'Free or Independent City,' was founded as a free-market town in the twelfth century. In 1368 it became part of the Habsburg Empire; indeed, the Habsburg coat of arms still adorns the city's Historisches Kaufhaus – a historical marketplace building completed in 1530. Other prominent buildings in the city's core are a Gothic cathedral built of red sandstone and the Albert-Ludwigs University founded in 1457. Today, Freiburg is somewhat of an *eco-city*. It is home to solar-power industries and its citizens are known for cycling and recycling.

The first ten houses in Chula Vista, meaning 'Beautiful View,' were not built until 1889, and the city was not incorporated until 1911. Nevertheless, by a quirk of history, the Rancho del Rey lands upon which the city sits also became part of Charles V's Habsburg Empire, just like Freiburg. The lands were claimed by the Spanish following Juan Rodríguez Cabrillo's arrival in San Diego harbour in 1542. In the early twentieth century, Chula Vista became one of the world's largest lemon-growing centres. During the First World War, the city produced some 21,000 tonnes of gunpowder for the British government. The population of the city began to rise significantly after the Rohr Aircraft company established itself there in 1941.

In the mid-1970s, concerned about traffic congestion and quality of life in its downtown core, the city of Freiburg took steps to restrict automobile use in its centre.[66] At first this involved closing a major north–south traffic route to motor vehicles, which subsequently led to the banning of automobiles in the city centre, high parking fees, and a prohibition on the construction of multi-storey parking garages. To provide access to the city centre, Freiburg built new streetcar lines and promoted walking and cycling. Nor was this all. Efforts to encourage alternatives to the automobile were also made in the suburban areas lying away from the city centre. The suburb of Rieselfeld, was planned to house 12,000 people on the city's western edge as a mixed-use, mixed-income development with single-family homes and apartment buildings of up to five storeys. The density of the development (68.5 persons/acre) was sufficiently high to extend an electric streetcar line from the centre to Rieselfeld. Moreover, shops, markets, and offices were developed at locations along the streetcar line, reducing the need for automobiles.

The result of Freiburg's planning policies was a shift in transportation away from cars. The number of cars registered in the city actually rose from 62,000 in 1979 to 78,286 in 1989, but the amount of vehicular traffic was unchanged at 232,000 car trips per day. All of the growth in transportation activity was accounted for by Freiburg's new transit systems and other sustainable modes. From 1976 to 1996, trips by public transit rose from 22 to 28 per cent, and by bicycle from 18 to 29 per cent; meanwhile, the share of trips by car fell from 60 to 43 per cent. As a former deputy mayor explained, 'The aim of Freiburg traffic policy is ... not the utopia of ousting the car from our reality, but ... pursuing policies of alternatives, creating conditions where the use of cars can be kept to a minimum.'[67]

Chula Vista also has a major north–south road running through its centre called the Interstate 805, which very much remains open to vehicular traffic. To the west of the I-805, the older (pre-1980s) side of the city is fairly typical of most American cities of its age, developed primarily around the automobile. It is predominantly composed of single-family detached houses and has a density of around 12.2 persons/acre. In 1990, 86 per cent of trips were taken by automobiles, 5 per cent by transit, and 9 per cent by other modes.

The post-1980s development to the east side of I-805 is an even more extreme example of an auto-dependent suburb. The density is just 5.6 persons/acre. Moreover, geographers S. Ryan and J.A. Throgmorton describe how, through the design of the street network for automobile travel, use of other modes has been thwarted:

> Many of the street network characteristics that facilitate automobile travel in the east, make travel by other modes inconvenient. Several six-lane primary arterials form the backbone of the street network in the east. Many of the developments along these arterials have only one point of access to the arterial street network. Each of the three completed neighborhoods in the East Lake project, for example, has only two points of access to the arterial network. Local streets inside the East Lake neighborhoods provide little internal connectivity. These factors make it difficult for pedestrians to access transit stops along the arterials. In addition, auto-speeds along the high-capacity arterials in the east make bicycle and pedestrian travel uncomfortable.[68]

With such an auto-focused design, a mere 1.7 per cent of trips occur by transit in eastern Chula Vista; 93 per cent of all trips are by automobile.

Just as Freiburg is a clean, attractive city, nestled in Germany's black forest, eastern Chula Vista is no doubt a desirable place to live. It is the sort of city that many Americans aspire to, with 'the quiet, safety and peace of semi-rural environments combined with the convenience of nearby urban amenities.'[69] With large detached houses typically spread out over 0.5- to 1-acre lots, here at last, in Chula Vista, California, we arrive at the American city envisaged by William Penn for Philadelphia, over three hundred years ago. Only, if you wish to go anywhere, you'd best take your car.

Consumptive Urban Form

The evolution of auto-dependent cities has had profound economic effects, which may be far greater than most economists recognize. Many people live in urban environments where basic activities like shopping for groceries, going to school, visiting a doctor, or simply getting a haircut require access to a car. Even those seeking exercise will get in the car to drive to the gym! Furthermore, given that many workers require use of a car for the tortuous trip to work – to make an income – it is clear that the car is a necessity for many urban dwellers.

Some might rightly argue that automobile ownership is a desirable thing, a luxury that people aspire to. This certainly was the case several decades ago – and it is still partially true today. After all, people spend significant amounts on luxury cars; we don't all drive Ford Fiestas! The sale price of a car clearly has an autonomous component – the price of a basic car – and a marginal component reflecting perhaps some additional functionality like quicker acceleration or space but mainly luxury and prestige.

Of course, car ownership also entails consumption of a whole range of other things, like gasoline, insurance, maintenance, parts, and parking. As such, the automobile systems in cities create employment for a wide variety of people: car salesmen, road- construction workers, gas-station workers, insurance brokers, mechanics, and even our beloved parking attendants. In many respects, the design of cities has made such employment a necessity, and many people receive an income because of our dependence on automobiles.

From the perspective of governments too, the auto-dependent city is a windfall. Not only do governments receive income tax from all the auto-related jobs, but then there is the sales taxes on the cars (new and used), the gasoline taxes, parking revenues for local government, and so on. Some of the revenues are required to build and maintain roads, but these turn out to be a small fraction of what is taken in. For example, in 1998, in the Greater Toronto Area (GTA), spending on roads by all levels of government was about $1 billion.[70] This may seem a lot, but in the same year residents of the GTA spent $14.8 billion on automobile-based transportation! This comprised $7.2 billion on vehicle purchases, $3.7 billion on fuel, $2.5 billion on maintenance and repair, and $1.45 billion on other insurance costs. Incidentally, spending on public transit, capital and operating, was about $1.5 billion that year. So what we really have is a virtuous cycle again; all government has to do is slap down some tarmac with a few bridges here and there and tax the public as it consumes.

The term *virtuous cycle* is perhaps unfortunate, since there is plenty of Ruskin's *ilth* associated with urban automobiles. Returning to the GTA example, in approximately the same year, 1998, there were about 98,000 traffic accidents, causing 220 deaths and 40,000 injuries.[71] Air pollution associated with road vehicles gave rise to about 400 premature mortalities and 1600 hospitalizations, just in the central city of Toronto alone. Annual greenhouse-gas emissions associated with automobile use in the GTA were of the order of fifteen megatons of CO_2. But, of course, dealing with such problems also provides jobs for doctors, coroners, body-shop repair workers, and research scientists – such is the nature of *ilth*.

The sprawling urban form that occurred in the second half of the twentieth century also entails high levels of consumption in sectors other than transportation. Automobile-based urban design has enabled lot sizes to grow, and hence house sizes are bigger. In the United States, the average single detached house increased from around 1100 square feet in the 1940s and 1950s to 2340 square feet in 2002.[72] House sizes more than doubled, and, given shrinking family sizes, the living area per family member actually increased by a factor of three. The mass of construction material – lumber, sheathing, and concrete – in homes is also estimated to have increased by a factor of three. Homes of the year 2000 are built to higher energy standards than those of mid-century, but, whether they are in Boston or St Louis, they use about 50 per cent more energy because of the increase in their size.[73] Of course, beyond the greater consumption of materials and energy in today's larger homes there is all the other stuff – paint, carpets, bathtubs, furniture, electrical and electronic equipment, garden shrubs, and paving stones. And don't forget all the clothes and shoes in the super-sized walk-in closets.

Now a naive economist might say that the increase in house size in American cities, and elsewhere, is simply a *result of* the increased wealth of these cities; however, there is more to it. The increase in house size is *part of* the economic growth, not just a result of it. Indeed, what I've described is perhaps the most significant virtuous cycle underlying economic growth in the second half of the twentieth century. Governments pay for arterial roads, water mains, and sewers in the countryside around our cities, developers construct neighbourhoods of palaces, and free-spending households move in with their 2.6 family members and 2.1 motor vehicles. The highly consumptive lifestyle associated with this urban form creates plenty of jobs. Then, whether it is through gasoline taxes, property taxes, or income taxes, all the above processes yield substantial revenues for governments, a small part of which is ploughed back into more pipes and roads.

By following this simple recipe over the past fifty years or so, the proportion of urban dwellers living in highly consumptive, auto-dependent city neighbourhoods has increased decade over decade. Thus, the fundamental process underlying the economic growth of cities has actually entailed their physical growth.

Robinson and Capital

The role of infrastructure and urban form is generally missing from most theories of economic growth, although there are glimpses of it. Keynes, for example, raises the following question, which is worth dwelling on: 'What will you do when you have built all the houses and roads and town halls and electric grids and water supplies and so forth which the stationary population of the future can be expected to require?'[74] In posing this question, Keynes alludes to the notion of a stagnant economy where all the capital investment, including government spending on infrastructure, has been made. Is such an economy possible and how would it be arrived at? There are several answers to these questions.

First, it should be recognized that, globally, urban populations continue to rise at a rapid rate. Where cities are growing, both in the developed and in the developing world, the form of the cities is often auto-dependent sprawl. In other words, houses, roads, town halls, electric grids, and water infrastructure continue to be built. Second, though, the scenario described by Keynes has, to some extent, come to fruition in some Western cities. In some parts of those countries where populations are relatively constant, much of the contemporary energy-supply systems, water pipes, and, to a lesser degree, housing was completed by the 1970s. Of course, some new infrastructure is still being developed, but, compared to the post–Second World War decades, infrastructure development in well-established Western cities has been modest. At the same time, Western economies have undergone a transformation of sorts, with less industrial production and a rise in service-sector jobs. So perhaps the answer to Keynes's question is the rise of the service economy.

Third, it is apparent that capital still has to be maintained. Whether it is machinery operated by ongoing private enterprises or infrastructure owned by governments, maintenance, repair, and replacement require substantial financial investments. Many cities throughout the world today struggle with the upkeep of their infrastructure systems. The market for rehabilitation of civil-engineered infrastructure in North America is as large as that for new infrastructure, even without considering a large suspected shortfall in maintenance budgets. Keynes himself recognized that providing net new capital investment is increasingly difficult the more capital there is to maintain.[75]

Then again, the problems of maintaining infrastructure are not at all new. Recall once more the 14 aqueducts of Rome, 317 miles in length, started around 300 BC, with major additions by emperors Augustus, Claudius, and Trajan. Urban historian Peter Hall makes a pertinent observation on the reign of Hadrian: 'The reign of Hadrian was unspectacular in terms of construction, but significant in maintaining the system: less than twenty years after Trajan's death the big conduits were again in disrepair, with leaking channels, broken bridges, and unstable arches; under Hadrian they were reconstructed and restored, and across the Campagna long lines of reinforcing arches and walls supported the older structures. And this reflects the basic problem: the aqueducts presented serious maintenance problems and often required major repairs.'[76]

A fourth answer to Keynes's question is that new forms of capital continue to develop through the evolution of technology, as Schumpeter recognized. The fifty years or so since Keynes put the question has seen the development of a vast range of technologies: computers, satellites, lasers, the Internet, and so on.

Given all of this, it would seem that the challenge of developing a theory of the growth of cities requires attention to capital formation, capital maintenance, technology change, and evolving urban form. Several theories have already been discussed, all of which offer insights into the growth of cities, but there is one more important work to consider, Joan Robinson's *The Accumulation of Capital*. Like Keynes's theory, Robinson's was not specifically developed for cities, but its findings are applicable to urban economies. Moreover, since Robinson is concerned with the growth of capital – and not just income – her findings offer potential understanding of the growth of urban wealth.

The Accumulation of Capital is a prime example of the discipline of economics. Robinson is quick to recognize the intricacies and complexities of real economies and is somewhat sceptical of notions of equilibrium, but she recognizes that simplified economic models can offer valuable insights. Her own model is qualitatively described, at least in this particular book, though, as would be expected of an economist, it is structured and coherent. Her assumptions are clearly and methodically presented and many are softened as the treatise progresses.

Robinson's simplest model provides the most central findings of her work. She considers an economy comprising two classes of people: workers, who provide all the labour, and entrepreneurs, who essentially own all the capital of firms. The simple model assumes that all the consumption of goods is attributed to the workers. (This could essentially mean that the number of entrepreneurs is small, but the assumption is relaxed later in the book.) The economy is assumed to be strictly laissez-faire, with no role for government. It is also considered to be closed (initially), meaning there is no trade. With respect to labour, however, the economy is essentially open, with the potential to recruit labour from a neighbouring self-sufficient peasant economy. It is also important to note that the workers can be employed either in the production of consumable goods or in the manufacture of capital equipment.

The relationship between the wages of workers and the profits of entrepreneurs is an important determinant of the accumulation of capital. The output of consumer goods has to be greater than the wages paid to workers making consumer goods in order for entrepreneurs to make profits. Without profits, there is no capital investment. Moreover, since capital equipment will deteriorate over time, zero profit would mean a gradual decline in capital. When profits are made, these translate into wages for workers employed in the manufacture of capital equipment. Thus, in the simple model, the total sale of consumable goods is equal to the sum of the wages for labour producing goods for consumption and wages for labour producing capital machinery.

Robinson describes how two types of stagnation in capital accumulation can arise, largely depending on wage rates. If wages are too low, barely providing subsistence, then consumption will also be low, and thus entrepreneurs do not have the necessary incentives to invest. Robinson notes a paradox of capitalism: 'Each entrepreneur individually gains from a low real wage in terms of his own product, but all suffer from the limited market for commodities which a low real-wage entails.'[77] If, alternatively, wages are so high that they approach the level of output, then entrepreneurs will not make sufficient profit to maintain investment in capital and thus accumulation falls.

There are potentially steady paths. If the ratio of accumulation to the stock of capital, the rate of profit, and the real wage is constant, then in theory accumulation can go on indefinitely. Note, however, that this assumes no technical change, so that in fact output per head is constant; that is, there is no real growth. This steady state also requires population to grow at about the same rate as capital accumulation. If, alternatively, the total labour force remains constant, then a steady state might be reached where all labour is employed in producing goods for consumption while capital is maintained at a constant level. Robinson describes this as a *state of economic bliss*, where consumption is at its highest sustainable level given a fixed level of technology.

Introducing technical change into the model, Robinson identifies conditions by which stable economic growth can occur.[78] The stock of capital, that is, machinery for production, has to grow at a rate commensurate with the increase in output per person to achieve steady employment.[79] Competition must also be such that prices move relative to money wages, with real wages rising to meet the 'ever growing output of the ever growing stock of capital.'[80] Without disturbance from political events and with entrepreneurs who remain optimistic about the future, it would be theoretically possible to have stable economic growth. Robinson describes this as a 'golden age' – a mythical state that she recognizes is not likely to occur.[81]

In her later work, Robinson also describes a 'bastard golden age' as one in which every scrap of consumption out of profits is directly at the expense of accumulation.[82] What she is suggesting is that it is possible to have *too much* consumption in an economy. In the short run, output can be high and many people gainfully employed, but unless there is sufficient saving and hence investment, there is no accumulation of capital. This is an important point and one to which we will return in chapter 7: *consumption* is an equal partner to *production* in the growth of cities. Is it possible for cities to develop such highly consumptive urban forms that their wealth is diminished in the long term? Might the Chula Vista model be proved wrong, and the Freiburg model right, in the twenty-first century?

Conclusion

Residents of cities are more productive and have higher average incomes than their country cousins. This could simply be a result of agglomeration effects, the higher place of cities in a hierarchy relative to other settlements, and/or the complexity of cities stemming from sheer size. It might also be argued that cities are centres of knowledge and innovation and thus attract smart and highly skilled workers, and perhaps that competition for such workers is such as to raise wages. Historically, it may also be the case that cities were safe places to accumulate stock and thus begin Gras's four-phase development process, leading to their emergence as financial centres, which was discussed in chapter 4. All of the above may help explain why city residents have higher incomes, but to understand fully how cities grow we must consider other factors as well.

From Xenophon to William Petty to Jane Jacobs and others, many have inquired as to the growth of cities. Several theories, all offering important insights, have been reviewed here. Can we, by piecing these together, provide a fuller understanding of the growth of cities? Increased productivity through capital investment and the division of labour, as famously described by Adam Smith, is certainly important. To this may be added Jane Jacobs's recognition that growth also involves *new work*, which cities generate by epigenesis. Through Keynes's insights into macroeconomic processes, though, we can recognize that growth of cities must also entail increased consumption. Some of this increased demand no doubt comes from the desire for luxury, as argued by David Hume. But there is more to it than that. The level of consumption in cities is also a reflection of urban form. Cities evolve such that certain technologies become locked in, necessitating high levels of consumption for urban survival. The auto-dependent cities of the twentieth century are a prime example.

Is there a theory that fully explains the growth of cities? Keynes's macroeconomics certainly helps in that it brings the production and consumption sides together. It captures the macroeconomic circular flow of money, but herein lies a problem: a complete explanation of urban growth requires a theory that breaks out of the macroeconomic cycle. Such a theory must explain how aggregate demand and supply increase together over the long term in an urban economy, not just how they reach equilibrium.

The question still remains as to how a theory of urban growth that captures phenomena such as capital formation, capital maintenance, technology change, and evolving urban form might be developed. The work of Joan Robinson, not specifically developed for cities, has certainly made progress in this direction. Robinson made a well-positioned, fine slice through a complex world and offered some enlightening findings about the growth of economies. Her models, however, are abstract and idealized; they are simplified down to reveal essential dynamics but still leave a need to postulate a fuller theory to describe the growth of complex economies.

Here the story of London's growth after the Great Fire of 1666 – interconnected as it is with far-reaching changes to the city's physical shape – offers helpful hints. By clearly demonstrating the ties between infrastructure and economic growth, London's rebirth in the late seventeenth century underlines the complexity of urban economies, a complexity so great that cities resemble not things but living organisms, in all their diversity and intricacy. If there is a kernel of truth in this analogy, perhaps it supplies the key to the theory we are seeking. Such is the challenge that we take up in the next chapter.

6 The Ecology of Urban Economies

The Mecca of the economist is economic biology rather than economic dynamics.

Alfred Marshall[1]

Driving through downtown Detroit, a keen observer can spot trees and shrubs sprouting from the roofs and ledges of skyscrapers. Two hundred and forty miles away, in Chicago, the city has an aggressive green-roofs agenda, exemplified by the 20,300 square feet of garden on the roof of city hall. Growing vegetation on roofs is all the rage these days, as green-building designers seek innovative ways to reduce energy demands, retain storm water, and make our cities more adaptable to climate change. The cases of Detroit and Chicago, however, are fundamentally different. The tree-topped skyscrapers of central Detroit are not some architect's bold design for saving the planet – far from it. The growth in vegetation is nature's response to the abandonment and decay of the city's towers. The vacant skyscrapers are just some of the many relics of the spectacular decline – some might say the *death* – of the city of Detroit.

When the French founded Fort Pontchartrain du Détroit in 1701, it was but a small garrison and trading post set against a forested lakefront landscape. The land where the city lies today was densely forested, likely populated with beech and sugar maple, black ash or mixed hardwood swamps, a few conifers, and perhaps a few patches of wet prairie.[2] The local natives, Ottawa, Huron, and Potawatomi, cleared a few trees to plant corn, trapped fish, and hunted game. The soggy woodlands were rich with wildlife such as 'badger, bear, fisher, fox, mink, muskrat, porcupine, rabbit, raccoon, weasel, wild-cat, wolf and woodchuck.'[3] In 1760 the English took over the fort and soon fought a three-year-long battle, known as Pontiac's Rebellion, against the local Ottawa – a foreshadowing perhaps of racial conflicts to follow. The outpost then became part of the United States under the 1794 Treaty of London, also known as Jay's Treaty.

Detroit's initial growth towards becoming an industrial centre began with the 1825 opening of the Erie Canal. Its strategic position on the headwaters of Lake Erie enabled Detroit to become a key port for the exploitation of Michigan's substantial natural resources, in iron, copper, and lumber. A shipbuilding industry soon developed and the manufacture of railroad cars followed. By the end of the century, the city had spawned a rich network of related wood- and metal-working industries. Particularly important for the subsequent rise in automobile manufacturing was the existence of a subcontracting tradition, by which many small, independent enterprises had the tools and skills to manufacture subcomponents of final products.[4]

The city's emergence as the world's leading centre for manufacturing automobiles was remarkably rapid. As an infant industry with few entry barriers, many short-lived automobile production companies started up and fizzled out. From 1902 to 1926, some 169 new companies were formed in the United States, but 139 of them disappeared; the median life was just seven years.[5] In 1900 New England companies focusing on steam-powered and electric cars were in the lead; Michigan was ranked lower than seventh among the states in terms of automobiles produced.[6] Detroit, however, had a sufficiently high number of pioneering entrepreneurs – men like David Dunbar Buick, Horace and John Dodge, Henry Ford, Charles Brady King, Henry M. Leland, and Ransom E. Olds – who were able to learn from each others' trials and errors. These men were also lowering their costs by assembling similar parts – springs, ball bearings, and so on – made by assorted manufacturers in the city. Such agglomeration effects soon drew others, such as Packard (originally based in Ohio), to move their production to Detroit. Moreover, the city had well-established financial resources and bankers with good business sense. By the end of 1903, Michigan was producing half of the vehicles in the United States, and Detroit was established as the centre of an innovative cluster;[7] it was the Silicon valley of the early twentieth century.

Among all of Detroit's automobile entrepreneurs, Henry Ford was particularly special. In some respects, he did not actually invent anything new. Even his methods of mass production had been previously established – applied to sewing machines, for example.[8] He did, however, apply mass production to a much larger product and combined it with a modular approach to manufacturing. Ford's marketing strategy was brilliant. Unlike the east coast manufacturers who were producing touring cars for the top of the market, Ford focused on basic, rugged cars for the market's lower end, particularly targeting farmers. In producing lower-cost cars, he was following the likes of Oldsmobile and Cadillac, who were producing cheap 'runabouts.' Ford, however, learned from the experiments of those who went before him, and in the Model T he produced a cheap car that was also of high quality.[9]

Adding to Ford's business savvy was an enlightened understanding of macroeconomics. He recognized that substantial profit could be made from large-volume and low-margins sales, and he continued to increase his volume by pushing his prices down. Yet Ford did not lower his prices by squeezing his labour costs. On the contrary, he surrounded himself with exceptional engineers and hired highly skilled workers, and insisted on paying all of them well. His reasoning was that, by paying high wages, he increased the consuming power of his workers and, via multiplier effects, that of the community at large. Thus, he increased the demand for his auto sales. Indeed, by 1914, Ford had a 48 per cent share of the US automobile market.[10]

With its leadership in automobile manufacturing, Detroit grew rapidly in size. From 1900 to 1920, its population increased from 300,000 to just under 1 million.[11] General Motors, and to a lesser extent Chrysler, would soon rise in Detroit as well, adding to the city's dominance of the auto industry. During the roaring 1920s, Detroit's population increased by more than 50 per cent again, reaching 1,568,000 at the end of the decade.[12]

To facilitate such rapid growth, Detroit planners offered ambitious and innovative ideas for expanding the city's transportation infrastructure. Interestingly, a plan presented in 1923 included some of the 'most advanced concepts in rapid transit design.'[13] The plan proposed a series of subway lines underneath the central city and a further sixty-five miles of surface rapid-transit lines, all to be integrated with 563 miles of trolley lines by 1950. The part of the plan that caught most attention, though, was the dovetailing of the surface rail transit with superhighways for moving automobiles. The idea was to have a radial pattern of 205-foot-wide corridors extending from downtown. The central 84 feet was to accommodate the high-speed rail transit, leaving 121 feet of width for limited-access highways. However, the head of the transit commission, Sidney Waldon, a retired automobile executive, hinted that the rail lines might play a secondary role in the overall plan. In 1926 the mayor and city council balked at a scaled-down version of the original plan, with just 46.6 miles of rapid-transit line, projected to cost $280 million. Transportation engineers Henry Miller and Nicholas Schorn argued for a much cheaper system just for surface vehicles, clearly as an alternative to the subway. Then, in 1929, Detroit voters rejected a proposed $54-million bond issue for the subway lines. Property owners near the proposed subway were concerned that the increase in the value of their assets would also entail higher property taxes. By 1930, it was clear that any chance of Detroit constructing a subway or substantial surface rapid transit had passed. The subway was never built, and the city proceeded to develop in a totally auto-dominated fashion.[14]

The post-war years of the 1940s and 1950s were heralded as a golden age for Detroit, but underneath the hood the city's chassis was rusting through with deep and bitter social ills. In 1951, celebrating the 250th anniversary of Detroit's founding, a prominent Detroit banker boasted how the 'city of destiny' was a 'nursery of inventive and technical genius.'[15] Four years earlier, the city was home to 647 manufacturing firms supplying 280,000 manufacturing jobs,[16] and the population had reached close to 2 million. The auto industry was still by far the main industry in town, and, because of their powerful union, the predominantly white and male members of the United Auto Workers Union were among the highest paid industrial workers in the country. In contrast, the disproportionately black, or female, non-union members received low wages and were lucky to get any benefits at all. Deep-seated racism was not restricted to the auto industry, or even to the workplace; it was endemic in the schools, the churches, the police force, and Detroit society as a whole. Many African Americans were confined to poverty in downtown ghettoes, shunned and excluded from the prosperous, charming, all-white neighbourhoods. Moreover, despite the rhetoric of the golden age, Detroit's economy had begun to decline. From 1947 to 1963, the number of manufacturing jobs fell by 134,000. It was the disadvantaged, poorly trained, and racially discriminated blacks that bore the brunt of early deindustrialization – stripped of jobs and increasingly marginalized in the central ghettoes.[17]

As black poverty intensified, the inner-city anger and frustration exploded with the Twelfth Street Riots of 1967. The five days of rioting saw 2000 buildings burned, causing President Lyndon Johnson to bring in the National Guard and US. Army. Forty-three people died in the riots, thirty-three of them black.[18] Some suggested that there was a political undertone to the event. Others saw it quite simply as a spontaneous protest against poverty, discrimination, and police abuse.[19]

The result of the 1967 riots was a rapid increase in the exodus of whites from the city. In truth, whites had been leaving the city for the growing suburbs for many years. Encouraged by federal housing and transportation policies, planners had bulldozed once vibrant neighbourhoods to make way for the freeways that facilitated the white flight to the suburbs. Between 1950 and 1970, the central city's white population decreased by 700,000.[20] But the 1967 riots were a watershed. The following year, 80,000 left the city – four times the number of two years earlier; and the number of registered handguns went up by 23,000.[21] Within six years of the riots, Detroit had a black majority and had elected in Colman Young its first black mayor. The white exodus continued throughout Young's almost twenty years in office. He would later remark in his autobiography: 'It's mind-boggling to think that at mid-century Detroit was a city of close to two million and nearly everything beyond was covered in corn and cow patties. Forty years later, damn near every last white person in the city had moved to the old fields and pastures – 1.4 frigging million of them. Think about that. There were 1,600,000 whites in Detroit after the war, and 1,400,000 of them left.'[22]

Meanwhile, the collapse of the city's auto industry continued. Unemployment in the city at the time of the riots was just 4.8 per cent, but from 1969 onward the auto industry slashed jobs. By 1975, the unemployment rate had risen to 18 per cent, the Detroit economy being particularly vulnerable to the oil crisis. By 1982, the city had half the number of manufacturing jobs as in 1963 – and that number was halved again by 1992.[23]

Depopulation and deindustrialization meant that thousands of buildings were left abandoned and decaying in Detroit. As well as the derelict downtown skyscrapers, there were vacant homes, schools, churches, libraries, and other municipal buildings. The twenty-five-storey landmark building of J.L. Hudson and Company, once the second-biggest-grossing department store in the United States, was closed in 1983 and lay abandoned for fifteen years before being demolished.[24] Today, other abandoned buildings include the once grand Michigan Central Depot train station, with its adjoining eighteen-storey office building, and Tiger Stadium, home of the baseball team from 1901 to

5 The abandoned central train station, with its adjoining office tower, is among the thousands of derelict buildings in Detroit. (© Photo: Lance Rosol)

1999 (demolition completed in 2009). One section of the city has almost an entire neighbourhood of formerly luxurious nineteenth-century mansions sitting derelict. Except for a small waterfront enclave housing corporate headquarters and casinos, there are abandoned buildings throughout the city.

Detroit's largest abandoned building is the 3.5-million-square-foot former Packard automobile manufacturing complex.[25] Comprising forty-seven connected buildings, five storeys high and almost one mile in length, it was once the production site for one of the most classic US cars. With its luxury styling, high-quality engineering, and monstrous V12 engine, the Packard had been the car of choice for royalty and movie stars before the Second World War. Even Henry Ford was carried in a Packard hearse at his funeral in 1947. The Packard plant closed down, however, in 1956, leaving to this day a 'labyrinth of rusted steel, shattered glass (and) crumbling concrete.'[26]

The scope of the dereliction and abandonment of Detroit is stagger-ing. In 1989 a count of the city's abandoned structures by the *Detroit Free Press* came to 15,215 buildings, of which 9017 were single-family homes.[27] Of course, some of the abandoned buildings are eventually demolished. Between 1978 and 1998, some 108,000 demolition permits were issued by the city, compared to just 9000 new building permits.[28] To put the abandonment in perspective, consider that the area of De-troit is 137 square miles. In 1993 there were forty square miles of vacant, abandoned land, and a later estimate suggests that the amount may now exceed sixty square miles!

Adding to the misery of derelict homes, vacant lots, drugs, and crime was the death of trees in many neighbourhoods. On Detroit's east side, for example, there had been vibrant, working-class neighbour-hoods, with streets of well-tended homes shaded by rows of stately elms. Dutch elm disease tragically wiped out many of the trees, leav-ing the sun-baked neighbourhoods devoid of shade.[29] It was a typical Detroit tale; lack of diversity in tree species made the neighbourhoods vulnerable.

Nature's overall response to man's abandonment of land is, of course, to grow back. It did not take long for the weeds to grow over the seats at Tiger Stadium, and one writer describes the former Packard auto plant as follows: 'Sturdy trees, some three storeys tall, grow from numerous places on Packard's roof, their seeds dropped by birds or carried by the wind. Green moss spreads along the floors in some areas, and oozes out of walls in others. Chalky stalactites, several inches long, hang from the ceilings on some floors, apparently the result of rainwater coursing through the walls.'[30] Large tracts of the city now razed of man-made structures have 'devolved into lush fields of lamb's quarters, spread-ing knotweed, milky pursland, spready spurge and russian thistle.'[31] Ringed-necked pheasant can occasionally be spotted in the tall grass. Much of the city is turning back into farmland and prairie.

What is particularly intriguing about the return of countryside into the city is that a green post-industrial economy has begun to take root in Detroit's core. Travelling through the city's streets, writer Rebecca Solnit noted 'a lot of signs that a greening was well under way, a sort of urban husbandry of the city's already occurring return to nature.'[32] She went on to report:

I also saw the lush three-acre Earth World Garden, launched by Capuchin monks in 1999 and now growing organic produce for a local soup kitchen.

I saw a 4-H garden in a fairly ravaged east-side neighborhood, and amid the utter abandonment of the west side, I saw the handsome tiled buildings of the Catherine Ferguson Academy for Young Women, a school for teenage mothers that opens on to a working farm, complete with apple orchard, horses, ducks, long rows of cauliflower and broccoli, and a red barn the girls built themselves.[33]

Yet, despite these few promising signs, the overall decline in the wealth of Detroit is tragic. The population of the city has fallen by more than 50 per cent since the 1950s, with most of the wealthy fleeing to the suburbs. In 2004 some 34 per cent of the remaining Detroiters were living below the poverty line – a higher percentage than in any other US city. The majority of families are headed by a single parent, and nearly half of the children under eighteen live in poverty. Of the seventy-seven largest cities in the United States, Detroit ranks seventy-third for median income and seventy-seventh for the value of owner-occupied housing. The 'city of destiny' is now the poorest city in the country.[34]

In analysing the demise of Detroit, we can point to a multitude of factors. The decision of the late 1920s not to build subways or other substantial urban transit meant that the city failed to establish a strong nucleus of wealth in urban real estate at the city core. The eventual 'superhighways' decimated the neighbourhoods through which they passed and assisted in the mass exodus to the suburbs. Detroit perhaps provides a prime example of a city that strangled itself, as Lewis Mumford had predicted.[35] How ironic that the city's decline would be so inextricably linked to the automobile, once the basis of its wealth. Of course, another aspect of Detroit's fall – white flight from the downtown – was the result of another factor entirely, racial conflict. The exodus of whites was common in many US cities, but it was extreme in the case of Detroit. The excessive power of the United Autoworkers Union may possibly also have been significant, too. Wages may simply have been so high that they eroded corporate profits to the extent that capital could no longer accumulate in the city, a process described, as we have seen, by Joan Robinson. Deindustrialization was certainly another, and important, cause of Detroit's decline. In its case, the impact of deindustrialization was particularly devastating because it was just a one-industry city. Detroit, as Jacobs argued, lacked the diversity necessary to provide resilience in the midst of changing economic times.

The tale of Detroit's fall has many hints suggesting that we need a dose of biology in order to arrive at a more comprehensive theory of how urban economies function. All the themes we have addressed so far – the accumulation of assets, the role of markets, the importance of physical form in general and infrastructure in particular – take us a long way in the quest to understand the process of urban growth. To complete the journey, however, we need to place all these themes in a larger context. Enter biology. The evolution of the Model T by a process of trial and error; the lack of diversity in the auto-dominated economy, making it as vulnerable as the elms of Detroit's east side; and the minor rebirth of a post-industrial economy akin to the weeds in Tiger Stadium – all point to a biological metaphor. Indeed, the whole notion of an urban economy growing and dying has a distinctly natural ring to it. The purpose of this chapter, therefore, is to deepen our understanding of urban economies by viewing them not as inanimate objects but as living ecosystems. This perhaps might seem like a strange twist in our inquiry; seeking metaphors in the biological world lies far from mainstream economics. It is a direction, however, whose value was recognized many decades ago by a most eminent economist.

Marshall's Challenge

Alfred Marshall was a giant among economists. As professor of political economy at Cambridge, Marshall is said to have dominated the British economics profession from the 1880s until his death in 1924.[36] In some respects, he helped shape the discipline of economics into what it is today. Before the neoclassical revolution at the end of the nineteenth century, there were those who studied *political economy* but no *economists*. Of particular significance in changing this state of affairs was Marshall's textbook *Principles of Economics*. Upon its first publication in 1890, it became the textbook of choice, replacing Mill's *Political Economy*.[37] It helped to establish mathematics and diagrammatic analysis as central tools of economic method – although these were initially confined to appendices and footnotes in line with Marshall's desire to write a practical book accessible to businessmen. That Marshall's text was still used by some schools as late as the 1950s says much about his influence.[38]

Marshall also contributed greatly to the body of economic theory. He is credited with translating Mill's utility theory into a mathematical form – using it to derive demand curves that he solved with supply curves in his partial-equilibrium analysis.[39] He was not the first to solve supply and demand curves together, but he took them from mathematical abstraction closer to practical application. Marshall also did early work on business cycles, suggesting that confidence was the main factor underlying fluctuations in the economy. His earlier training was in psychology. Marshall also helped in the early development of welfare economics, by adopting and promoting Jules Dupuit's theory of consumer surplus for measuring benefits to society.

There are, however, some interesting ambiguities in Marshall's legacy. While he was able at mathematics and used it in his work, he was sceptical about its applications in economics, concerned that it could produce theoretical results of no practical relevance.[40] He pronounced a need to use statistical methods in economics, although rarely doing so himself. Of particular interest to the current inquiry is that, while the most enduring aspects of Marshall's work are arguably of a mechanistic nature, he long argued that biological metaphors were necessary for understanding economics.[41]

Marshall's underlying philosophy conceived of society as a complex evolutionary process of multiple interactions between individuals and the wider economy. He recognized that there was an analogy between what he called the earlier stages of economic reasoning and physical mechanics, but that analogies for later stages would be better made with biology than physics. He wrote: 'In earlier stages of economics, we think of demand and supply as crude forces pressing against one another, and tending towards a mechanical equilibrium; but in the later stages, the balance or equilibrium is conceived not as between crude mechanical forces, but as between the organic forces of life and decay.'[42] Marshall recognized that mechanics was not sophisticated enough to represent social and industrial evolution. Mechanical analogies could handle changes in the quantity of forces at work, but not the character of those forces.[43]

The notion that economic theory has largely been developed by analogy with physics has been rigorously pursued by the economic historian Peter Mirowski in his provocatively entitled *More Heat than Light*. His thesis is that both classical and neoclassical economic theory have been established in imitation of physical theory – and that this ultimately constrains them. A large part of Mirowski's book is devoted to explaining the roots of neoclassical theory, synonymous with Léon Walras, William Stanley Jevons, Vilfredo Pareto, and Francis Ysidro Edgeworth at the end of the nineteenth century. Walras, incidentally, was somewhat of a failed physicist, his contribution being the development of general equilibrium theory by which supply and demand curves for all markets in an economy are solved simultaneously; it was not a theory much to Marshall's liking.[44] As Mirowski explains, neoclassical economics was developed on the mathematical foundations that evolved in the 1840s with the discovery of the conservation of energy.[45] The fundamental notion of *value* (of a thing) came to be to economics what energy was to physics. Moreover, just as energy was first conceptualized as a substance and then as a field, so too was value.[46] The most explicit example of the physical basis of neoclassical economics was perhaps Irving Fisher's doctoral thesis of 1891, which provided a clear translation between mechanics and economics. In fact, Fisher's thesis advisers included the great thermodynamicist Josiah William Gibbs.[47] Much of economic theory has its roots in physics.

Mirowski also remarks at the frequent occurrences of scientists in the twentieth century who had independently kindled a belief that energy is the true measure of economic value. Since the energy theory of value was never developed with a serious, concerted effort and was never adopted within an academic discipline, it was continually rediscovered.[48] There are some variations. Mirowski distinguishes between *neo-energists*, who literally believe that energy is identical to economic value, and *neo-simulates*, who regard it merely as a metaphor.[49]

The one economist who arguably explored the neo-energist notion further than others was Nicholas Georgescu-Roegen – and he found it wanting. Georgescu-Roegen identified several reasons why energy equivalency could not be taken as a literal representation of economic value: it ignores the heterogeneous nature of matter; it lacks a rigorous definition of net energy; and it neglects the second law of thermodynamics – that useful energy is expended in the form of heat.[50] These are points worth considering in pursuing the main objective of this chapter, which is essentially to take up Marshall's challenge.

The aim here is to describe the economic workings of a city in a fashion that sees them as analogous to the workings of a biological system, so that phenomena such as the growth and accumulation of wealth can be explained by more comprehensive means than existing economic theory. To achieve this aim, the *ecosystem* shall be used as the basic analogy upon which the workings of an urban economy will be *metaphorically* described.

Before explaining the analogy between an urban economy and an ecosystem, it should be noted that others have followed Marshall in describing economic phenomena in biological terms. For example, the set of equations developed by A.J. Lotka and V. Volterra to describe the growth of species populations has been used by many to describe the growth of technologies. The well-known technology S-curve essentially follows the same mathematical model as a biological population, growing exponentially at first but then at a slower rate until reaching a constant level dictated by carrying capacity.

The use of biological metaphors in economics was relatively common in the period between 1880 and 1914.[51] Thorstein Veblen discussed Darwinian principles in his *Theory of the Leisure Class* and proposed a research program to restructure economics along these lines.[52] Ellis Powell described the process by which banks formed a financial structure, with London at its centre, using terms such as *natural selection* and *survival of the fittest*.[53] John Bates Clark is said to have 'laced his *Philosophy of Wealth* (1885) with organic metaphors and images from Spencerian biology.'[54] The integration of ideas from biological and social sciences during this period was strongly driven by the philosophy of Herbert Spencer, whose work influenced Marshall. After the First World War, however, references to biology in economics were sporadic and infrequent.

After a lengthy hiatus, the 1980s produced a landmark work in evolutionary economics, Richard Nelson and Sidney Winter's *Evolutionary Theory of Economic Change*. The authors regarded the operation of markets as analogous to the process of natural selection, with profitable firms surviving in a fashion akin to successful organisms. They saw the regular routines performed by firms, such as producing things, hiring staff, ordering inventory, research, advertising, and the like, as being analogous to genes.[55] Based on this genetic interpretation of firm behaviour, Nelson and Winter used computer models to simulate a variety of micro and macro economic behaviours, including economic growth.

A notable recent book, emanating from the business community, is Eric D. Beinhocker's *The Origin of Wealth*.[56] Beinhocker provides a synthesis of the emerging field of complexity economics, which encompasses ideas from the area of evolutionary economics. He describes wealth as being the result of a three-step process – differentiate, select, and amplify – which he characterizes as a generic formula of evolution. Economic evolution is regarded as the result of evolution in three design spaces – physical technologies, social technologies, and business plans – with the last of these being a key ingredient to achieve a successful fit between technology and society. Like Nelson and Winter, Beinhocker sees markets as the selection mechanism for successful businesses. Moreover, the break with neoclassical economics is clear: 'Markets win over command and control, not because of their efficiency at resource allocation in equilibrium, but because of their effectiveness at innovation in disequilibrium.' Another intriguing notion, with Spencerian undertones, is that of niche construction, which holds that, as organisms evolve, they have an impact on their environment, which subsequently influences their own evolution. Through such evolution, Beinhocker argues, business plans and the needs/tastes of society co-evolve together.

A further analogy of particular value to the present analysis is Jane Jacobs's idea that the diversity of urban economies is key to their growth and stability.[57] Jacobs makes this observation by drawing a parallel with a swamp, rich with a wide variety of flora and fauna. Such an idea is consistent with the direction to be taken shortly, but first it is necessary to explain the essential details of how ecosystems function.

Ecosystems

The term *ecosystem* is recognized to have first been used by the colourful English ecologist Sir Arthur Tansley.[58] A student of University College, London, and Trinity College, Cambridge, Tansley became chair of botany at Oxford University in 1927. He was the founder of the British Ecological Society and first editor of the *Journal of Ecology*. Tansley had broad interests in many academic disciplines and even studied for some time with Sigmund Freud. He was known as a charismatic entertainer who apparently loved fast cars. He was also a great popularizer of the topic of ecology, having written classic books such as *The British Isles and Their Vegetation*.[59]

Tansley's development of the ecosystem concept followed from his experimental studies of competition between plant populations under unfavourable environmental conditions, much like Detroit rooftops![60] He regarded the ecosystem as a complex of interactions both within communities of organisms and with their physical non-living (abiotic) environment. These interactions he saw as a 'system in the sense of physics'[61] and were the basis for defining community structure and function.

The reference to 'physics' here is intriguing. It seems that, in following Marshall's notion that economics should be based on biological principles, one cannot avoid returning to physics to some degree. Indeed, the principles of conservation of mass and energy are important for understanding ecosystem function, as will be discussed presently. Nevertheless, there are further key concepts in ecosystem theory that make it quite distinct from physics. These include Charles Elton's concept of the food chain, Frederick Clements's theory of succession, and, of course, Charles Darwin's theory of evolution.

The simple concept of the food chain recognizes that the feeding patterns of populations of organisms are a basis for describing the structure of biological communities. For clarity, note that an *organism* – plant, animal, bacteria, or virus – is a living thing. A *population* is a group of individual organisms that can breed with one another, and a *community* is a group of populations that exist together in a defined location, for example, within an ecosystem. At the bottom of the food chain are the plants,[62] which perform the fundamental role of synthesizing organic material, that is, food, from inorganic inputs by using solar radiation. Above the plants are further levels of populations which feed on the level below. The second level is composed of primary consumers that graze on vegetation, while carnivores enter at the third level. There can be several layers of carnivores before reaching the top of the food chain, which is often humans.

The actual structure of ecosystems is more complex still, generally described by *food webs* composed of overlapping food chains. As an example, consider the food web of the organisms of the Antarctic Ocean.[63] At the bottom of the web are algae, which by performing photosynthesis provide the fundamental source of food for the whole web. The first consumers in this case are tiny shrimp-like krill, which feed upon the algae. The krill, in turn, are food for a variety of fish and also baleen whales. Now a whole bunch of creatures feed on Antarctic fish and thus create multiple food chains; these include penguins, killer whales, leopard seals, and squid and sperm whales. These five are on different food chain levels, since the killer whale will eat the penguins, leopard seals, and squid. Sperm whales also feed upon squid, as do baleen whales. Joining killer whales at the top of the web are humans, which certainly feed upon fish. Although now banned by many countries, the practice of commercial whaling also places humans above sperm whales and baleen whales in the web. There is also a small, but growing, human fishery for those tiny krill, the herbivores way down near the bottom of the web. Thus, there is interaction on multiple levels in a food web.

There is a crucial further category of organisms in a community structure – the detrivores. These are the fungi, bacteria, vultures, and worms that feed upon the dead tissue and excrement of the other organisms in ecosystems. The detrivores play an important role by recycling mass in an ecosystem, transforming dead material into a non-biological form, which is then used again by plants.

Because of the activity of detrivores, mass is often approximately conserved in ecosystems. Plants construct biomass, which is typically composed of at least 90 per cent carbon, hydrogen, and oxygen, along with macro-nutrients (nitrogen, phosphorus, and so on) and a variety of trace elements.[64] The mass accumulates in organisms throughout the food web. The detrivores recycle the dead biomass, breaking it down into basic compounds ready for the reconstruction of living biomass. Mass can enter or leave an ecosystem by the movement of animals, or by erosion and transportation by wind and water. Ecosystems are generally not closed like a flask in a chemical laboratory experiment – they are open systems allowing for the potential for mass to come and go. Generally speaking, however, the boundaries of an ecosystem might be approximately defined so that much of the mass is maintained.

The conservation of the mass of nutrients in tropical rain forests is particularly interesting. Of the three main types of forest ecosystem, tropical rain forests typically have a far greater diversity of species than the coniferous and temperate broadleaf forests. One acre of rainforest typically supports four to ten times more species than an acre of forest at temperate latitudes.[65] An amazing characteristic of rainforests, however, is that the red tropical soils upon which they root are typically poor in nutrients. The dousing of the soils by large volumes of warm water during tropical storms has removed the flinty silicates that give a grey tint to northern soils.[66] The remaining red soils are less capable of bonding with metal ions, and in particular nutrients. As a result, most of the nutrients in tropical rainforests are stored within the biomass of the trees themselves. When a great tree dies and falls to the forest floor, an elaborate network of roots, aided by attached fungi, rapidly retrieves the nutrients. There is no build-up of thick, brown, nutrient-rich humus as in northern forests. The living communities rapidly recycle and hoard the nutrients in the rainforest. Thus, much of the mass is conserved.

Ecosystems can also be analysed in terms of energetics. Unlike mass, which is approximately recycled, energy flows *through* ecosystems. The plants perform the first, all-important step of transforming solar radiation into useful chemical-bond energy (sugars and starches) by photosynthesis. In this process, and in all subsequent transfers through the food chain, there are significant heat losses. Conservation of energy always holds, but by the second law of thermodynamics there is always loss of useful energy at each transfer. Animals spend significant amounts of energy chasing prey and processing food, not to mention all their other activities. Consequently, decreased amounts of useful energy remain at higher levels of the food chain.

As a consequence of the heat loss at each level of the food chain, there are decreasing amounts of energy available to organisms at each trophic level. Energy pyramids typically show about an order-of-magnitude reduction in the energy flow per square metre with each higher food-chain level.[67] At the top of the food chain, then, there is not much energy available. In the example of the Antarctic food web, there is far more chemical-bond energy in all of the ocean's krill than there is in all of the fish, and still less again in all of the whales. Energy pyramids give a clear indication, as Paul Colinvaux puts it, of why big, fierce animals are rare.[68] Tigers, grizzly bears, killer whales, and other top-level predators are rare because there is not enough energy in upper food-chain levels to support a large amount of biomass.

Of course, the observant reader may recognize that humans are also at the top of the food chain and, at over six billion in population, we are not so rare! This is because we have interfered in the natural ecosystem in several ways. For example, by mining fossil fuels and using them to produce fertilizers in large amounts, we have increased the productivity of agriculture. Perhaps as significantly, by our very own growing and harvesting of crops, we have learned to make exploitative use of allogeneic forces. These are environmental shocks to an ecosystem, and they play a role in ecosystem succession, in which communities of organisms are progressively replaced with others. The shocks may be of a periodic nature, such as those associated with seasonal weather patterns, or be intermittent events such as forest fires, floods, earthquakes, or volcanic eruptions. Following a catastrophic disturbance such as a volcanic eruption, an ecosystem will be essentially destroyed and the area will revert back to the initiation stage of ecosystem succession.[69] The bare surface will first be colonized by a small number of specialized highly stress-tolerant plants, such as mosses and liverworts, that can grow in cracks between rocks without need of soil. As these first colonizers die and soil formation begins, the ecosystem moves to a further developmental stage of succession. The specialized stress-tolerant species are replaced by more productive and competitive species such as grasses and weeds. As the ecosystem matures, stable soil, nutrient, and water conditions exist, supporting bushes, small trees, and higher organisms up the food chain. At the final stage of succession – the climax – the vegetation is dominated by large, long-lived trees.

Life in an ecosystem near climax can be highly competitive. In the tropical rainforests, for example, which are known for their high biodiversity, plant species survive by growing as tall as possible to out-compete neighbouring plants for incoming solar radiation. Little sunlight reaches the forest floor. Moreover, so much of the available nutrients are sequestered in the trees' biomass that the soil below the canopy is often lacking nutrients. Thus, only low-energy organisms are able to survive.

Not all ecosystems reach climax. The environment may be too stressful, for example, with low temperatures, lack of rain, or high evaporation; or there may be periodic allogeneic forces that cause the ecosystem to spend energy repairing biomass. Coniferous and temperate boreal forest ecosystems typically do not reach the diversity of tropical rainforests, because they have to cope with seasonal cold temperatures. Grazing by animals and fires, the latter often caused by humans, keep moorlands at a pre-climatic stage.[70] A further example is estuaries – waves and tides, by raising and lowering water levels and varying salt concentrations, keep estuaries in a developmental stage of succession.

The use of energy in ecosystems near climax is different from that in earlier stages. In the tropical rain forest, most of the energy is used to service the large amounts of existing biomass; there is relatively little net growth. Estuaries, however, are so frequently disturbed that much of the energy they receive is used to build new biomass. In fact, estuaries are such vibrant ecosystems that they are net energy producers. Sea creatures will travel to estuaries for feeding or breeding before leaving for deeper aquatic ecosystems.

In a similar fashion, man has learned to apply allogeneic forces in near optimal fashion in the farming of crops. Were a field of wheat to be left unharvested it would likely be colonized by shrubs, bushes, and small trees until some climax state is reached and no further net growth occurs. Humans, however, have learned to harvest wheat just after the ecosystem's most productive period of growth, when energy captured via photosynthesis is used to grow new biomass.

From this brief introduction, it is apparent that ecosystems can differ greatly in their characteristics and that ecologists have developed sophisticated theories to explain ecosystem function. There is rarely a single straightforward explanation of ecological phenomena. Consider the matter of what limits growth in some of the main types of non-forest land ecosystems: tundra is limited by cold temperatures; temperate grasslands are constrained by precipitation and periodic drought; tropical savannas are subject to extreme seasonal precipitation and low nutrients; and deserts have rates of evaporation several times higher than of precipitation. There are also exceptional cases within ecosystems. Some parts of forest ecosystems on the Pacific coast of North America have higher productivity than tropical rain forests because of a high loading of nitrogen coming from the dung of bears feeding in salmon-rich rivers. Another case is surface ocean waters, which are typically depleted of nutrients, but which may, as a result of the upwelling of nutrient-rich deep ocean waters, support a tremendous diversity of sea life. Ecosystems are complex and diverse; hence, our knowledge of them may help in understanding other complex systems, such as urban economies.

The Ecological Basis of Urban Economics

Having explained the fundamental functioning of ecosystems, we can now turn to the analogous operation of urban economies. The theory to be discussed here may also serve to explain the nature of larger economic entities – such as nations. The analogy is developed, however, in terms of the economies of cities based on consideration of spatial dimensions. The argument is not that typical cities and typical ecosystems are necessarily of the same size; this is not the case. Rather, urban economies and ecosystems can both be defined by spatial areas that include commonly interacting populations of people or populations of organisms, respectively.

Firms operating in an urban economy can be seen to be analogous to organisms in an ecosystem. They are the basic units of an economy – independent entities that typically survive on their ability to be competitive or collaborative. Yet firms are also dependent on the overall state of the economy, just as organisms are dependent on their host ecosystem. In many respects, a theory that sees firms as being as complex and diverse as organisms is far more suitable than the conventional microeconomic models, which usually consider homogeneous firms selling identical goods in perfect markets. Microeconomic theory typically assumes that, for firms to survive, they have to be economically efficient, that is, produce good and services of a required quality at competitive prices. Firms differentiate themselves, however, in many ways: through special product features, timing and locations of sales, branding and reputation, product mixtures, and cooperation or strategic alliances with other companies.[71]

One ecological theory of species survival, CSR theory, distinguishes between species that are able to survive in highly stressed, highly disturbed, and highly competitive environments.[72] Highly stressed environments include those with extreme temperatures or extremely high or low levels of rainfall, such that growth of biomass is hindered. Some species are able to survive by adapting to stressful environments. Coniferous trees, for example, developed long needle-like leaves with low surface area as a strategy against losing heat in cold climates. Highly disturbed environments are those in which biomass is damaged or destroyed, for example, by grazing, forest fires, or unstable substrate. Some disturbance-tolerant trees have developed coatings of bark that are more resilient to burning. Australian Eucalyptus trees even emit a blue haze of flammable oils, encouraging the occurrence of periodic forest fires, to which they are well adapted. Another example is lichen, which have an ability to survive on moving scree slopes. Stress-tolerant and disturbance-tolerant organisms do not necessarily have to be competitive with many other organisms – there is less competition in their difficult environments. It is in the low-stress and low-disturbance environments where most species are found, and so it is in such environments that an organism's ability to compete is essential to survival.

In an analogous fashion, there are firms that survive in difficult economic environments, where achieving economic efficiency in the face of competition is less essential. Mining or construction companies working in some stressful developing world countries may develop ways of interacting with non-democratic governments and are less concerned with market forces. In other cases, markets may be so highly disturbed that firms survive by continual adaptation; firms in the fashion industry or some consumer-electronics markets may be primarily concerned with producing goods that are trend setting, rather than necessarily being price competitive. Economic efficiency helps, but it is not necessarily essential for a firm's survival.

Another ecological theory, known as r-K theory, is concerned with the reproduction aspects of organism-survival strategy.[73] At one extreme are the r-strategists, which rapidly produce large numbers of offspring that are widely dispersed in an ecosystem. These are often small and vulnerable; many fail to survive, but, by virtue of their numbers, the species survives. Conversely, K-strategists put more energy into producing and nurturing a small number of large offspring. These organisms are much better at competing for necessary resources and tend to live longer.

Similar strategies can also be seen in the business world. Venture capitalists, for example, use something of an r-strategist approach. They typically invest relatively modest amounts in many small promising entrepreneurial companies in a few select areas of technology, with the expectation that perhaps one in ten might grow to be lucrative in the long term. The opposite case is a state-owned company, such as an airline or oil company, created by governments to fulfil a key national need. Such companies might be nurtured by subsidies in early years and later perhaps privatized once market conditions are favourable.

While firms can range in size from single-person businesses to large multinational corporations, it is remarkable that their distribution in large urban economies is similar to that often found with organisms in an ecosystem. There are many more smaller firms than large ones, and more people overall are employed in smaller firms. As an example, analysis of a 2001 dataset of 19,000 firms in the Toronto region, with ten or more employees, showed that 17,043 firms employed between 10 and 100 people; 1887 firms had 101 to 1000 employees; 105 firms had 1001 to 10,000 employees; and just 7 employed over 10,000.[74] This data set excluded government workers, educational establishments, and firms with fewer than ten employees. Of the seven large firms, five had fewer than 17,000 employees.[75] Clearly, in this urban economy, big, fierce companies are rare.

Numbers of organisms and their total mass typically decrease in a similar fashion at higher levels of food chains. For example, a study of a Kentucky bluegrass grassland ecosystem found 14,300,000 plants/hectare; 1,700,000 herbivores/hectare (mainly insects, but also a few large mammals); 900,000 primary carnivores/hectare (mainly spiders and insects); and just seven secondary carnivores/hectare (for example, weasels).[76] In a study of a Wisconsin freshwater lake, the biomass of producers (plankton and macrophytes) was 1700 kg/hectare; primary consumers (invertebrates), 220 kg/hectare; and primary carnivores (fish), just 23 kg/hectare.[77] These distributions have some similarities with those observed for firms in urban economies.

The structural relationship between firms in an economy might also be seen to have some similarities to a food web. The analogy is not that firms go around eating one another, although this does happen in a sense when firms are taken over by others.[78] Rather, it is that firms provide capital goods and services for one another and that these are generally passed upwards through a structural hierarchy. The relationships between firms are fairly complex, as can be partially seen at the industry level in input-output tables similar to those devised by W.W. Leontief. Indeed, the relationships in economies may be considered more complex than a food web in that firms can exchange goods and services, whereas mass in ecosystems usually goes up food chains. Nevertheless, there is within economies a general tendency to pass labour-embodied capital up through hierarchies. For example, a mining company produces iron ore, which is processed by steel manufacturers; the raw steel is then moulded by a machine maker into a device used to produce some good. It is also intriguing to note some of the findings from eco-industrial parks, in which co-located firms exchange products and by-products. Studies have found that the degree of connectedness between industrial tenants in eco-industrial parks is about the same as that typically found in biological systems.[79] Overall, while the detailed structures of ecosystems and urban economies may differ, they are similar in the sense that both are hierarchical. Moreover, it would seem there is a potentially useful analogy between capital and mass.

Not only is the capital of economies analogous to the mass of ecosystems, but both come in a variety of forms. Physical capital is like organic biomass. Yet there is more to capital than just buildings and machinery, as was explained in the review of Adam Smith's classifications in chapter 5. Take human capital, for example: technical knowledge and management skills are less tangible, but these are just as important to the continued success of firms as physical capital. They are in a sense the nutrients of firms: their nitrogen, phosphorus, sulphur, and other elements – small in mass relative to the major constituents of biomass (carbon and water), but essential nonetheless.

How, then, does capital get recycled in an urban economy? The answer is somewhat bizarre. It has to be recognized that the products of capital are the goods and services consumed by households, which require them to sustain human capital. Households are like detrivores, consuming the goods excreted by capital production, using them for sustenance, entertainment, and whatever else, but eventually generating the knowledge and skills necessary to renew capital formation.

So, if capital is analogous to mass, what is the equivalent to energy? The answer in simple terms is money. Recall how neoclassical economics is based on a parallel between conservation of energy and conservation of value. In our metaphorical system, it is apparent that the flow of energy has parallels with financial transactions or simply cash flows.

A strict analogy between energy and value, however, cannot be drawn for two reasons. First, value is a complex three-headed beast, encompassing utility, scarcity, and embodied labour, as discussed in chapter 2. Perhaps more to the point is concern over applying the principle of conservation of energy. Energy is always conserved, but *useful* energy is not. This is the second law of thermodynamics that so concerned Georgescu-Roegen. In an ecosystem, useful energy is continually being lost as heat.

Nevertheless, just as an ecosystem requires energy to build and maintain biomass, so do economies require cash flows to build and maintain capital. Perhaps one potential weakness in the parallel is that energy flows through ecosystems, whereas money circulates in economies. There again, from the perspective of an individual organism, significant amounts of energy are transferred to the greater environment to build and maintain mass. Similarly, individual firms must make payments to society, for example, via taxes, as well as finding ways of receiving cash flows from society. Moreover, urban economies are typically very open, with significant cash flows entering and leaving through trade and government interactions. The key point is that, in the absence of evolution, ecosystems approach a limiting state at which all energy is required to maintain net biomass; and, similarly, an urban economy may approach a state at which all incoming cash flows are required just to maintain a net amount of capital.

Urban economies are also subject to external allogeneic forces, which may be random or periodic in nature, just like those that have an impact on ecosystems. The most significant periodic allogeneic forces influencing ecosystems are typically seasonal fluctuations in climate. The periodic fluctuations most affecting cities, however, have longer cycles of twenty to twenty-five years; they are known as Kuznets waves.[80]

Kuznets waves, named after Nobel Prize–winning economist Simon Kuznets, are part of an empirically supported theory which suggests that there are rhythms in long-term economic behaviour. National-level data indicate that economies move through cycles of expansion, overshoot, and collapse, with a total cycle duration of twenty to twenty-five years. Such cycles have been shown to describe growth in real per capita GDP, population growth, and industrial production.[81] The Kuznets cycle may be linked as well to the phenomena of baby boom generations.

The long-wave theory also includes phenomena that follow a longer cycle of approximately fifty to fifty-five years. In particular, the life cycles of technologies are considered to follow a fifty- to fifty-five-year Kondratiev cycle, named after their Russian inventor, Nikolai Kondratiev, but popularized by Austrian economist Joseph Schumpeter. The basic idea is that technologies can be grouped into periods of major innovation, for example, the early Industrial Revolution (1770s–1840s), steam power and railways (1840s–90s), electrical and heavy engineering (1890s–1940s), Fordist mass production (1940s–90s), and information and communications (1990s–).[82] The other important phenomena following a fifty- to fifty-five-year cycle are prices, that is, patterns of inflation. There are approximately two Kuznets cycles to one Kondratiev cycle. This means there is a period of deflationary growth and a period of inflationary growth within each Kondratiev wave. New technologies are established during the deflationary phase and there is accelerating accumulation of associated infrastructure. During the inflationary growth phase, the established technologies reach market saturation and infrastructure accumulates at a decreasing rate.[83]

These long-term rhythms in economic behaviour have a profound effect on the growth of cities. Many studies conducted over almost a century have shown that city building booms follow the twenty- to twenty-five-year Kuznets cycle.[84] Periods of rapid urban development typically accompany the rapid growth that occurs in each Kuznets cycle. Increasing employment opportunities and rising wages draw in population. Demand for housing fuels urban development. This induces consumer spending along with both public and private investment, which continues until overshoot and collapse.[85]

The twenty- to twenty-five-year patterns of building booms in cities are similar to the annual cycles of ecosystems. During periods of low energy, vegetation sheds its leaves; firms in economies lay off excess labour. Come spring, however, the growth of new biomass occurs; capital investment spurs growth until the summer climax is reached. Yet changes in technology and urban design practices can significantly affect the nature of urban building booms, and there is often evolution in urban form from one cycle to the next.

Reinterpreting the Growth of Cities

With an ecological basis for urban economies now set out, we can return to the central issue posed in chapter 5 of how the growth of cities can best be understood. We find that the ecosystem model, with its associated theories of energetics, structure, competition, succession, and evolution, provides a comprehensive way to capture the biology of capital formation and urban economic growth. Let us put the answer to Marshall's challenge to the test.

Consider first the remarkable economic growth of London following the Great Fire of 1666, recounted in the previous chapter. London experienced a catastrophe akin to a forest ecosystem being burnt to the ground. The ecosystem was moved from a semi-climatic state back to the first stage of succession, that is, initiation. Most Londoners survived the flames and saved their personal money bags too. There was also sufficient skilled labour for rebuilding. Analogously, the ecosystem had sufficient nearby energy and nutrients for rapid recolonization. The first firms to benefit most in the early phase would be the builders, carpenters, roofers, stonemasons, ironmongers, and so on. After five years, when most of the non-religious buildings were replaced, there would still be much work for a next wave of craftsmen – the furniture makers, household appliance makers, and interior decorators of the day. London was speedily rebuilt as an ecosystem in its early stages of succession, with large quantities of energy being used to produce new biomass.

As well as reverting to an early stage of succession, London also went through evolution. There is some irony in the observation that London was reconstructed in a fashion similar to that of an ecosystem rapidly producing biomass. While there were large quantities of timber used in the reconstruction, the regulations in response to the fire actually required all outside building walls to be faced in brick or stone. The only external woodwork allowed was for window frames, door cases, and breastsummers on shop fronts.[86] The new regulations must have prompted massive growth in industries supplying the new construction materials. Bricks, tiles, and lime were produced in or close to London – thus boosting the local economy. Timber, lead, and coal (to power the kilns) came from farther away.[87] The evolution in London's building technology moved it to higher standards, thus rapidly expanding the industries required to supply the new materials.

There were further aspects of the new building regulations that would similarly expand various sectors of London's economy. Fleet Street, Cheapside, Cornhill, and many other eminent streets were required to be wider[88] – and, when paved, this would increase the demand for stone. The wider streets also led to an increase in the amount of travel by horse-drawn taxis. Where previously water from rooftops had cascaded out from gutters above the street, all the new roofs were required to have proper downspouts[89] – thus spurring downspout production. The new regulations in building heights would have had particularly strong effects. Buildings in 'by-streets and lanes' had to be of two storeys plus garrets, while those on streets and lanes of note, or facing the river, were required to be of three storeys plus garrets.[90] All buildings on 'high and principal streets' and 'mansion houses for citizens and other persons of extraordinary quality' were to be of four storeys. Rebuilding the houses to be taller and grander than before meant that not only more construction materials but also more furnishings and more coal for heating would be required. London undertook rapid evolution to a higher standard of living. Its economy grew as a result of its change in urban form.

Now move the clock forward about 260 years to New York City during the Great Depression, when another revolution in urban form occurred. As discussed in chapters 1 and 4, New York experienced a shock to its economy perhaps almost comparable to London's in 1666, only clearly without the catastrophe of being burnt to a cinder. In ecological terms, what New York experienced was not a backwards move to an earlier phase of ecological succession, but a huge step forward to a new stage – again caused by technological evolution.

New York had come to a point at which much of its manufacturing industry was redundant. Its financial institutions were sufficiently powerful that they could now provide the backbone to the New York economy. The factory workers had become excess labour. With repayment of European war debts to New York banks and the infusion into the city of a billion or more dollars under Roosevelt's New Deal, New York was not short of cash. It was akin to an ecosystem with readily available energy for growth of biomass and an excess of the necessary nutrients. The city grew physically like a great forest. The new infrastructure – buildings, bridges, tunnels, airports, piers, and transit – was briefly described in chapter 1. It was the development of New York's suburban highway system, however, that perhaps constituted the most significant technological evolution.

New York is the home of the world's earliest motorways. With bridges and tunnels separating it from local roads, William Vanderbilt's Long Island Parkway, built from 1906 to 1911, may possibly claim to be the world's first motorway.[91] Yet the Long Island Parkway and the Bronx River Parkway, finished in 1923, were but early experimental pieces of a massive metropolitan highway system – a system for which substantial construction began in earnest about 1930.

The key last volumes of New York's *Regional Plan*, written by Thomas Adams between 1929 and 1931, proposed the development of satellite communities and industrial parks served by 2527 miles of new highways.[92] The plan also called for improved suburban rail, especially radial services, although this never came to fruition. The plan was a reflection of the trend towards mass car ownership. It was strongly backed by the Regional Plan Association – which was dominated by company directors, presidents, and chairmen of big business. Moreover, under the directorship of Robert Moses, with substantial work by the Port Authority, the implementation skills were there. By 1942, more than 54 per cent of the proposed 2527 miles of highway were completed. This included the Southern State, Hutchinson River, Saw Mill River, Cross County, and Henry Hudson parkways and the Triborough Bridge system.[93] 'New York, long before Los Angeles, [was] the first motorway metropolis in the world.'[94]

New York's period of massive physical growth continued well into the 1960s, but then, like an ecosystem approaching climax (or awaiting further evolution), it slowed. With so much energy spent constructing infrastructure, the new biomass needed to be maintained. Of course, the new jobs created were not just in road repair, vehicle sales and servicing, automobile insurance, and the like. The highway network supported a whole new type of economy, as was discussed in chapter 5.

The case of Detroit can also be explained in ecological terms, as was suggested earlier in this chapter. At the end of the nineteenth century, the city had numerous small, independent, highly skilled, and innovative companies; it was akin to a flourishing ecosystem with a rich diversity of species. Indeed, the conditions in Detroit – its energy and nutrients – provided the special circumstances for the evolution of an organism – the automobile manufacturing company – into a newer form. Then, through the first decades of the twentieth century, the city grew rapidly, attracting further financial investment and skilled workers. The problem, however, was that the burgeoning auto manufacturers began to dominate Detroit's economy. Through consolidation and vertical integration, the diverse mix of companies performing bits-and-pieces work was gradually replaced with a few large corporations. The same can happen in ecosystems when one dominant species out-competes all others. Sea urchins, for example, or some shellfish, can dominate bay areas if there is an absence of a keystone species such as star fish or sea otters to keep their numbers in check.[95] Similarly, when an invasive species is introduced into some ecosystems, it out-competes native organisms, leading to an unhealthy, low-diversity ecosystem.

In the case of Detroit's economy, the effects of the auto sector's dominance were particularly extreme. The products of Detroit autoworkers' own labour influenced the shape and urban form of the city itself. Healthy parts of the city were destroyed to build superhighways to the suburbs, and the city, now poisoned by racism, stopped accumulating capital. Then, to make matters even worse, the Detroit economy confronted a changing environment – the beginnings of competition from Japanese auto manufacturers. In the face of this, Detroit proved helpless: its golden age was at an end. As in any ecosystem subject to blight, though, there are some hardy species that live on and new ones that can tolerate the extreme conditions – Detroit still maintains some components of its manufacturing heritage, and there are some signs of a post-industrial economy springing to life.

Moving beyond these three specific examples – London, New York City, and Detroit – how well does the ecosystem analogy generally describe urban evolution? In particular, recall the work of urban historian Peter Hall discussed in chapter 1. Why was it that technological innovation in manufacturing occurred in fringe cities such as Manchester, Glasgow, Detroit, and San Francisco, while innovation in infrastructure mostly occurred in large established power centres such as Rome, London, Paris, and New York? Hall offers a range of explanations, including socio-economic, political, and cultural factors. Our aim here is not to contradict Hall – after all, we are only working with a metaphor – but to see what insights the ecosystem model provides.

First, the evolutions in urban infrastructure were more likely to happen in capital cities with large populations, where the stresses were such that the risks of urban breakdown were greater. Moreover, such innovations in infrastructure required huge amounts of capital investment, which only the most wealthy cities could at first afford. In ecological terms, huge amounts of energy were required to fuel the substantial growth in biomass.

The innovations in industrial processes, however, required something finer. They occurred in cities with a suitably skilled workforce, a few innovative individuals, and a lack of stuffy, hierarchical control. In ecological terms, these cities possessed a rare and subtle mixture of nutrients from which the new innovative technologies could grow. Perhaps the right blend of nutrients could not occur in the larger financial centres, because, as in a tropical rainforest, the nutrients were already bound up in the trees.

Conclusion

It is suggested here that the most comprehensive way to understand an urban economy is to regard it as an ecosystem composed of a heterogeneous mix of competing firms, each with niches that they seek to fill as they provide value to citizens. Cities grow in complex ways, with the lock-in of infrastructure and the strategic fit of one type of firm providing opportunities for other firms. By this evolving process, firms build up the capital of cities, akin to mass in ecosystems.

Were it not for major innovations, the city might approach some form of dynamic equilibrium analogous to an ecosystem in its most advanced stage of succession. The structure of the city has developed such that most labour is employed merely maintaining the existing system. This means more than just maintaining the roadways, water pipes, and other physical infrastructure; it includes all the jobs and activities that enable cities to maintain the status quo – provision of food and housing, policing, emergency services, medical treatment, and so on. Such a city would be like an ecosystem at climax: all the energy is used to maintain the current amount of biomass and there is no net new growth.

Most cities, however, continue to grow. This is because they are subject to waves of innovation – waves of creative destruction, as Joseph Schumpeter famously put it – and are also innovative themselves. The greatest waves of all are those in urban form, such as those experienced by London after the Great Fire and New York during the Great Depression. These cities were like grass meadows, which had built up enough nutrients, or were subject to a sufficiently favourable change in condition, to move to the next level of succession. They offer a stark contrast to Detroit, a city whose rise and fall is akin to the story of an ecosystem which first flourishes before experiencing a long, slow decline.

7 Conclusion: The Wealth of Cities

> The city sat like a spider in the web of the American economy, drawing resources into the metropolis, transforming them, and sending them to places near and far.
>
> S.B. Beckert[1]

In 1976 the world came to Montreal. The games of the 21st Olympiad were held in one of the world's most modern, technologically advanced cities. The main arena for the games was a boldly designed stadium with a plastic roof supported by the world's longest inclined tower; it was actually late in its construction and proved to be very expensive.[2] A fourteen-year-old Romanian, Nadia Comăneci, became the first gymnast in Olympic history to score a perfect 10.0, a feat she achieved seven times at the Games. Montreal was a proud, confident city; it had been selected ahead of Moscow and Los Angeles to host the Games. Just nine years after hosting the world exhibition of 1967, Montreal's global presence was far greater than that of any Canadian city before her, or any since. Ironically though, the census of 1976 showed that the city that for over a century had been Canada's largest metropolitan area had been caught and surpassed in terms of population by its close rival, Toronto.

The 1960s were sumptuous years of prosperity for Montrealers.[3] Under the visionary leadership of Mayor Jean Drapeau, the city was transformed into a twenty-first-century city ahead of its time. The year 1962 saw the opening of the Place Ville Marie, to rival New York's Rockefeller Center. The same year saw completion of the forty-three-storey CIBC bank tower – then the world's tallest prefabricated building – and the new Champlain bridge crossing from Montreal island over the

St Lawrence. The following year Montrealers had a new concert hall and expanded boulevards in the downtown. In 1964 the CIBC tower was surpassed by the 623-foot Stock Exchange Tower, this time the world's tallest reinforced concrete building. With new computers and other electronic devices, the Montreal exchange had the most modern facilities anywhere in the world.[4]

But it was the world exhibition of 1967 that really put Montreal on the map. In typically extravagant Montreal fashion, an artificial island was constructed in the St Lawrence, using fill excavated from the tunnelling of the city's brand new subway system. Fifty million people visited Expo 67 at a time when the metropolis had a population of 2.6 million. American visitors must have been impressed, for the following year Montreal was awarded the first major league baseball team outside the United States, to be named the Expos. Adding to the spectacle of Expo 67 was the visit of French president Charles de Gaulle on board the French ship *Colbert*. General de Gaulle, however, added fuel to the delicate question of Quebec's possible separation from Canada – an issue that would prove to be significantly tied to the decline of Montreal, as will be elaborated below. From the balcony of Montreal's city hall, de Gaulle greeted a large crowd with the inflammatory words 'Vive Montréal! Vive le Québec! Vive le Québec libre!'[5]

The movement for Quebec independence had been growing for several decades and was in some regards a consequence of the growth of Montreal.[6] From 1941 to 1971, the city had added two million people, the major influx being from rural and small-town Quebec. During the 1940s and 1950s, Montreal quietly fostered French culture – the growing population making new expressions in politics, art, education, and everyday life. In the 1960s, the energy burst into a flowering of French theatre, music, film, and television. Montreal was transformed from an English city with many French speakers into a French city with many English speakers. With this growth in a distinct culture came calls for autonomy from a predominantly English-speaking Canada.

The separatist movement included an extreme faction that turned to violence.[7] In 1969 a bomb exploded in the house of Mayor Drapeau; he and his family were unharmed. Further bombings occurred in the rich Westmount area the following May. That year, 1970, was the year of the October Crisis, which saw the kidnapping of British diplomat James Richard Cross and Quebec labour and immigration minister Pierre Laporte. The latter was tragically killed. Many Montreal citizens were arrested under the War Measures Act under suspicion of being terrorists.

It was the political wing of the separatist movement that proved to have the greatest impact on the Montreal economy. Upon gaining power in the provincial elections of 1976, René Lévesque's Parti Québécois (PQ) passed Bill 101, the Charter of the French Language. French was already the official language of Quebec. The change from official bilingualism (English and French) had been made in 1974, under the Liberal government of Premier Robert Bourassa. Bill 101, however, was more forceful in promoting the French language. In its original form, the charter made it illegal for commercial signs outside of business establishments to be in any language other than French. Children attending public schools were also forced to receive education in French (unless a parent had received his or her education in English in Quebec). Some of these rules were subsequently challenged by the Supreme Court of Canada and slightly softened, but at the time the new laws were strictly enforced by what the English media considered a near-fascist-style language police.

The response was a flood of companies moving their headquarters out of Montreal, predominantly to Toronto. One of the most public moves was that of Canada's largest insurance company, Sun Life, which saw eight hundred white-collar jobs leave the city.[8] The Sun Life Building had been a prominent, long-standing landmark in downtown Montreal; its vaults had been the secret hiding place of the Bank of England's gold bullion and the British crown jewels during the Second World War. In January 1978 the company announced that it would move its headquarters to Toronto, acknowledging that the decision was a response to Bill 101. A study by a Liberal Party member showed that forty-two major companies had moved all or a major part of their head-office operations out of the province. These included Allied Chemical Canada, BP Canada, MacDonald Tobacco, Standard Brands, and Redpath Industries. Most relocated to Toronto.

Even the Bank of Montreal, Canada's oldest chartered bank, effectively moved to Toronto.[9] Formed in 1817, the Bank of Montreal had served as Canada's central bank until 1935, playing a role in financing the first transcontinental railway in the 1880s. By 1977, however, Toronto's Bay Street was seen as the country's future financial centre and so the bank moved its operational headquarters to Ontario's capital. As a face-saving measure, the bank's legal head office remained in Montreal, but the chairman, president, and senior executives all moved to the new office at First Canadian Place in Toronto.

Toronto had always been just a bit smaller in size than Montreal, but through the twentieth century it began to grow at a substantially higher rate. In 1900 Toronto was two-thirds the size of Montreal, and from a national perspective the latter was more important for finance, publishing, wholesaling, retailing, manufacturing, and entertainment.[10] Toronto's industrial base was growing faster, though, especially in clothing, printing, metal fabrication, and food processing, and subsequently in automobile manufacturing. From 1911 to 1931, the population of the Toronto region doubled from 409,000 to 818,000. During the Second World War, Toronto was a major centre for industrial production; by 1943, eighty-seven large plants and many smaller ones in the Toronto region were mobilized for the war effort. There was a further surge in population during the post-war decades, with growth between 4 per cent and 5 per cent per year, again driven by a successful manufacturing-based economy.[11]

While Montreal was breaking world records for its buildings in the 1960s, Toronto's downtown cityscape also grew impressively. From 1962 to 1982, the central corridor's office space grew from twenty million square feet to fifty million square feet.[12] Prominent buildings included First Canadian Place (1972), with over two million square feet, and the Toronto-Dominion tower (1967) and Ontario Hydro building (1975), both with over one million square feet. In 1977 Torontonians were also treated to the fabulous new Eaton Centre, a four-level indoor shopping centre, with a glass-domed ceiling running the length of two city blocks, complete with a flock of sculpted Canadian geese by artist and filmmaker Michael Snow. All the new office towers, however, were surpassed in height by the 1976 opening of the CN Tower; the 1814-foot-high communications tower with revolving restaurant was, until 2007, the tallest free-standing structure in the world. At the same time, responding in part to Montreal's Expo 67, the Ontario government financed a significant number of entertainment venues in Toronto: the Ontario Place amusement park, the Ontario Science Centre, additions to the Royal Ontario Museum and Art Gallery of Ontario, the Roy Thompson concert hall, and renovations to Exhibition Stadium were all completed within a few years.[13]

Toronto managed to balance its growth with a strong social agenda. For a few years in the early 1970s, a reform group in power at city hall, concerned about protecting neighbourhoods, imposed height restrictions on new buildings. Most significantly, in June 1971, the province abandoned plans to build an expressway on the west side of downtown, opting to preserve older middle-class neighbourhoods, and later extended the subway system.[14] The campaign to scrap the Spadina Expressway, led by, among others, urbanist-author-turned-activist Jane Jacobs, has become part of Toronto folklore. While many US cities suffered from inner-city blight, Toronto managed to maintain strong, safe, and affluent inner-city neighbourhoods. With clean streets and low crime, it became recognized as 'the city that worked.'[15]

The spectacular growth in Toronto's downtown core continued until about 1991. Major buildings in the later era included the Scotia Plaza (1988), the Bay/Wellington tower (1991), and the Canada Trust tower (1990), all over one million square feet. These were linked to the surrounding buildings in the downtown core by a complex of attractive, subterranean, pedestrian walkways. Lined with four million square feet of shops and cafés, the sixteen miles of luxury walkways enable Torontonians to stroll throughout the downtown core protected from the harsh Canadian winters. In 1987 visiting British actor Peter Ustinov appropriately remarked, 'Toronto is a kind of New York operated by the Swiss.'[16]

While Toronto managed to get most of its infrastructure investments right, Montreal struggled. Toronto's $600-million SkyDome stadium with retractable roof, built for the Toronto Blue Jays baseball club, was perhaps lavish and overpriced. Montreal's Olympic stadium, however, had ended up costing $1.61 billion, an incredible twelve times over budget! There were many reasons for the overruns: a labour strike delayed the tower; the 60,000-square-foot Kevlar roof, sixty-five tons in weight, languished in a warehouse in France until 1982 and, when installed, was torn in heavy winds. It took until December 2006 to pay off the costs of the stadium. Currently, without a major professional sports franchise (the baseball team left in 2004), the stadium is now closed for four months every winter because of concerns that the roof will collapse under snow loads. The Montreal Games, still the most expensive in Olympic history, took place in a half-built stadium.

Montreal's other great infrastructure extravagance was its vastly underused Mirabel International Airport.[17] In 1967 there were calls for a second Montreal airport. It was somehow determined that Montreal's existing Dorval Airport was too small for the confident city's expected growth, and that, even if Dorval was expanded, it would reach a maximum capacity of twenty million passengers per year by 1985.[18] With the decision to build a second airport made, political squabbling about its location began. The Canadian government wanted it on the west side of Montreal, close to Ottawa; the Quebec government preferred the east side, closer to Quebec City. In the end, the compromise was the current Mirabel site in St-Scholastique, some thirty-four miles north of Montreal.

Grand plans were made for the new airport. Mirabel was to be a great new terminus for North America, drawing passengers from competing airports in Boston, New York, Pittsburgh, and Toronto. It was to be developed in three phases, with six terminals and six runways costing $1 billion, by the year 2000.[19] The federal government expropriated 88,000 acres of farmland, even though only 5200 acres were required for phase 1 and 17,000 acres for the full plan; the airport was to be surrounded by a vast industrial park and linked to downtown Montreal by a six-lane toll highway and a high-speed electric train. Mirabel's first phase opened in October 1975, one year late, and at a cost of $600 million, double the budget.[20] The rail and road links were not completed, however, so it was hard for Mirabel to compete with Dorval, which, being situated much closer to Montreal, still carried 8.7 million passengers per year. Mirabel lost $115 million in the first two years of operation.

Moreover, by the late 1970s and into the 1980s, the Montreal economy was in decline. The separatist PQ government was in power and Toronto had become the larger city. Unemployment in Montreal was over 9 per cent in 1981, compared to just 4 per cent in Toronto; by the late 1980s, Montreal unemployment's rate was over 13 per cent. With a struggling economy, Montreal's airline passenger traffic remained stagnant at under ten million passengers per year throughout the 1980s and 1990s. Dorval continued to carry more than double the passenger traffic of Mirabel, the latter mainly focusing on carrying freight. By 1998, however, it was clear that Mirabel was an economic disaster, and most of the remaining passenger flights and even more of the freight switched to Dorval. By year 2000, Mirabel carried merely one million passengers, on charter flights, and had half the cargo freight of Dorval. Meanwhile, most of the transatlantic airlines had determined that Toronto was the preferred hub for Canada. Passengers flying out of Toronto's airport numbered twenty million in 1990, and, following the opening of a new terminal, the total increased to over twenty-five million per year by the end of the century. By 2009, two older terminals had been replaced with another new terminal and over thirty million passengers per year were using Toronto Pearson airport.

In becoming Canada's main transportation hub, Toronto also went one step further in becoming the country's financial centre, again at the expense of Montreal. The competition between the two cities had been long and drawn out.[21] Montreal was seemingly ahead during the first half of the twentieth century. Its St James Street exchange specialized in railway securities and industrial stocks, housing traders with a desire for high technology. However, it either overlooked, or could not attract, the mining industry, which was centred in Ontario.[22] Thus, from early on, Toronto became the financial centre for mining stocks.

For much of the twentieth century, Canada's major banks were also split between Montreal and Toronto.[23] In 1898 the Merchants Bank of Halifax moved from Canada's early financial centre to Montreal, where it changed its name to the Royal Bank of Canada. And so, along with the Bank of Montreal, the city was home to Canada's two largest banks. Yet in 1900, when the Bank of Nova Scotia left Halifax, it chose to relocate in Toronto, where, in later years it became a major Canadian bank, along with the Canadian Imperial Bank of Commerce and the Toronto Dominion Bank. Canada then had two banking centres; even the country's money market was peculiarly said to be 'centred' in Toronto 'and' Montreal.[24] In 1983, when the Toronto Stock Exchange relocated to new premises in First Canadian Place, it was clear that Toronto had emerged ahead of Montreal as Canada's financial centre. According to the *Financial Post*, of the 278 Canadian-owned industrial companies, 197 now had headquarters in the Toronto area. Measured in terms of the assets of corporations that had moved to Toronto between 1970 and 1981, Toronto gained $31.4 billion while Montreal lost $20.5 billion.[25] Forty-five out of fifty-seven banks operating in Canada chose to locate in Toronto. Meanwhile, by 1999, over 90 per cent of the value of shares traded in Canada were on the Toronto Stock Exchange. That year, $529 billion worth of shares were traded on Bay Street, compared to just $42 billion in Montreal.[26] Moreover, in a more open and competitive globalized financial system, Toronto had found a niche as the world's centre for mining stocks.[27] Toronto achieved a feat which, while not unprecedented in history, is rare. It overtook the largest city in the same country in terms of population and became the wealthier metropolis. By 2001, the Toronto metropolitan area had a population of 4.9 million, compared to 3.5 million in the Montreal metropolitan area. In 2000 the average household income in Toronto was $80,194, compared to just $52,965 in Montreal.[28]

The story of Toronto's rise relative to Montreal includes several of the themes addressed in this book. Most notably, it exemplifies Gras's four-phase theory of how a financial metropolis develops. For decades, Montreal was wealthier than Toronto, but, having established itself as a commercial centre, Toronto proceeded to surpass its rival first as an industrial city, then as a transportation hub, and soon after as a financial centre. Of course, Bill 101 and the Quebec independence movement added a layer of complexity that is beyond Gras's model. It may be argued, rightly or wrongly, that Bill 101 was a response to discrimination by the rest of Canada. Nevertheless, to pass a bill that discriminated against a large part of the hard-working business class of Montreal was, in economic terms, sheer lunacy. The resulting move of so many businesses from Montreal to Toronto sealed the decline of the former's stock market and status as a financial centre.

It seems incredible that Quebecers actually voted to ship so much of their wealth and prosperity down Highway 401 to Toronto. As far back as Xenophon, there was recognition of the importance of tolerance and openness to foreigners for urban prosperity. Several examples where such openness helped build the wealth of cities have been seen in previous chapters. Amsterdam was noted for its acceptance of other Europeans, such as French Huguenots and Spanish Jews. London, too, was always a melting pot; the rich men of the city came from many parts of Europe. It is no coincidence that one of the main streets passing through the city is called Lombardy Street. (Of course, there were times when Catholics were persecuted in these two cities, and slavery was accepted; let us not wear rose-coloured glasses.) Another example is the rise of the wealthy Chinese in Hong Kong, an indication of the tolerance of the British rulers there. Furthermore, New York City's liberal world view was a benefit not only to itself but to other cities worldwide.

Beyond the insights of Xenophon and Gras, however, this inquiry offers a more theoretically rich understanding of how the wealth of cities evolves. There are three key elements to this theoretical model. The first is a means for measuring the wealth of cities through the assets of citizens. There is no more practical way to gauge how the wealth of cities changes than through real estate and financial assets – the primary two components of urban wealth; the value of real estate in particular will change over time as cities physically grow, or the building stock is renewed. As discussed in chapter 3, these components of urban wealth are valued by a complex of interacting markets, through drivers that are both internal and external to the city. All cities, of course, have real estate markets, but the wealthiest cities are those that out-compete others to host financial markets.

The second element is the principle that the ways in which cities physically evolve profoundly influence economic growth. Citizens become locked in to lifestyles that are a determined by urban form; hence, consumption in cities is a function of urban design. Finally, to understand how changes in urban form and urban economies occur requires a biological perspective. The third main element of this book, then, has been a description of how urban economies can be understood in terms analogous to those of natural ecosystems. These three key elements of the theoretical model set out here are elaborated on below.

The Wealth of Citizens

Wealth is power over the goods and services that people need or desire. Large corporations, small corporations, national governments, and local governments – all have power; indeed, they supply most of the goods and services that people require. Ultimately, though, corporations and other businesses are owned by people, and governments are an embodiment of people. So, when it comes to the tricky question of quantifying the wealth of a city, what we are really getting at is the wealth of its citizens.

Chapter 2 recounted the case of sixteenth-century Seville, which, despite all the gold and silver landing at its port, did not become as wealthy as it might. Seville was a large and important European city, without doubt. Earlier, in 1400, with a population of 70,000, it had been Europe's ninth-largest city.[29] Yet, in spite of then establishing itself as the transportation centre for the New World, Seville did not become Europe's financial centre; Antwerp and later Genoa were ahead in that respect. Furthermore, most of Seville's assets were owned by the citizens of other cities. What became of Seville after the sixteenth century? It continued to be a significant centre for the arts, culture, and, above all, religion, but a series of unfortunate events seriously eroded its economy. In the seventeenth century, as Spain's economy was in crisis, Seville became a monastic city – a city driven by zeal for the Counter-Reformation – home to the Franciscan, Dominican, Augustine, and Jesuit orders. The terrible plague of 1649 was devastating, halving the population of the city. Then, in 1717, the administration of the Indies was moved downriver to Cadiz. This was partly for political reasons, but the silting up of the Guadalquivir River had also made navigation difficult. The great Lisbon earthquake of November 1755 also affected Seville. It was said that the bells of Seville Cathedral pealed on their own, as the quake left many buildings and monuments in ruins. By 1750, Seville's population was still just 68,000, making it only the twenty-fifth-largest city in Europe.[30]

The twentieth century brought better years for Seville. In 1899 one of its most famous heroes returned to the city. The remains of Christopher Columbus, Admiral of the Atlantic, were moved from Havana, Cuba, to lie in the transept of the Seville cathedral. In 1929 the city hosted the World Exposition in the marvellously constructed Plaza de España. Its economy was boosted yet again as the World Exposition returned in 1992.

As we learned from Seville, the wealth of a city is determined by the net assets of its citizens: their property and investments. The value of such assets is ultimately measured through markets. Yet markets can take on a life of their own, rising and crashing based on the rash expectations of human beings. We recounted the roller-coaster rides that Paris and London went through during the Mississippi and South Sea bubbles of 1720. Some citizens came out much wealthier, like the mysterious Richard Cantillon, while others such as Isaac Newton and the Duke of Portland lost a bundle. When the net value of all citizens' assets is considered, however, urban wealth is found to be much more steadfast. Peaks in real estate markets and equity markets run counter to each other, with an overall upward trend in wealth. Even in New York City after the great crash of 1929, real estate value rose and peaked two years later in 1931.[31] The financial crisis of 2008 was an exception, producing a flight to gold. This notion of conservation does not mean that the wealth of individual cities cannot have occasional sporadic gains or losses. Berne made a handsome profit from the South Sea bubble, while Hong Kong took a considerable correction to its wealth when the Asian financial crisis of 1997 transferred value from Asian real estate to Western technology stocks. Nonetheless, such fluctuations in the wealth of cities are likely far less severe than those experienced by individual citizens.

Some cities have risen above others to become very wealthy, reaching near to the top of a hierarchy of cities. These are the cities that host and thus control markets. Whether involving eastern spices, Baltic lumber, Eurodollars, or blue-chip stocks, different tactics have been taken by cities to establish and maintain their markets. Venice forced much of Europe's trade to be conducted through its port by controlling the activities of foreign merchants and subsidizing its own merchants with the protected convoys of the *galere da mercato*. Amsterdam similarly achieved entrepôt status by the sheer number of its ships. Antwerp was entrepreneurial in establishing its wholesale market. New York, as the 1920s Pujo Committee found, had an exclusive club controlling much of the city's enormous wealth. There is more to it than simply laissez-faire.

To become a financial metropolis a city must first pass through three other phases. London was the first city to reach phase four, according to Gras, but the process is also well demonstrated by the case of Toronto described in this chapter. Toronto, the capital of Ontario, was already a commercial centre (phase 1) in the nineteenth century; indeed, the native meaning of Toronto is 'meeting place.' In the twentieth century, Toronto grew through the second phase as a major industrial centre, and then, from the 1970s onward, it finally overcame the competition of a weakening Montreal to reach the status of national transportation hub (phase 3) and dominant financial centre (phase 4) within a few short years.

A particularly key step in becoming a financial metropolis seems to be the establishment of a transportation network centred on a city. London did this with its port, railway network, and telegraph cables. New York achieved a superior geographical position through its financing of the Erie Canal. The Gotthard tunnel helped to establish both Zurich and Milan, while Frankfurt benefited from its airport. In addition, to make it through to the fourth phase – to become a financial metropolis – usually requires overcoming fierce competition. New York overtook Philadelphia after the Bank War of the 1830s. Liverpool and Manchester, though, could not move from under London's wing. The case recounted in this chapter was quite remarkable; Quebecers actually helped the rise of Toronto, relative to their own city of Montreal, by electing a separatist government.

The wealth of cities is reflected in the assets of citizens, but the value of such assets also relates to the incomes of the citizens. Whether through commercial activities, industry, transportation-related employment, or financial services, the incomes that citizens earn have a bearing on our measurement of urban wealth. Keynes recognized that those with greater incomes have a greater propensity to save. Thus, the equities, bonds, and other financial assets held by citizens of high-income cities would be expected to be greater than those of lower-income cities. Household incomes, moreover, have a strong bearing on the value of urban real estate. As household income rises in cities, so too does the value of homes. This is apparent from the positive income elasticity of demand for housing. Essentially, affluence increases competition between households for desirable property, thereby raising prices. Other factors, as discussed in chapter 3, also affect housing prices. Supply constraints or really low interest rates, as in Hong Kong in the mid-1990s, can send market prices soaring. Over time, however, markets will respond to short supply and correct for changes in interest rates, and so income is, not surprisingly, the most important determinant of the wealth of cities.

Of the various forms that urban wealth can take, a particularly important one is real estate. There is interplay between real estate markets, financial markets, and other forms of wealth, such as gold. When investors in financial markets see few opportunities, or are uncertain, or are just looking to spend their gains, often it is real estate that ends up storing the wealth. The recent financial crisis of 2008 was somewhat of an exception, but, taking a longer historical perspective, it is clear that real estate is a physical manifestation of the wealth of cities.

The storage of wealth in real estate is exemplified by the history of New York's Fifth Avenue – the richest street in the world. The spine of Gotham has been the home to some of New York's, indeed the world's, wealthiest citizens – the likes of the Astors, Carnegies, and Vanderbilts. In the late nineteenth and early twentieth centuries, Fifth Avenue grew at a tremendous rate, but its growth was no mere matter of simple expansion – it was a vibrant, often chaotic, process of destruction and rebuilding.[32] The avenue witnessed a physical manifestation of Schumpeter's 'creative destruction,' or, as Marx put it, 'All that is solid melts into the air.'[33] This is true of any street under reconstruction, but for Fifth Avenue it was particularly dramatic.

In less than one hundred years, Fifth Avenue was transformed from an empty country road into a paradise of millionaires' mansions and then into a dense collection of luxury shops and apartments.[34] The avenue had been laid out in 1824, but development above 14th Street did not occur until the 1850s. Growth in New York's industry and commerce swallowed up serene residential neighbourhoods, such as Washington Square, encouraging the city's elites to move uptown.[35] Exquisite mansions built by the country's finest architects for New York's wealthy elite soon made Fifth Avenue a sought-after address. Yet, as building of the mansions peaked in the 1890s, others were being demolished to make way for luxury apartments.[36] The south end of the avenue, below 42nd Street, was also soon invaded by manufacturers. The garment industry in particular benefited by following the luxury-clothing stores that were now also moving up the avenue. New York had a great diversity of other small manufacturers too, for which, in the 1920s alone, between fifty and sixty million square feet of industrial loft space was erected.[37] Half of the fifty-eight brownstones that, in 1902, had lined the avenue between 34th and 42nd streets were gone by 1910, and nearly all were demolished by 1930.[38] The pace of change was so rapid that some houses were replaced within a decade of construction. Few of the mansions in 'millionaires' mile' alongside Central Park stood for more then forty years, and those that did survive changed hands frequently.

Many of New York's wealthiest citizens multiplied their fortunes through real estate holdings yet battled in vain to preserve the serenity of Fifth Avenue against the tide of reconstruction – the physical reality of the city's accumulating wealth. With profits from their equity holdings in steel making and railroads, men like Carnegie and Vanderbilt built luxurious homes on the avenue. To avoid the threat of encroachment by towering apartment buildings and lofts, Andrew Carnegie built his estate far up the Avenue at 90th Street.[39] The Astors, by contrast, 'skipped their way up the Avenue' from Washington Square, moving first to 34th Street and then to 68th Street.[40] Indeed, the last of these moves to the heart of the upper avenue was said to have caused a mass exodus of the wealthy from the lower avenue. Others, however, dug in and attempted to preserve stable residential enclaves. The Vanderbilts in particular spent a fortune to purchase large quantities of land surrounding their various mansions between 51st and 59th streets.[41] Some of their lands they also sold with restrictive covenants to ensure that they remained for low-rise residential use. Such covenants, however, sometimes merely stalled development – and some vacant lots under covenant found no buyers owing to the threat of taller buildings progressing up the avenue. Then, of course, there was always the enticement to join the windfall of the real estate boom. From 1901 to 1907, property values along the avenue increased by an average of 250 per cent.[42] The typical 25-by-100-foot lot costing $125,000 in 1901 rose to $400,000 in 1907. The market slowed down during the First World War, but bounced back spectacularly in March 1920, when the Astors sold 141 lots in the city for $5 million.[43] Eventually, the force of the market was too great even for the Vanderbilts, whose grand mansion at 58th and 5th was torn down in 1924. There was a tweaking of legislation that year, causing a demolition spree; at least a further twenty-six mansions above 59th Street were torn down and replaced mainly with apartment buildings.[44]

Efforts to restrain the destructive dynamic of the real estate market did eventually succeed. Though it did little for the mansions, zoning legislation of 1916 prevented manufacturing firms from invading the avenue between 42nd and 90th streets. Behind this legislation – the country's first comprehensive zoning law – was a powerful coalition known as the Fifth Avenue Association.[45] Where individual millionaires had failed, an association of property owners, residents, and retailers succeeded in its objective of maintaining Fifth Avenue as an exclusive retail and residential area. Through a long, concerted, and unified approach, courting and embracing municipal authority, they established one of the earliest formal business districts and achieved the zoning legislation. A bastion of conservatism, the Fifth Avenue Association managed to tame a rampant property market to the great benefit of its members. To this day, Fifth Avenue, from 42nd to 90th streets, remains the most expensive retail street in the world.

What the history of Fifth Avenue reveals is a natural force underlying the growth in urban wealth. As the physical shape of cities evolves over time, so does the wealth of cities as reflected by the value of real estate. Yet, while the construction or sale of each building may be carefully planned and conducted by individual citizens, the real estate market as a whole has a wild, rampant physicality to it, which in the case of Fifth Avenue was eventually tamed.

The Physical Shape of Urban Economies

Beyond the manifestation of urban wealth in real estate, this book has pointed to a yet deeper link between the growth of urban economies and their physical urban form. One of the most central goals of the discipline of economics is to explain the phenomenon of economic growth. The notion developed in this book is that economic growth, as measured by changes in per capita income, has been inherently tied to changes in the physical shape of cities. Urban form is very much dependent on changes in technology, which many recognize as fundamental to economic growth. Most growth theories consider technological innovation, perhaps accompanied by changes in management practices, to have been responsible for increasing productivity. This is certainly the case. But what we have added is the idea that application of technology in changing types of urban form has induced increases in consumption, which are as important as increases in output for growth to occur.[46]

This key insight came from Keynes, who noted that 'a man's habitual standard of life usually has the first claim on his income.'[47] Our habits are shaped by the environment around us; our consumption is governed by the size and shape of the physical space that we inhabit and the paths and distances we must travel to satisfy human wants and needs. The fundamental shapes and forms of our cities have usually evolved slowly, on time scales similar to the life of a person. This is similarly the case with other subjective factors that govern consumption. To quote Keynes again: 'The subjective factors ... include those social practices and institutions which, though not unalterable, are unlikely to undergo a material change over a short period of time except in abnormal or revolutionary circumstances. In an historical enquiry or in comparing one social system with another of a different type, it is necessary to take account of the manner in which changes in the subjective factors may affect the propensity to consume.'[48]

What Keynes is getting at is that the factors that affect our propensity to consume – and hence overall economic growth – usually change slowly and thus are difficult to discern. My argument is that one of the most important of these factors is the physical shape of cities, and that, while it is true that changes in urban form usually occur so slowly over time as to be imperceptible, such is not always the case. Consider the story of London after the Great Fire of 1666, recounted in chapter 5; the reconstruction of the city after that catastrophe amounted to a rapid, revolutionary change in urban form that was evident to the people who lived through it. But there are other examples too. One is London again, this time in the nineteenth century; the other is New York in the first half of the twentieth century. These two case studies reinforce the link between urban form and the propensity to consume, and hence the wealth of cities.

In the nineteenth century, London went from being a compact city of one million people, most of whom could make all their journeys by foot, to a sprawling metropolis of six million teeming with taxicabs, omnibuses, and trains. At the heart of the transformation lay, once again, decisions about the city's infrastructure. The main barrier to London's economic growth at the beginning of the century was quite simply the inadequacy of its streets. At that time, London, which stretched from Buckingham Palace to about a mile past the Tower of London, was traversed by only three east–west routes.[49] The Strand / Fleet Street route had bottlenecks at the west end of the Strand and another at Temple Bar. The middle route along Oxford Street and High Holborn (before New

Oxford Street was constructed) had narrow deviations along St Giles High Street and Broad Street, plus a tricky descent into the River Fleet valley. Moreover, the High Holborn and Fleet Street routes merged together at St Paul's Cathedral, making Cheapside the worst bottleneck of them all. Only the New Road (now the inner North Circular Road: Marylebone, Euston, and Pentonville roads) was uncongested, other than perhaps for the animals going to market. Travelling north to south was even more difficult. There was no Regent Street, Charing Cross Road, Shaftsbury Avenue, or Kingsway or Farrington Roads. Indeed, there was no immediately obvious major north–south thoroughfare.[50] And then, of course, there was the River Thames, which was crossed by only three narrow bridges. All of this had serious consequences. The vehicle technology to support suburbanization – and thus economic growth – already existed in the form of the long stagecoach, later called the omnibus.[51] But London's streets had too many blockages to cater for omnibuses, and so the dirty, old Hackney carriages – which could be afforded only by the wealthy – had a legally enforced monopoly on public transportation within most of the city.[52]

Between 1814 and 1830, London's main thoroughfares were substantially improved.[53] The majestic Regent Street was cut through dilapidated housing, completing a link from the New Road to the top of Whitehall. The west end of The Strand was improved and Fleet Street widened near Temple Bar. The High Holborn route was helped by construction of Skinner Street. Moorgate Street was also built in the city, linking the Bank of England to Finsbury Square. Three new bridges were opened across the Thames – Vauxhall (1816), Waterloo (1817), and Southwark (1819) – although these did levy expensive tolls. Most important, the new London Bridge, with a wide carriageway of fifty-two feet, was opened in 1831. Many turnpike gates were removed, freeing up the movement of vehicles. Moreover, in 1826, the turnpike trusts north of the Thames were consolidated under the control of Sir John McAdam's new commission, which soon set about macadamizing – that is, paving with small broken stones – many of the main roads through London. With all these changes, the capacity of London's street system was dramatically increased.

It might be noted that the motives behind London's street improvements went beyond just meeting the needs of traffic. The 1814 construction of Regent Street, for example, provided better access between Westminster and the crown's large Marylebone Park estate, thereby substantially increasing the value of the crown lands.[54] Moreover, the route was chosen partly to destroy derelict housing, but also in a manner that clearly separated the nobility and gentry on the west side from an area populated by mechanics and traders to the east. In many of the other nineteenth-century street improvements, however, slum clearance was a major objective. Financial expediency was required for all of London's road improvements, and there were usually more proposed schemes than finances available. Hence, schemes that removed 'hotbeds of disease, misery and crime' were often chosen.[55] Routes were selected so as to improve buildings, construct sewers, and open up access to crowded areas, as well as to provide access across the city.

In September 1831 the government repealed the Hackney carriage legislation and encouraged a major improvement in London's public transportation by permitting licences for omnibuses. The omnibuses were long, covered stagecoaches with capacity for about twenty people inside, and often pulled by three horses abreast. The government's change in legislation was likely influenced by the opening of ten omnibus routes in Paris in 1828.[56] George Shillibeer had also, from 1829, run omnibuses along the New Road, which lay outside the Hackney carriage monopoly.[57] As a result of the change in legislation, there were 825 licensed omnibuses on London's streets by 1839.[58] While fares were perhaps still too expensive for London's working class, the omnibuses dramatically increased the mobility of the growing middle class. Moreover, with their monopoly removed, the 1100 dirty Hackney carriages essentially disappeared, unable to compete with new hansom and brougham cabs, which numbered 2450 by 1844.[59]

The 1830s also heralded the emergence of two other new modes of public transportation in London. At Easter 1835, a relatively cheap steamboat service began operating between London Bridge and Greenwich.[60] Smaller steamboats began to run between London Bridge and Westminster in 1837. Then, by 1843, eight iron steamboats operated between London Bridge and Chelsea, carrying two million passengers that year. The first railway line into London, the elevated London and Greenwich, opened in 1836, soon to be followed by many others.[61] Initially, the railways mainly carried passengers from destinations outside London. The London Bridge Station and Fenchurch Street Station were the only ones to handle much short-distance commuter traffic in the 1840s. In many cases, though, the railways helped to generate business for the omnibus companies, since passengers needed to travel from the ring of railway stations to their final destinations.

The economic impacts of these three new modes of urban transportation were considerable. An 1854 study of daily commuting into the city recorded 200,000 persons arriving by foot and 15,000 by steamboat. Estimates by T.C. Barker and M. Robbins suggest that a further 6000 arrived by train, and about 20,000 by omnibus, each day.[62] Walking was clearly still the most common mode, for it was free; many of the working class would walk up to an hour or more to get to work each day. Yet it is the 40,000 or so other commuters who were so significant. Fifty years earlier, there would have been very few people commuting into the city by public transportation. These 40,000, plus others working elsewhere in London, were now living a suburban lifestyle. Such suburbanization clearly was a boost to the home-construction sector of London's economy. Moreover, these middle-class Londoners were becoming locked in to residential locations that required them to pay for vehicular transportation services as a regular part of their daily routine. There had been a change in the subjective factors affecting the propensity to consume. Payments for transportation services by the middle class provided jobs and income for other Londoners – not just the drivers, conductors, and managers of the transportation vehicles, but also those involved with grooming horses, selling feedstock, and maintaining buses, and perhaps some local manufacturing. The growth in the transportation sector of London's economy was substantial, and this would lead to even more profound changes in other sectors as the transportation system grew during the second half of the nineteenth century.

The world's first underground railway, the Metropolitan, was opened on 10 January 1863, linking Paddington Station to Farrington Street (in the city) via King's Cross.[63] Before the opening, an article in *The Times* reflected the scepticism many felt as to whether the subterranean railway would pay for itself. Yet it was a great success. Indeed, as suburban commuter traffic grew on the Great Northern line into King's Cross, and with the arrival of the Midland Railway into St Pancras, the Metropolitan line was rapidly doubled from two to four tracks and extended to Moorgate in the heart of the city.

Meanwhile, between 1860 and 1866, bridges were built that brought the south London railway lines over the river to new stations at Victoria, Charing Cross, and Cannon Street. These stations were subsequently linked by a second underground railway, the District line, which, with extensions to the Metropolitan line, formed a loop around inner London.[64] Inside the loop, travel by omnibus continued to rise, but only after an intervention from Paris![65] In December 1855 the Compagnie

Générale des Omnibus de Londres was formed, in Paris, with a capital of twenty-five million francs (£1 million), much of it thought to have come from the Crédit Mobilier. Within five months, the French company had bought half of the omnibuses in London, and soon afterwards it owned 600 of the 810 vehicles on her streets. Despite its near monopoly, which helped lower the cost of feeding horses, the company proved to be untenable. The remaining independent British operators cut their fares and, supported by a patriotic public, squeezed the French profits. On 1 January 1859 the French company was taken over by the British London General Omnibus Company (LGOC). In 1860 the LGOC carried forty million passengers,[66] and this number rapidly increased as the costs of horse feed continued to decline. By 1885, the LGOC was carrying 76.6 million passengers, and this grew dramatically to 112 million in 1890.[67] By this time, a smaller rival, the London Road Car Company, had formed and was carrying a further 37 million passengers.

While omnibus traffic grew in central London, after 1870 the inner suburbs began to be dominated by horse tramways.[68] The trams were more efficient than the omnibuses and could carry twice as many passengers using the same number of horses. The tram tracks were not allowed into central London, however, for fear of causing traffic congestion. Suburbanization soared in the second half of the century, and as it did businesses replaced residences in the central area. The residential population of the city fell from 128,000 in 1851 to 75,000 in 1871 and just 27,000 in 1901. Decreases were similarly observed for Westminster, Holborn, and Finsbury after 1870. The number of businesses in central London, however, continued to increase. Thus, while the residential population declined, the day population of the city increased from 170,000 in 1866 to 300,000 at the turn of the century.[69] Commuting had become routine for many Londoners.

The fundamental significance of urban transportation in London's economic growth cannot be overstated. As the population of Greater London grew from 4.2 million in 1875 to 6 million in 1895, the number of journeys by train, tram, and omnibus increased almost fourfold, from 275 million to 1 billion trips per year.[70] Every movement of a vehicle is a small dynamic of the economy at work. Furthermore, as transport-driven suburbanization mushroomed, so did London's economy. The 1880s and early 1890s were particularly dynamic, with real per capita income growing at a rate of 25 per cent per decade.[71] This corresponded to a massive increase in road and bridge construction beginning in the late 1870s.[72] The number of licensed cabs, mainly hansoms, reached

6 Over the nineteenth century London grew from a compact, walking city of one million people to a metropolis of six million, teeming with taxicabs, omnibuses, and trains. Its revolutions in transportation infrastructure underlay the creation of new economic sectors in retail, tourism, and entertainment. (Photo courtesy of David Gregory, Postcards of the Past)

10,500 by 1884[73] – a fourfold increase in forty years. Rows and rows of relatively cheap terrace houses, plus growing areas of detached and semi-detached housing, were fed by rail and tramways. A favourable national tax system also boosted housing supply. The window tax was removed in 1851, as were duties on bricks (1850), glass (1860), and timber (1866).[74] The cheap construction costs for terrace houses kept rental costs low, and hence wages in London remained competitive. The increase in London's population and concentration of businesses in its centre also no doubt had agglomeration effects. The recipe was right for economic growth.[75]

Yet there was more to it. London's growth also entailed social change and the creation of new economic sectors, enabled by its new transportation system. Besides the increases in commuter trips, there was also a huge increase in travel for other purposes. London's first department stores developed mid-century and grew rapidly in number towards the end of the century.[76] Together with the expansion of specialized shops, the large department stores prompted many shoppers to travel into central London from the suburbs and beyond. The volume of purchasing was much greater than that of previous generations. Employment expanded both in retailing and in the consumer-goods industry. Travel for pleasure also emerged as a new industry. Londoners left at weekends to visit the countryside or seaside, while others would travel into the city to visit exhibitions. There was also growth in travel for entertainment. Masses of Londoners travelled during the evening to attend music halls and theatres; the rate of attendance was unparalleled elsewhere in the United Kingdom.[77] In the early 1890s, London had thirty-five substantial music halls, which altogether entertained around 45,000 people per night. London's new urban form enabled new types of consumption and new industries, or, as Jane Jacobs would simply put it, new work.

On the other side of the Atlantic, a different phenomenon occurred – the great twentieth-century transformation of cities into sprawling automobile-based metropolises. New York led the way. Other cities, such as Los Angeles and Detroit, were also growing rapidly into auto-dependent cities in the early twentieth century, but New York is especially noteworthy because of its particular regional-planning decisions – decisions that were necessary to change the physical form of such a massive and complex region – and the momentous, yet ambiguous, role of Robert Moses in making the city's plans a reality, as outlined shortly below.

From 1900 to 1930, the number of registered motor vehicles in the United States increased from a mere 8000 to 26.75 million.[78] Over the same period, the average hourly wage of Americans increased by 313 per cent.[79] The connection between the revolution in transportation system and US economic growth is clearly strong. By 1926, Americans were spending 18 per cent of their take-home income on car payments, many of which had been purchased on credit.[80] The automobile was well on its way to becoming a significant component of autonomous consumption. In 1938 President Roosevelt noted that the automobile had become an integral part of the daily lives of millions of ordinary American families.[81]

With just over 10 per cent of the US population, New York State had a higher number of automobiles and more miles of highway than any other state. The number of vehicles registered in the state increased from 1,815,434 in 1926 to 2,584,123 in 1939.[82] A great many of these would have been in the metropolis. New York City alone had 600,000 registered autos in 1930.[83] By 1939, New York State also had 12,652 miles of state roadways, a little more than California, which had 12,097.[84] The New York total includes some of the 2527 miles of suburban highways that had been envisaged in the 1929 regional plan (other parts were in New Jersey and Connecticut; some were yet to be completed). A map of the highways from the regional plan shows a metropolitan loop, twenty to thirty miles in diameter, a further outer metropolitan bypass, great radial arteries spreading out from the central city, and a host of other highways including waterfront routes along the shores of Manhattan.[85]

The formation of New York's regional plan was in itself a remarkable achievement. In the early decades of the century, the metropolis was a region under stress. Every day, millions of commuters headed into Manhattan, where masses of migrants packed into overcrowded tenements. Meanwhile, skyscrapers, sweatshops, and classy hotels grew uncontrolled and uncoordinated, all adding to extreme congestion in the downtown. Such regional issues needed regional solutions. The early planning profession recognized that it was necessary to understand the region as a whole – to see it as an evolving organism. Decision making, however, was fragmented. The New York metropolis had a population of ten million people living over an area of 5528 square miles. It was governed by three states and 436 local governments.[86] Moreover, for the first thirty years of the century, power in the central city remained divided between the five borough presidents on the Board of Estimate.[87]

There were some early successes in planning. At the turn of the century, a group of exceptional engineers had, in laying out its rail system, understood how the region functioned as a whole.[88] The introduction of zoning in 1916 was another notable milestone in the city's planning. Yet set against this were mayors such as John Hylan, who in November 1917 abolished the city's planning committee.[89] In the early 1900s, New York City really had no plan –nor did the larger metropolitan area.

The driving force behind the regional plan was actually a Chicago business executive, Charles Dyer Norton. In 1918 he persuaded the Russell Sage Foundation to take up the role of the defunct city planning committee, but in the context of the wider region. There was more to the plan than just a vision of suburban highways forming the basis of an automobile city. It had a coordinated system of classified highways integrated with land-use plans for the entire region. The work in preparing the plan had included advances in understanding of the regional economy; Columbia University economist Murray Haig explained the process of industrial decentralization as crowding out by other industries. The regional plan achieved, as director of research Thomas Adams put it, an understanding of how the parts of the city were interrelated.[90]

While the regional plan was influential, perhaps even enlightening, it by no means had any authority, and it was regarded by some – including Robert Moses, the man who actually made much of it come to fruition – with disdain. Moses had no use for planning, seeing himself much more as a 'doer.' Yet the man who was responsible for directing the construction of numerous highways and bridges (not to mention swimming pools and housing projects) largely did so within the spirit of the regional plan. Over a forty-year period, Moses was the administrator behind the highways which rapidly propelled the New York region into the auto age. He did it by appropriating the plans and innovations of others, in particular the Regional Plan Association. His skill was an incredible ability to accumulate institutional power while harnessing finances from ever-shifting streams.[91] From 1924, he was chair of the State Council of Parks and the Long Island State Park Commission. He used his authority to create beautifully landscaped 'parkways' through the green areas in his jurisdiction. This was in the era when automobile ownership was still a desirable luxury pastime, before it had become autonomous consumption for the masses, as discussed in chapter 5. In the depression years of the 1930s, Moses drew upon the huge amounts of public works funding available under the New Deal, but also sustained his expanding highway empire with toll revenues from his bridges and highways. After the Second World War, Moses primarily hired engineers, rather than landscape artists, to construct more cost-effective, but ugly, expressways. In the 1950s and early 1960s, he oversaw completion of some of his largest highway projects, drawing upon federal interstate highway funding, and in the process became a controversial figure because of his willingness to raze whole neighbourhoods in pursuit of his vision.

The growth of sprawling auto-dependent suburbs that began with New York was gradually replicated in Los Angeles and other American cities. This highly consumptive urban form was a necessary ingredient for the rapid economic growth of the twentieth century. The proliferation of the urban automobile, and the spacious suburban lifestyle it enabled, provided employment and income for many. The physical growth of cities was a necessary ingredient for the increased wealth of cities over the century.

We should be careful, however, in drawing hasty conclusions from our understanding of the impact of urban form on urban economies. It does not necessarily follow that cities will become wealthy by sprawling in the manner of Chula Vista, as opposed to the transit-oriented Freiburg. Herein lies a tale of two types of cities. The massive increases in consumption associated with auto-dependent cities may well have fuelled twentieth-century economic growth, but in addition to the sprawling, highly consumptive cities, there are also *investing* cities. Such cities are those that achieve a different balance between accumulation of financial capital and physical expansion, where citizens typically save more of their income and are on average slightly more modest in their purchasing of automobiles, suburban palaces, and associated goods. This may not be a matter of choice, or deliberate policy. Some cities, such as some older European ones, may be physically constrained, for example, limited in space in which to grow; others cities may have deliberately restrained growth through greenbelts or other forms of planning constraints. Whatever the reason, these are the cities where citizens derive a higher percentage of their income from their investments. They invest in multinational corporations and other businesses that derive profits from the growth of highly consumptive cities. Indeed, one might suspect that the world's wealthiest cities – London, New York, and Tokyo – maintain their wealth because they achieve an appropriate balance between citizens' consumption and investment. In its period of rapid physical growth, nineteenth-century London maintained a high level of investment. As for New York, even though it was the first automobile metropolis and built hundred of miles of suburban highways, it did so after already establishing the exceptionally dense and wealthy nucleus of Manhattan. Tokyo, though perhaps now suffering along with all of Japan from the country's economic malaise, remains a model of restrained consumption and vigorous investment.

One of the best examples of an investing city is Singapore. From 1960 to 2003, the ratio of real private consumption to GDP in Singapore fell from 0.80 to 0.42.[92] Such a low rate of consumption makes the citizens of Singapore the stingiest consumers in the developed world. Of course, it also means that they are great at saving, and hence at investing. With high levels of investment, the wealth of Singapore has grown substantially since 1980, albeit with a sharp correction during the Asian financial crisis of the late 1990s.[93] Much of the wealth of Singapore is tied up in real estate. The island has a limited supply of land, and the citizens are partially forced to save because of the high costs of housing.

The city-state's transportation policies also contribute to the low levels of consumption. Singapore has an excellent and extensive subway system, which is used by most citizens. Travel by automobile is deterred by massive vehicle-registration costs and car prices that are the highest in the world.[94]

In comparison to Singapore, auto-dependent cities in North America and elsewhere have not done well in terms of savings. In recent decades, household savings rates, which are a key determinant of investment, have significantly fallen in several Western countries. From 1984 to 2004, savings as a percentage of disposable household income fell from 11.2 per cent to 1.9 per cent in the United States, from 17 per cent to 2.7 per cent in Canada, and from 12.4 per cent to –3.7 per cent in Australia! Note that these are the countries with the most sprawling cities. By contrast, savings rates in France went from 11 per cent in 1984 to 12.4 per cent in 2004, and in Germany from 13 per cent in 1991 to 10.65 per cent in 2004. These are countries with less sprawling cities and higher levels of transit use. It appears that sprawling cities may well be over-consuming at the expense of investment. Have the citizens of such cities been living in what Joan Robinson labels a Bastard Golden Age?

There is a further reason why urban societies may wish to reconsider the twentieth-century recipe of economic growth through urban sprawl – that is the emergence of the twenty-first-century *creative city*. Contemporary scholars such as Richard Florida are of the view that the already successful cities of this century are those that have attracted creative, innovative, artistic workers.[95] This trend will likely persist in the future. The leading cities will continue to be those that produce the goods and services of the latest new technology wave – in IT and biotechnology – and those that have artists and designers producing unique, individualized goods in a world of post-Fordist flexible specialization.[96] It is further argued that such cities will physically regenerate, repairing the damage of twentieth-century sprawl. The creative class wants to live in green, healthy, and visually stimulating cities. No more bumper-to-bumper commuting on congested highways; no more smog. These entrepreneurial workers reject the monotonous, cookie-cutter suburbs in favour of interesting, vibrant, walkable city quarters, with café culture. Old manufacturing buildings are converted into artists' studios and lofts. Physically, the creative city entails large-scale urban regeneration.

How will these creative cities generate new wealth? Certainly attracting high-tech companies is good for urban economies, as they provide investment, jobs, and incomes. Jacobs might argue that it entails more than just attracting companies. Creative cities will replace their imports with their own new innovations, which will subsequently generate new exports. It is even possible that, in the process of urban regeneration, truly creative cities may do the ultimate in import replacement and relinquish their reliance on automobiles. The important point, though, is that the citizens in cities where new technologies are created are more likely to have ownership of the firms that produce the new technologies. Wealth is all about ownership of assets.

Yet we should also ask questions here. What are the citizens of the twenty-first-century creative cities going to consume? Which technologies will they be locked in to? These are pertinent questions. Consider, for example, that since the 1980s the trajectory of London's creative industries – in the audio-visual sector, the music industry, publishing, design, the visual and performing arts – has to some extent gone up and down with swings in the economy.[97] Is this all just luxury spending – important in the eyes of Hume, but not generating real new wealth in the eyes of Smith? Perhaps new media has yet to develop a 'killer' application that hooks us all, beyond televisions and PCs, that is. There are signs, however, that consumers in the twenty-first century might already be replacing their slavery to car payments and walk-in closets with a lock-in to caffeine and the Internet. Will creative cities of this century go so far as to replace their addiction to gasoline with addiction to coffee shops and technological gadgets?

The Biology of Cities

We began this book by discussing cities where the streets were paved with gold. The metaphor is apt for a few real cities today, such as London and New York. These are cities that host major markets, where citizens own substantial amounts of the world's financial assets and make large incomes, thereby increasing the value of real estate. There have also been imaginary, fantastical cities proposed by thinkers for which such levels of extreme wealth have been suggested – the city-state of Plato's Republic or Rousseau's Utopia, for example. From our understanding of the functioning of urban economies, we can reject such idealistic models of cities as being counter to the true nature of cities. They have none of Ruskin's *ilth*; Plato and Rousseau ignore all the dirt, the grime, and the stench of cities; there are no detrivores. Their cities are clinical, mechanical, and stagnant perfections of urban life. Real cities are not like that; they are complex, evolving systems comprising self-organizing, adaptive agents – the households and firms – all trying to make a buck in order to survive. In other words, they are much like ecosystems.

Urban economies are, of course, complex, and we have argued that understanding the long-term economic phenomena of capital formation and maintenance, and of evolving urban form under technological change, requires a biological perspective. Our model sees urban economies as comprising complex heterogeneous firms interacting in ways that are somewhat akin to those of organisms, often in competition and yet largely interdependent. The urban economy evolves over time because of physical changes in cities based on technological change, just like ecosystems undergoing succession. Urban economies are also subject to allogeneic forces – typically periodic, but sometimes sporadic – similar to those that stress or disturb ecosystems.

Just how helpful is this metaphor for understanding cities? What use is it for urban decision makers? Our outline of the evolution of urban economies based on ecosystem theory was inspired by Alfred Marshall. He noted that 'economic problems are imperfectly presented when they are treated as problems of statistical equilibrium, and not of organic growth.'[98] Other economists, though, are sceptical of the usefulness of biological analogies. There may be too many loose analogies made between economic and biological systems. Evolutionary economics is some way from the mainstream of economic thought. Of what use, then, is the metaphor?

A first, simple answer is that we may need the metaphor to be able to perceive something for the first time. We have already discussed how neoclassical economics drew upon analogies with physics at its formative stage – it was a necessary step in the development of the science. A more sophisticated answer is that cities and ecosystems are both just special cases of general, complex, evolutionary systems. Researchers at the Santa Fe Institute in New Mexico, and elsewhere, are of the mind that there are general universal principles governing complex evolutionary systems. As E.D. Beinhocker argues, economic and biological systems are just subclasses of a more universal class of evolutionary systems. They share the same algorithm of evolution and have some similarities, even though the realizations of that evolution are very different.[99] In other words, there is something more fundamental beyond the metaphor.

To provide a short example of complex systems theory, we might consider Arthur Koestler's model of Self-regulating, Open, Hierarchic

Order (SOHO).[100] Drawing upon Ludwig von Bertalanffy's general systems theory, Koestler argues that all complex structures and processes with relatively stable characteristics must have some sort of hierarchical organization. By hierarchy he does not mean something rigid like a ladder, but a multilevel system, with branching into subsystems. Both food webs in ecosystems and the structure of firms in an urban economy are of a hierarchical order. To describe subassemblies within the hierarchy, Koestler introduces the term 'holon' – which provides a bridge between atomism and holism. Each holon can function as a quasi-independent whole – like our firms or organisms. Hence the system is open and self-regulating. Each holon is still a dependent part of the assembly above it, and is still subject to a set of fixed rules or canons, which account for its coherence and stability. Such rules determine only the invariant characteristics of the system. A signal passed down from a higher level may not necessarily dictate what a holon is expected to do; it may merely trigger some form of action. This quasi-independence of holons also means that SOHO systems are adaptive and can evolve; there should perhaps have been an 'E' for evolving added in the acronym.[101] The main point, then, is that firms, institutions, and other actors in cities should be seen not merely as analogous to organisms but as holons.

The proposition that follows from the above is that, by continuing to study complex systems such as ecosystems, we should expect to gain understanding of other complex systems – and in particular cities. To give an example, we might consider a question debated by ecologists with regard to energy flow through ecosystems. As ecosystems approach the climax stage of succession, they use an increasing amount of their energy for maintenance rather than for net growth of new biomass. The question is whether natural ecosystems grow to a point where the ratio of biomass to energy flow is maximized, or whether the energy flow itself is maximized.[102] The equivalent question in economics is whether economies grow to a point where the ratio of capital to output is maximized, or whether output (and hence income) is maximized. One can imagine that Keynesians and monetarists might disagree on this one. Perhaps the ecologists have the answer!

A further matter on which insights from ecology might inform urban economics is that of diversity. We noted in chapter 5 how Jacobs's theory of economic diversity had proved to be the better of three contenders for explaining urban economic growth. We also saw how lack of diversity played a significant role in the decline of Detroit. Ecologists have long been interested in understanding why biodiversity is different in some ecosystems than in others. The answer is not straightforward – and is still being studied. Nevertheless, empirical observation suggests that a bell-shaped model of species diversity with respect to stress and/or disturbance is quite typical. As noted in chapter 6, at high levels of stress or disturbance, the only organisms that persist are the few stress- or disturbance-tolerators. Thus, diversity is low. It also turns out, however, that at very low stress or disturbance conditions, the most competitive species of organisms are able to dominate the readily available resources to such an extent that less competitive species cannot survive and biodiversity again declines. Thus, it is at medium levels of stress and/or disturbance that the highest levels of biodiversity are achieved.[103] On this note it is interesting to recall Peter Hall's observation that the world's most creative cities, at the times of their greatest cultural expression, were nothing like utopias but rather were uncomfortable places. Pericles' Athens, da Vinci's Florence, and Shakespeare's London were turbulent cities undergoing social transformation. They were subject to substantial levels of stress or disturbance, yet not so disturbed as to be physically destroyed, as in the cases of Pompeii, Dresden, or Hiroshima.

Focusing on economic matters, a major source of stress on businesses – the organisms of the urban economy – are the cyclical waves that affect economies. Businesses have to be fit enough to survive times of recession when consumer spending is weak. Governments and central banks try to soften the impacts of such cyclical waves by, for example, changing levels of government spending or interest rates. Yet it would seemingly be undesirable if governments and central banks became too skilled at managing the business cycles in economies. With every downturn, a few of the less efficient or over-stressed companies become insolvent. If the stress of business cycles were entirely eliminated, a possibly undesirable consequence might be a long-term decrease in the diversity of economies.

Another issue in urban economics that is in need of some insights from ecology is the impact of transportation infrastructure projects. We have seen many important contributions of transport infrastructure to the growth of cities: such infrastructure has created new consumer markets, expanded existing markets, sparked agglomeration effects, supported suburbanization, provided a means of dominating hinterlands in cities' progression towards the status of financial centres, and constituted a fundamental part of the evolution of new urban form. Transportation economists, however, have yet to establish techniques that incorporate such profound effects into the analysis of the benefits and costs of urban transportation projects. Benefits are typically calculated at the microeconomic level from part of the area under a demand curve known as Dupuit's surplus. This is despite the fact that real demand curves are rarely known and have to be approximated. Benefits are also sometimes estimated by valuing the travel-time savings that follow from new transportation infrastructure. In the long run, however, firms and households typically take advantage of the new infrastructure and relocate such that travel time remains unchanged. The microeconomic methods of evaluating the benefits of transportation infrastructure are really quite inadequate.

On first glance, the costs of transportation projects seem more straightforward to calculate, simply reflecting the costs of labour, materials, and design, but this depends again on whether a micro or macro economic perspective is taken. In microeconomics, costs are costs. In macroeconomics, however, spending money on construction workers' salaries can under some circumstances be a way of boosting an economy or generating regional income, and can thereby be considered entirely beneficial. Whether construction counts as a cost or a benefit depends on whether the activity is in an underemployed or fully employed economy.[104]

Final Reflections

It is apparent from this discussion that there is still much we have to learn about how urban economies function. How should urban economies be managed to encourage diversity? How should urban transportation projects be evaluated? Our current economic methods for supporting decision making in cities have questionable foundations. The objective pursued by early-twentieth-century New York planners of *understanding the city as an organism* is still a work in progress. If this book has done nothing more than open the door to further understanding of the complex working of cities, and of the biological nature of urban economies, then it has played its part.

There is perhaps, however, a further lesson to be taken from Arthur Koestler and other complex-systems theorists. If cities are considered as systems of self-organizing adaptive agents, this suggests that there are significant limits to decision making in cities. Again, to recall the experience of New York in the mid-twentieth century: the planners had no power of implementation; the agent Robert Moses took and adapted the regional plan to suit his purposes. Moreover, while the rise of Toronto as Canada's financial centre neatly reflects Gras's theory, it had much do to with the folly of Montreal and was hardly the result of deliberate policy on the part of Torontonians.

Urban leaders, whether elected officials or influential bureaucrats, can perhaps at best help generate future visions of cities; others may be able to direct budgets towards projects that are deemed to be important. And so, even if this book has helped to explain what underlies the wealth of cities, it does not claim to offer a prescription as to how cities, or rather their citizens, can increase their wealth. That is something they will have to work out for themselves, like any ecosystem and its organisms adapting to an ever-changing environment.

Notes

Introduction

1 World Bank Databank, World Development Indicators for China, 2009 http://databank.worldbank.org.

2 J.E. Fernandez, 'Resource Consumption of New Urban Construction in China,' *Journal of Industrial Ecology* 11, no. 2 (2007): 99–115.

3 London: Bloomsbury Publishing Plc, 2009.

4 J. Friedmann, 'The World City Hypothesis,' *Development and Change* 17 (1986): 69–83.

5 S. Sassen, *The Global City* (Princeton, NJ: Princeton University Press, 1991).

6 Vol. 1, Berkeley: University of California Press, 1995; vol. 3, London: William Collins and Sons, 1984.

7 N.S.B. Gras, *An Introduction to Economic History* (repr. New York: Augustus M. Kelley, 1969).

8 Joan Robinson, *The Accumulation of Capital* (London: Macmillan, 1956), 24.

9 See, for example, L. Kamal-Chaoui and A. Robert, eds, 'Competitive Cities and Climate Change,' OECD Regional Development Working Papers, no. 2 (OECD, 2009).

10 R.R. Nelson and S.G. Winter, *An Evolutionary Theory of Economic Change* (Cambridge, MA: Harvard University Press, 1982).

11 The theory in chapter 6 has a limited relationship to the contemporary discipline of ecological economics (e.g., see H.E. Daly and J. Farley, *Ecological Economics: Principles and Applications* [Washington, DC: Island Press, 2004]). The discipline of ecological economics aims to place economic activities in the context of a larger global ecosystem, containing cycles of carbon, nutrients, water, metals, and so on. It is concerned with understanding how economies extract scarce natural resources and produce pollutants

requiring assimilation by natural ecosystems. The author has elsewhere made contributions to this discipline through studies of urban metabolism (C.A. Kennedy, J. Cuddihy, and J. Engel Yan, 'The Changing Metabolism of Cities,' *Journal of Industrial Ecology* 11, no. 2 [2007]: 43–59) and the development of macroeconomic models for predicting greenhouse-gas emissions (M. Fung and C.A. Kennedy, 'An Integrated Macroeconomic Model for Assessing Urban Sustainability,' *Environment and Planning, B* 32, no. 5 [2005]: 639–56). The theory in chapter 6 merely uses the language and relationships of ecosystem theory as a metaphorical basis for understanding urban economies. The contribution perhaps lies closer to the emerging field of evolutionary economics (e.g., see K. Dopfer, ed., *The Evolutionary Foundations of Economics* [Cambridge: Cambridge University Press, 2005]), the focus of which is on the biology of urban capital formation.

Chapter 1: Where the Streets Are Paved with Gold

1 Forbes 2009 World Billionaire list: http://www.forbes.com/2009/03/11/worlds-richest-people-billionaires-2009-billionaires_land.html.
2 Braudel, *Civilization and Capitalism*, 31, notes that Alonso Morgado's *Historia de Sevilla* claimed that every street could have been paved with gold and silver.
3 Ibid., 120.
4 Adam Smith, *An Inquiry into the Nature and the Causes of the Wealth of Nations* (1776; London: Penguin, [1982]), 502.
5 Lewis Mumford, *The City in History* (New York: Harcourt, Brace and World, 1961).
6 Paul Bairoch, *Cities and Economic Development: From the Dawn of History to the Present* (Chicago: University of Chicago Press, 1988).
7 Spiro Kostof, *The City Shaped: Urban Patterns and Meanings through History* (Boston: Little, Brown, 1991).
8 Peter Geoffrey Hall, *Cities in Civilization: Culture, Innovation, and Urban Order* (London: Phoenix, 1999).
9 Ibid., 'Book One: The City as Cultural Crucible,' 3–288.
10 Ibid., 281.
11 Ibid., 286.
12 Ibid., 'Book Two: The City as Innovative Milieu Hall,' 291–500.
13 Berlin's dominance in electrical engineering was a casualty of the First World War.
14 Hall, *Cities in Civilization*, 'Book Four: The Establishment of the Urban Order,' 611–939.

15 Ibid., 932.

16 Ibid., 938.

17 N. Ferguson, *The Ascent of Money: A Financial History of the World* (London: Penguin, 2009), 67, 128, 191.

18 Braudel, *Civilization and Capitalism*, 21–2, distinguishes between the world economy, which applies to the whole planet, and a world-economy, which refers to an economically autonomous section of the world able to provide for most of its own needs.

19 Note that Gras, in his *Introduction to Economic History*, does not consider Athens, Rome, and Constantinople to be financial centres. I consider Gras's theory in chapter 4.

20 Youssef Cassis, *Capitals of Capital: The Rise and Fall of International Financial Centres, 1780–2009* (Cambridge: Cambridge University Press, 2010).

21 The following descriptions of Venice, Antwerp, Genoa, and Amsterdam draw upon chapters 2 and 3 of Braudel, *Civilization and Capitalism*.

22 Lewis Mumford, *The Culture of Cities* (New York: Harcourt and Brace, 1938), 3.

23 In the *Meaning of the City* (trans. Dennis Pardee; Grand Rapids, MI: W.B. Eerdmans, 1970), the French theologian Jacques Ellul interprets many biblical references as evidence that cities were seen as sources of conflict.

24 Braudel, *Civilization and Capitalism*, 120.

25 Ibid., 125.

26 Ibid., 126.

27 Ibid., 123.

28 Ibid., 149.

29 Ibid., 150.

30 Ibid., 152.

31 Ibid., 165.

32 Ibid., 180.

33 Ibid., 191.

34 Ibid., 207.

35 Ibid., 213, 224.

36 Ibid., 216–20.

37 See ibid., 249, 256, 260.

38 P. Jay, *Road to Riches, or The Wealth of Man* (London: Orion Books, 2000), 198.

39 Braudel, *Civilization and Capitalism*, 246, 266–76.

40 Ibid., 262.

41 M. Ball and D. Sunderland, *An Economic History of London, 1800–1914* (London: Routledge, 2001), 42.

42 Ibid., 4.
43 Ibid., 82.
44 E.A. Wrigley, *People, Cities and Wealth: The Transformation of Traditional Society* (Oxford: Blackwell, 1987), 133–56.
45 W.D. Rubenstein, *Elites and Wealthy in Modern British History: Essays in Social and Economic History* (Sussex, UK: Harvester Press; New York: St Martin's, 1987).
46 Ball and Sunderland, *An Economic History of London*, 208.
47 Ibid., 222.
48 Ibid., 213.
49 Ibid., 83.
50 Ibid., 345.
51 Ibid., 346.
52 Ibid., 351.
53 Ibid., 354.
54 Ibid., 356.
55 J.R. Kurth, 'Between Europe and America: The New York Foreign Policy Elite,' in M. Shefter, ed., *Capital of the American Century* (New York: Russell Sage Foundation, 1993), 74–7, provides this explanation for the Great Depression, drawing on C.P. Kindleberger and R.Z. Aliber, *Manias, Panics and Crashes: A History of Financial Crises*, 5th ed. (New York: Palgrave Macmillan, 2005).
56 M. Shefter, 'New York's National and International Influence,' in Shefter, ed., *Capital of the American Century*, 6–8.
57 G.L. Lankevich and H.B. Furer, *A Brief History of New York City* (New York: Associated Faculty Press, 1984), chap. 7; and Shefter, 'New York's National and International Influence,' 6–8.
58 The La Guardia era is described in Lankevich and Furer, *A Brief History of New York City*, chapter 8.
59 Kurth, 'Between Europe and America,' 81–2.
60 Shefter, 'New York's National and International Influence,' 12.
61 Lankevich and Furer, *A Brief History of New York City*, 263.
62 M.P. Drennan, 'The Decline and Rise of the New York Economy,' in J.H. Mollenkopf and M. Castells, eds, *Dual City: Restructuring New York* (New York: Russell Sage Foundation, 1991), 27.
63 Ibid., 26.
64 Ibid., 31–8, and D. Vogel, 'New York as a National and Global Financial Centre,' in Shefter, ed., *Capital of the American Century*, 56–9, describe New York's economy in the 1980s.
65 Allen J. Scott, *Social Economy of the Metropolis: Cognitive-Cultural Capitalism and the Global Resurgence of Cities* (Oxford: Oxford University Press, 2008).

66 A.D. Aschauer, 'Is Public Expenditure Productive?' *Journal of Monetary Economics* 23, no. 2 (1989): 177–200, is an often quoted study. Also useful is D.W. Gillen, 'Transportation Infrastructure and Economic Development: A Review of Recent Literature,' *Logistics and Transportation Review* 32, no. 1 (1996): 39.

67 The rent curve describes how the price and demand for real estate change with increasing distance from a central business district.

Chapter 2: A Theory of Urban Wealth

1 H. Thomas, *Rivers of Gold: The Rise of the Spanish Empire* (London: Weidenfeld and Nicholson, 2003), 94.

2 Ibid., 458–74.

3 Ibid., 122.

4 Ibid., 373.

5 H. Kamen, *Spain's Road to Empire: The Making of a World Power, 1492–1763* (London: Penguin, 2002), 99–105.

6 Ibid., 105–9.

7 Ibid., 88.

8 Ibid., 154.

9 Ibid., 285–6.

10 Ibid., 286.

11 Ibid., 292–6.

12 Ibid., 293.

13 Ibid., 436.

14 Braudel, *The Mediterranean and the Mediterranean World in the Age of Phillip II*, 517–42.

15 Ibid., 519.

16 R.E. Cameron, *A Concise Economic History of the World: From Paleolithic Times to the Present* (Oxford: Oxford University Press, 1997), 107.

17 J.K. Galbraith, *A History of Economics* (London: Hamish Hamilton, 1987), 31–45.

18 Biographies of Cantillon include Anthony Brewer, *Richard Cantillon: Pioneer of Economic Theory* (London: Routledge, 1992); and A.E. Murphy, *Richard Cantillon: Entrepreneur and Economist* (New York: Oxford University Press, 1986).

19 Marginalism is an integral component of conventional economics. It recognizes that many economic decisions are made at the border or margin. For example, the cost and benefit or revenue from producing a good determines whether such production is worthwhile.

20 W.S. Jevons, 'Richard Cantillon and the Nationality of Political Economy,'

Contemporary Review, January 1881, repr. in *Essai sur la nature du commerce en général, by Richard Cantillon*, edited and translated by Henry Higgs (London: Frank Cass, [1931] 1959), 342.

21 *Essai sur la nature du commerce en général*, 3.

22 P. Jay, *Road to Riches, or the Wealth of Man* (London: Orion Books, 2000), 2.

23 T. Veblen, *The Theory of the Leisure Class: An Economic Study of Institutions* (1899), Rev. ed. (New York: B.W. Huebsch, 1918), 29.

24 K. Marx, *Capital: A Critique of Political Economy*, vol. 1 (London: Penguin, 1976), 799.

25 R.E. Backhouse, *The Ordinary Business of Life: A History of Economics from the Ancient World to the Twenty-first Century* (Princeton, NJ: Princeton University Press, 2002), 155.

26 J. Robinson, *The Accumulation of Capital* (London: Macmillan, 1956), 15.

27 J.M. Keynes, 'The General Theory of Employment,' *Quarterly Journal of Economics* 51, no. 2 (1937): 213.

28 J. Ruskin, *The Genius of John Ruskin: Selections from His Writings*, ed. J.D. Rosenberg (New York: George Braziller, 1965), 262.

29 Ibid.

30 Ibid., 258.

31 C. Jones, *Paris: Biography of a City* (London: Allen Lane, 2004), 40.

32 Ibid., 55.

33 Ibid., 43–4.

34 G. Leff, *Paris and Oxford Universities in the Thirteenth and Fourteenth Centuries: An Institutional and Intellectual History* (New York: John Wiley and Sons, 1968), 15–16.

35 Jones, *Paris*, 44.

36 Ibid., 49.

37 R. Florida, *The Rise of the Creative Class: And How It's Transforming Work, Leisure, Community and Everyday Life* (New York: Basic Books, 2002); and *The Flight of the Creative Class: The New Global Competition for Talent* (New York: Harper Business, 2004).

38 A. Nichols, *Discovering Aquinas: An Introduction to His Life, Work, and Influence* (Grand Rapids, MI: W.B. Eerdmans, 2003), 3–18.

39 J.W. McConnell, *Basic Teachings of the Great Economists* (New York: Garden City Publishing, 1943), 21.

40 See P. Hall's introduction to *Von Thünen's Isolated State: An English Edition of Der Isolierte Staat*, trans. C.M. Wartenberg, ed. P. Hall (Oxford: Pergamon, 1966), xii–xviii; and Backhouse, *The Ordinary Business of Life*, 147.

41 A.H. Maslow, *Motivation and Personality* (New York: Harper-Collins, 1954).

42 The information on Philadelphia's city hall is from http://www.phila
.gov/virtualch/ and http://www.geocities.com/Athens/Delphi/2115/
Mainframeset.html.

43 M.M. Dunn and R.S. Dunn, 'The Founding, 1681–1701,' in R.F. Weigley,
ed., *Philadelphia: A 300-Year History* (New York: Norton, 1982), 6–10.

44 Ibid., 14–16.

45 G. Fallis and L.B. Smith, 'Uncontrolled Prices in a Controlled Market: The
Case of Rent Controls,' *American Economic Review* 74, no. 1 (1984): 193–200.

46 Ibid., 198–9.

47 These data, obtained from Statistics Canada, omit some assets, including
home contents, collectibles and valuables, and annuities and registered
retirement income funds.

48 J.D. Benjamin, P. Chinloy, and G.D. Jud, 'Why Do Households Concentrate
Their Wealth in Housing?' *Journal of Real Estate Research* 26, no. 4 (2004):
329–31.

49 'Going through the Roof,' *The Economist*, 28 March 2002.

Chapter 3: Markets

1 The founding of Hong Kong is described in F. Welsh, *A History of Hong
Kong*, rev. ed. (London: HarperCollins, 1997), 11–131.

2 Ibid., 80.

3 Ibid., 78.

4 Ibid., 86.

5 Ibid., 87.

6 Ibid., 104.

7 Ibid., 109.

8 Hong Kong's population statistics are given ibid., 137, 253, 404, 438, 478.

9 B. Renaud, F. Pretorius, and B. Pasadilla, *Markets at Work: Dynamics of the
Residential Real Estate Market in Hong Kong* (Hong Kong: Hong Kong University Press, 1997), 85.

10 A. Rabushka, *Hong Kong: A Study in Economic Freedom* (Chicago: University
of Chicago Press, 1979).

11 Welsh, *A History of Hong Kong*, 461–4.

12 Ibid., 475–502.

13 Ibid., 480.

14 Ibid., 495.

15 Rabushka, *Hong Kong*, 24–5.

16 Renaud, Pretorius, and Pasadilla, *Markets at Work*, 27.

17 Ibid., 27.

18 Ibid., 13, table 1.1.
19 Ibid., 20–1.
20 Ibid., 68.
21 Ibid., 78, figure 5.7.
22 Ibid., 76.
23 Y. Fu, 'Hong Kong: Overcoming Financial Risks of Growing Real Estate Credit,' chapter 7 in K. Mera and B. Renaud, eds, *Asia's Financial Crises and the Role of Real Estate* (New York: Sharpe, 2000), 142, figure 7.1a.
24 Renaud, Pretorius, and Pasadilla, *Markets at Work*, 52, table 4.1.
25 Ibid., 65.
26 Ibid., 55–6.
27 Fu, 'Hong Kong,' 146.
28 Ibid.
29 Mera and Renaud, eds, *Asia's Financial Crisis*.
30 Fu, 'Hong Kong,' 153.
31 Elasticity of demand is calculated as the percentage change in demand divided by the percentage change in price at a given point on the demand curve.
32 This section describes the model of D. DiPasquale and W.C. Wheaton in 'The Markets for Real Estate Assets and Space: A Conceptual Framework,' *AREUEA Journal* 20, no. 1 (1992): 181–97, drawing largely upon Renaud, Pretorius, and Pasadilla, *Markets at Work*.
33 Residential space can be either rented or owner-occupied. It turns out that both can be understood in relatively similar terms. Homeowners face a user-cost of occupation, for example, mortgage payments, taxes, and maintenance cost, which in theory are equivalent to the costs of renting if equilibrium is reached between these two markets. Home ownership is less desirable if equivalent properties can be rented at lower rates. Conversely, renting is less attractive if the monthly costs of owning property are much lower.
34 Renaud, Pretorius, and Pasadilla, *Markets at Work*, 34.
35 The vacancy rate actually falls below some natural rate relating to turnover in the market.
36 R. Peng and W. Wheaton, 'Effects of Restrictive Land Supply on Housing in Hong Kong,' *Journal of Housing Research* 5, no. 2 (1994): 111, 263–91, 282 (table 4).
37 Ibid., 282, table 4.
38 Renaud, Pretorius, and Pasadilla, *Markets at Work*, 41.
39 Ibid., 45–64.
40 In the case of private housing, the value of the asset is the user-cost of

owner occupation discounted by the rate of borrowing adjusted for the expected rate of housing appreciation. So again, interest rates, by way of their impacts on mortgage rates, are a determinant of the value of buildings.

41 Renaud, Pretorius, and Pasadilla, *Markets at Work*, 55.
42 Ibid., 65–82.
43 The supply curve of the development industry may be considered upward sloping with a fixed-cost component, that is, independent of the amount of space provided, and a variable-cost component that depends on the amount of new space provided.
44 Renaud, Pretorius, and Pasadilla, *Markets at Work*, 83–93.
45 S. Griffith-Jones, *Global Capital Flows: Should They Be Regulated?* (New York: St Martin's Press, 1998), 53, presents data reported by InterSec: Global Research and Consulting Group.
46 Ibid., 53.
47 Ferguson, *The Ascent of Money*, 67.
48 Bill Gross, quoted ibid., 69.
49 Ibid., 66.
50 Ibid., 128–9.
51 W.M. Clarke, *How the City of London Works*, 5th ed. (London: Sweet and Maxwell, 1999), 36–44.
52 A. Damodaran, *Corporate Finance: Theory and Practice* (New York: Wiley, 1997), 619.
53 Ibid., 620.
54 Kindleberger and Aliber, *Manias, Panics and Crashes*, 99.
55 Ibid., 27.
56 G.M. Trevelyan, *Illustrated History of England* (London: Longmans, 1956), 494.
57 J. Carswell, *The South Sea Bubble*, rev. ed. (Gloucestershire, UK: Alan Sutton, 1993), 30.
58 Ibid., 23–6.
59 Ibid., 45.
60 Ibid., 58.
61 Ibid., 5, 65–8.
62 Ibid., 68–9.
63 Ibid., 70–81.
64 Murphy, *Richard Cantillon*, 82.
65 Ibid., 79.
66 Ibid., 131.
67 Carswell, *The South Sea Bubble*, 87.

68 Ibid.,103.
69 Ibid., 100.
70 Ibid.,117. Some outlandish firm names may well have been satirical.
71 Ibid., 129.
72 Ibid., 150.
73 Ibid., 170.
74 Kindleberger and Aliber, *Manias, Panics and Crashes*, 256–65.
75 C. Borio and P. McGuire, 'Twin Peaks in Equity and Housing Markets?' *BIS Quarterly Review*, March 2004, 79–93. There are a few cases where two equity-price peaks occur in a period before a new housing-price peak is reached.
76 Black Thursday (24 October) was the peak of market; the collapse that day was followed by a recovery; the following Black Monday (28 October) and Black Tuesday (29 October) were two of the worst days in the history of the New York Stock Exchange.
77 Redistribution may involve some getting richer and others getting poorer. The wealth of any individual may remain unchanged through appropriate portfolio balancing between real estate, financial assets, and other forms of wealth.
78 Carswell, *The South Sea Bubble*, tells the remarkable story of the hunt for prominent South Sea director Robert Knight, who had escaped to Europe and been captured in the Austrian Netherlands. The official government investigative body sought to have Knight extradited home to explain his role in the issue of illegal South Sea shares. Meanwhile, a secret group within Parliament dissuaded the Austrians from returning Knight for fear that he would implicate the king, thereby undermining the Hanoverian monarchy and perhaps allowing the Jacobites to return (207–18).
79 Ibid., 113.
80 Ibid., 108, 165.
81 Murphy, *Richard Cantillon*, 187.
82 Ibid., 187.
83 Carswell, *The South Sea Bubble*, 137; Kindleberger and Aliber, *Manias, Panics and Crashes*, 110.
84 See Wikipedia, 'Dot-com Bubble,' section 'Companies Significant to the Bubble.'
85 *Al Shindagah*, 'Dubai: City of Gold,' 46 (May–June 2002), www.alshindagah .com/mayjun2002/dubai.html.
86 Dubai Chamber of Commerce and Industry, 'Dubai's Trade in Gold and Diamonds Continues to Grow,' http://www.dcci.gov.ae/content/ Bulletin/Issue27/TradeMonEn_ISSUE27.pdf.

87 'History of Dubai, Dubai Places,' http://dubaiplaces.com.
88 M. Hvidt, 'Public-Private Ties and Their Contribution to Development: The Case of Dubai,' *Middle Eastern Studies* 43, no. 4 (2007): 557–77.
89 Dubai Gold and Commodities Exchange, 'An Introduction to DGCX,' http://www.dgcx.ae.
90 Kindleberger and Aliber, *Manias, Panics and Crashes*, 15.
91 http://en.wikipedia.org/wiki/List_of_most_expensive_paintings.
92 http://www.answers.com/topic/sotheby-s-holdings-inc (accessed 1 January 2011).
93 Borio and McGuire, 'Twin Peaks in Equity and Housing Markets?' 90.

Chapter 4: Competitive Financial Centres

1 R.V. Remini, *Andrew Jackson and the Bank War* (New York: Norton, 1967), 1.
2 R.E. Wright, *The First Wall Street: Chestnut Street, Philadelphia, and the Birth of American Finance* (Chicago: University of Chicago Press, 2005), describes the history of Philadelphia as a financial centre.
3 Ibid., 11–12.
4 Ibid., 67.
5 Ibid., 145.
6 Ibid., 11–12.
7 C. Sherrif, *The Artificial River: The Erie Canal and the Paradox of Progress, 1817–1862* (New York: Hill and Wang, 1996), 20–1.
8 Ibid., 21.
9 See ibid., 194n1.
10 Wright, *The First Wall Street*, 118–19.
11 Ibid., 147.
12 Ibid., 149.
13 Ibid., 150–5.
14 Ibid., 156.
15 Ibid., 157–8.
16 Ibid., 152–4.
17 Ibid., 160–3.
18 'Management Issues, London Bankers Set for Bonus Bonanza,' 30 October 2006, http://www.management-issues.com.
19 H.C. Reed, *The Preeminence of International Financial Centers* (New York: Praeger, 1981), viii. The Heckscher-Ohlin model of international trade uses David Ricardo's theory of comparative advantage to describe patterns of commerce and production based on the factor endowments of trading regions. Johann Heinrich von Thünen's distance-from-centre model

describes how rings of different agricultural or land-use activities will be formed around a central city based on profit maximization.

20 E.P. Davis's study 'International Financial Centres – an Industrial Analysis,' Bank of England Discussion paper, 1990, 51, is summarized in S. Bonetti and D. Cobham, 'Financial Markets and the City of London,' in D. Cobham, ed., *Markets and Dealers: The Economics of the London Financial Markets* (London: Longman, 1992), 18–20.

21 Reed, *The Preeminence of International Financial Centers*, 5–8.

22 A. Pred, *City-systems in Advanced Economies: Past Growth, Present Processes and Future Development Options* (London: Hutchinson, 1977), 9.

23 Ibid., 173 and 214.

24 Gras, *An Introduction to Economic History*, chap. 5.

25 Ibid., 187–208.

26 Ibid., 190.

27 Ibid., 209–18.

28 Ibid., 219–43.

29 Ibid., 243–69.

30 Ibid., 260–1.

31 Congressman Arsène Pujo of Louisiana headed a House of Representatives committee into the power of Wall Street financiers over the country's finances.

32 Gras, *An Introduction to Economic History*, 264.

33 Reed, *The Preeminence of International Financial Centers*, 2.

34 Ibid., passim.

35 Chapter 1 of P.J. Taylor, *World City Network: A Global Urban Analysis* (New York: Routledge, 2004) provides a concise overview of recent world-city theory.

36 Friedmann, 'The World City Hypothesis,' 69; also cited in Taylor, *World City Network*, 22.

37 Sassen, *The Global City*, 6; also cited in Taylor, *World City Network*, 25.

38 Sassen, *The Global City*, 12–13; also cited in Taylor, *World City Network*, 24.

39 Material in this section is based on C.P. Kindleberger, 'The Formation of Financial Centers: A Study in Comparative Economic History,' *Princeton Studies in International Finance* 36 (1974), reproduced as chapter 4 of Kindleberger's *Economic Response: Comparative Studies in Trade, Finance and Growth* (Cambridge, MA: Harvard University Press, 1978). See pp. 76–105.

40 Cassis, *Capitals of Capital*, 102.

41 Ibid., 4.

42 Ibid., 14.

43 Ibid., 11.

44 Ibid., 12.
45 Ibid., 25.
46 Ibid.
47 Ibid., 26.
48 Ibid., 20.
49 Ibid., 22–3.
50 Ibid., 28.
51 Ibid., 29.
52 Ibid., 60–1.
53 *Financial News*, 22 January 1934, 'Fiftieth Anniversary: The City 1884–1934,' 25, quoted in Cassis, *Capitals of Capital*, 61.
54 Cassis, *Capitals of Capital*, 48.
55 Ibid., 63.
56 Ibid., 65–6.
57 Ibid., 67.
58 E. Powell, *The Evolution of the Money Market (1385–1915): An Historical and Analytical Study of the Rise and Development of Finance as a Central, Coordinated Force* (1915) (New York: Augustus M. Kelly, 1966), 370.
59 Cassis, *Capitals of Capital*, 98.
60 Ibid., 78–9.
61 S.B. Beckert, *The Monied Metropolis: New York City and the Consolidation of the American Bourgeoisie, 1850–1896* (Cambridge: Cambridge University Press, 2001), 18.
62 Cassis, *Capitals of Capital*, 117.
63 Ibid., 121–2.
64 Ibid., 122.
65 Ibid.
66 W.L. Silber, *When Washington Shut Down Wall Street* (Princeton, NJ: Princeton University Press, 2007), 55–6.
67 Cassis, *Capitals of Capital*, 123.
68 Ibid., 106.
69 See Silber, *When Washington Shut Down Wall Street*.
70 Cassis, *Capitals of Capital*, 152.
71 Ibid., 156.
72 Ibid., 166.
73 M. Simon, 'The Pattern of New British Portfolio Foreign Investment, 1865–1914,' in A. Hall, ed., *The Export of Capital from Britain 1870–1914* (London: Methuen, 1968), 27.
74 R.C. Michie, *The London and New York Stock Exchanges, 1850–1914* (London: Allen and Unwin, 1987), 54.

75 Ibid., 223.
76 Author's calculation based on a total market value of NYSE securities of $26 billion, given by Michie, *The London and New York Stock Exchanges*, 230.
77 Data on the US and UK rail networks is from A. Grübler, *The Rise and Fall of Infrastructures* (Heidelberg: Physica-Verlag, 1990), 101, 108.
78 Cassis, *Capitals of Capital*, 182.
79 Ibid., 184.
80 Ibid., 185.
81 Ibid., 185–6.
82 Ibid., 200.
83 Ibid., 205.
84 Ibid., 207.
85 Bonetti and Cobham, 'Financial Markets and the City of London,' 7.
86 C.P. Kindleberger, *A Financial History of Western Europe*, 2nd ed. (Oxford: Oxford University Press, 1993), 440.
87 Ibid., 438.
88 Ibid., 439.
89 Bonetti and Cobham, 'Financial Markets and the City of London,' 7.
90 Ibid., 8.
91 Ibid.
92 Cassis, *Capitals of Capital*, 269.
93 Ibid., 346n7.
94 Ibid., 271.
95 Ibid., 265.
96 V.P. Carosso, *Investment Banking in America: A History* (Cambridge, MA: Harvard University Press, 1970), 151.

Chapter 5: Economic Growth, Production, and Consumption

1 E.A. Wrigley, *People, Cities and Wealth: The Transformation of Traditional Society* (Oxford: Blackwell, 1987), 133.
2 The progression of the fire is described in S. Porter, *The Great Fire of London* (Gloucestershire, UK: Sutton Publishing, 1996), 34–54.
3 Ibid., 3.
4 Ibid., 89.
5 Ibid., 72.
6 Ibid., 127.
7 D.W. Roberts, *An Outline of the Economic History of England* (London: Longman, 1962), 107.

8 S. Pollard and D.W. Crossley, *The Wealth of Britain, 1085–1986* (London: Batsford, 1986), 147.
9 Roberts, *An Outline of the Economic History of England,* 128, 131.
10 R.E. Backhouse, *The Ordinary Business of Life: A History of Economics from the Ancient World to the Twenty-first Century* (Princeton, NJ: Princeton University Press, 2002), 85.
11 Petty's Life is described in C.H. Hull, ed., *The Economic Writings of Sir William Petty* (Fairfield, NJ: A.M. Kelley Publishers, 1986).
12 Ibid., 107.
13 Ibid., 302.
14 Ibid., 308.
15 Ibid., 457–60.
16 Ibid., 469.
17 Ibid., 473.
18 Ibid. This quote has to be seen in its political context. Petty may well have been suggesting to the new king, James II, that England was strong enough to stand independently from France, a message that was also implicit in his *Political Arithmetick,* written for James II's father, Charles II; see ibid., lxi.
19 T.M.M. Baker, *London: Rebuilding the City after the Great Fire* (Chichester, UK: Phillimore and Company, 2000), 5.
20 Ibid., 8.
21 Xenophon, 'On the Means of Improving the Revenues of Athens,' in *Xenophon's Minor Works,* trans. J.S. Watson (London: George Bell and Sons, 1905), 248.
22 Ibid., 251.
23 Ibid., 262.
24 Ibid.
25 C. Cobb, T. Halstead, and J. Rowe, 'If the GDP Is Up, Why Is America Down?' *Atlantic Monthly,* October 1995, 59–78.
26 P. Jay, *Road to Riches, or The Wealth of Man* (London: Orion Books, 2000), 217.
27 L.A. Sveikauskas, 'The Productivity of Cities,' *Quarterly Journal of Economics* 89, no. 3 (1975): 393–413.
28 See Y. Lee, *Schumpeterian Dynamics and Metropolitan-scale Productivity* (Aldershot: Ashgate, 2003), chap 2.
29 J.E. McDonald, *Fundamentals of Urban Economics* (Upper Saddle River, NJ: Prentice-Hall, 1997), 37–43.
30 Ibid., 58–9.
31 W. Issacson, *Benjamin Franklin: An American Life* (New York: Simon and Schuster, 2003), 312.

32 E.C. Mossner, *The Life of David Hume*, 2nd ed. (Oxford: Oxford University Press, 1980), 596.
33 J. Rae, *Life of Adam Smith* (London: Macmillan, 1895), 284.
34 Smith, *An Inquiry into the Nature and the Causes of the Wealth of Nations*, 429.
35 Ibid., 371.
36 Ibid., 373.
37 Ibid., 374.
38 Ibid., 377.
39 Ibid., 121–6.
40 Backhouse, *The Ordinary Business of Life*, 128–9.
41 Smith, *An Inquiry into the Nature and the Causes of the Wealth of Nations*, 177.
42 Ibid., 192.
43 Ibid., 479.
44 Ibid., 496.
45 J. Jacobs, *The Economy of Cities* (New York: Random House, 1969), 82.
46 Ibid., 79.
47 Ibid., 40.
48 Ibid., 129.
49 Ibid., 233–5.
50 Ibid., 85.
51 Ibid., 86.
52 E.L. Glaeser, H.D, Kallal, J.A. Scheinkman, and A. Shleifer (1992), 'Growth in Cities,' *Journal of Political Economy*, Centennial issue, 100, no. 6 (1992): 1126–52.
53 Smith, *An Inquiry into the Nature and the Causes of the Wealth of Nations*, 109–10.
54 My account of Keynes's life is based on R. Lekachman, *The Age of Keynes* (New York: Random House, 1966).
55 J.M. Keynes, *The General Theory of Employment, Interest and Money* (1953; Orlando, FL: Harcourt, 1964), 89.
56 Ibid., 89–90.
57 Ibid., 98.
58 Ibid., 104.
59 Ibid., 115.
60 Economists typically now define marginal propensity to consume relative to disposable income, i.e., to after-tax income.
61 Keynes, *The General Theory of Employment, Interest and Money*, 91.
62 Ibid., 121.
63 Ibid., 120.
64 This increase in autonomous consumption related to the design of cities

may also contribute to explaining the growth in the per capita GDP of many countries over the past two centuries or so, although this is a bold assertion that goes beyond our focus here on cities.

65 D. Blanke, *Hell on Wheels: The Promise and Peril of America's Car Culture, 1900–1940* (Lawrence: University Press of Kansas, 2007), 32.

66 This comparison of transportation and land use in Freiburg and Chula Vista is based on S. Ryan and J.A. Throgmorton, 'Sustainable Transportation and Land Development on the Periphery: A Case Study of Freiburg, Germany and Chula Vista, California,' *Transportation Research*, part D, 8 (2003): 37–52.

67 Ibid., 42–3.

68 Ibid., 48.

69 This is a developer's description of the East Lake community in eastern Chula Vista. Ibid., 45.

70 C.A. Kennedy, 'A Comparison of the Sustainability of Public and Private Transportation Systems: Study of the Greater Toronto Area,' *Transportation* 29 (2002): 459–93.

71 Ibid.

72 A. Wilson and J. Boehland, 'Small Is Beautiful: U.S. House Size, Resource Use, and the Environment,' *Journal of Industrial Ecology* 9, nos. 1–2 (2005): 278.

73 Calculations based on Wilson and Boehland, 'Small Is Beautiful,' table 3, 282.

74 Keynes, *The General Theory of Employment, Interest and Money*, 106.

75 Ibid., 105.

76 Hall, *Cities in Civilization*, 636.

77 Robinson, *The Accumulation of Capital*, 78.

78 Ibid., 87.

79 An alternative is that people work fewer hours or retire early.

80 Robinson, *The Accumulation of Capital*, 89.

81 Ibid., 99.

82 J. Robinson, *Essays in the Theory of Economic Growth* (London: Macmillan, 1962), 63.

Chapter 6: The Ecology of Urban Economies

1 A. Marshall, *Principles of Economics: An Introductory Volume*, 8th ed. (London: Macmillan, 1898), quoted in A.C. Pigou, ed., *Memorials of Alfred Marshall* (New York: Kelley and Millman, 1956), 318.

2 R. Solnit, 'Detroit Arcadia,' *Harper's Magazine*, July 2007, 65–73.

3   Ibid., 65.
4   Hall, *Cities in Civilization*, 401.
5   Ibid., 399.
6   Hall lists the top-producing states in 1900 as Massachusetts, Connecticut, Illinois, New York, New Jersey, Ohio, and Pennsylvania. Ibid., 399.
7   Ibid., 401.
8   Ibid., 411–12.
9   Ibid., 404.
10 Ibid., 412–14.
11 M. Foster, *From Streetcar to Superhighway: American City Planners and Urban Transportation, 1900–1940* (Philadelphia: Temple University Press, 1981), 15.
12 Ibid., 46–7.
13 Ibid., 80.
14 Ibid., 80–6.
15 B. McGraw, 'Historians in the Streets: Life in the Ruins of Detroit,' *History Workshop Journal* 63 (2007): 296.
16 Ibid.
17 K. Boyle, 'The Ruins of Detroit: Exploring the Urban Crisis in the Motor City,' *Michigan Historical Review* 27, no. 1 (2001): 109–27.
18 McGraw, 'Historians in the Streets,' 291.
19 Boyle, 'The Ruins of Detroit.'
20 McGraw, 'Historians in the Streets,' 298.
21 Boyle, 'The Ruins of Detroit.'
22 Solnit, 'Detroit Arcadia,' 68.
23 Boyle, 'The Ruins of Detroit.'
24 McGraw, 'Historians in the Streets,' 295.
25 Ibid., 292.
26 Ibid.
27 Ibid., 294.
28 Solnit, 'Detroit Arcadia,' 68.
29 McGraw, 'Historians in the Streets,' 297.
30 Ibid., 292.
31 Ibid., 290.
32 Solnit, 'Detroit Arcadia,' 72.
33 Ibid.
34 Boyle, 'The Ruins of Detroit,' and McGraw, 'Historians in the Streets,' 300.
35 Mumford, *The Culture of Cities*, cited in J. Montgomery, *The New Wealth of Cities: City Dynamics and the Fifth Wave* (Aldershot, UK: Ashgate, 2007), 1.
36 Backhouse, *The Ordinary Business of Life*, 178.
37 Ibid., 154.

38 Ibid., 181.
39 Ibid., 179.
40 Ibid., 181.
41 Ibid., 179.
42 Marshall, quoted in Pigou, *Memorials of Alfred Marshall*, 318.
43 Ibid., 317.
44 Backhouse, *The Ordinary Business of Life*, 179.
45 P. Mirowski, *More Heat than Light: Economics as Social Physics, Physics as Nature's Economics* (Cambridge: Cambridge University Press, 1989), 35.
46 Ibid., 218.
47 Ibid., 222–4.
48 P. Mirowski, 'Energy and Energetics in Economic Theory: A Review Essay,' *Journal of Economic Issues* 22, no. 3 (1988): 816.
49 Ibid., 811.
50 Ibid., 822–5.
51 G.M. Hodgson, 'Decomposition and Growth: Biological Metaphors in Economics from the 1880s to the 1980s,' in Kurt Dopfer, ed., *The Evolutionary Foundations of Economics* (Cambridge: Cambridge University Press, 2005), chap. 5.
52 Ibid., 114.
53 E. Powell, *The Evolution of the Money Market (1385–1915): An Historical and Analytical Study of the Rise and Development of Finance as a Central, Coordinated Force* (1915; repr. New York: A.M. Kelly, 1966).
54 Hodgson, 'Decomposition and Growth,' 113.
55 Another routine followed by firms is to take strategic approaches to non-routine problems; this leads to routine-changing processes akin to biological mutation.
56 E.D. Beinhocker, *The Origin of Wealth: Evolution, Complexity, and the Radical Remaking of Economics* (Cambridge, MA: Harvard University Press, 2006).
57 J. Jacobs, *The Nature of Economies* (Toronto: Random House, 2001).
58 G. Dickinson and K. Murphy, *Ecosystems: A Functional Approach* (London: Routledge, 1998), 13.
59 A.G. Tansley, *The British Islands and Their Vegetation* (Cambridge: Cambridge University Press, 1939).
60 Dickinson and Murphy, *Ecosystems*, 12–13.
61 Ibid., 12.
62 Formally called *autotrophs*.
63 Dickinson and Murphy, *Ecosystems*, 58.
64 Ibid., 63–4.
65 D.S. Edwards, Earl of Cranbrook, *A Tropical Rainforest: The Nature of Biodi-*

versity in Borneo at Belalong, Brunei (London: Royal Geographical Society; Singapore: Sun Tree Publishing, 1994), 79.

66 P. Colinvaux, *Why Big Fierce Animals Are Rare: An Ecologist's Perspective* (Princeton, NJ: Princeton University Press, 1978), 79–80.

67 For examples, see E.P. Odum, *Basic Ecology* (Philadelphia: CBS College Publishing, 1983), 151–3; and Dickinson and Murphy, *Ecosystems*, 55–7.

68 Colinvaux, *Why Big Fierce Animals Are Rare.*

69 Dickinson and Murphy, *Ecosystems*, 102.

70 Ibid., 108–12.

71 J.B. Barney, *Gaining and Sustaining Competitive Advantage* (Reading, MA: Addison-Wesley, 1997), 220–7, 284.

72 See Dickinson and Murphy, *Ecosystems*, 36–7.

73 Ibid., 38.

74 Unpublished analysis conducted by the author. Small firms (10–100 people) employed a total of 522,431 people and had estimated sales of (Cdn) $216 billion. Both of these measures become smaller as one moves up through the ranges of firm size. The seven firms at the top employed a total of 202,000 people and had total sales of $54 billion.

75 It is also likely that some of these larger firms were counting employees outside the Toronto region.

76 Dickinson and Murphy, *Ecosystems*, 57.

77 While energy always decreases up the food chain, pyramids of organism numbers and biomass can be inverted; see Odum, *Basic Ecology*, 159–62. Inversion of pyramids of firms by employee numbers might also be expected.

78 Although this idea is not pursued any further here, it might be possible to develop a whole theory of economic growth essentially based around the processes of company start-up, mergers, and acquisitions.

79 C. Hardy and T.E. Graedel, 'Industrial Ecosystems as Food Webs,' *Journal of Industrial Ecology* 6, no. 1 (2002): 29–38.

80 B.J.L. Berry, *Long-wave Rhythms in Economic Development and Political Behavior* (Baltimore, MD: Johns Hopkins University Press, 1991), 80.

81 Ibid., 83.

82 Ibid., 47–8.

83 Ibid., 80.

84 Ibid., 82.

85 Ibid., 86.

86 Porter, *The Great Fire of London*, 106.

87 Ibid., 111.

88 Ibid., 105.

89 Ibid., 106.
90 Ibid., 107.
91 Hall, *Cities in Civilization*, 795.
92 Ibid., 786–95.
93 Ibid., 797.
94 Ibid., 795.
95 R.T. Paine, 'A Conversation on Refining the Concept of Keystone Species,' *Conservation Biology* 9, no. 4 (1995): 962–4.

Chapter 7: Conclusion – The Wealth of Cities

1 Beckert, *The Monied Metropolis*, 19, commenting on the economy of New York City in the 1850s.
2 The roof and tower were not completed in time for the Games; in fact, they were over a decade late in being finished.
3 R. Prévost, *Montréal: A History*, trans. E. Mueller and R. Chodos (Toronto: McClelland and Stewart, 1993), 386–98.
4 E.A. Collard, *Chalk to Computers: The Story of the Montréal Stock Exchange* (Quebec: Bibliothèque Nationale du Québec, 1974), 41–2.
5 Prévost, *Montréal*, 390.
6 J. Jacobs, *The Question of Separation* (New York: Random House, 1980), 11.
7 Prévost, *Montréal*, 393–4.
8 CBC Radio, 'The World at Six,' 6 January 1978.
9 Wikipedia, 'Bank of Montreal' (1 July 2006).
10 Jacobs, *The Question of Separation*, 13.
11 J. Lemon, *Toronto since 1918: An Illustrated History* (Toronto: James Lorimer and Co., 1985), 198, table XII.
12 Ibid., 160.
13 Ibid., 168.
14 Ibid., 151.
15 Ibid., 11.
16 Peter Ustinov's reference was reported by John Bentley Mays in the *Globe and Mail* on 1 August 1987.
17 This section on Mirabel International Airport draws upon facts collected by Sebastian Flasynski for a paper in my course on infrastructure economics at the University of Toronto. Data on passenger flights and urban employment are from Statistics Canada.
18 D. Masse, 'The Airport,' *Financial Times of Canada*, special edition, 'Perspective on Money,' 29 September 1975, 3–7.
19 Ibid.

20 W. Stewart, *Paper Juggernaut: Big Government Gone Mad* (Toronto: McClelland and Stewart, 1979), 30, 36.

21 Kindleberger, in 'The Formation of Financial Centers,' 105–14, was perplexed by the coexistence of Montreal and Toronto as financial centres.

22 Jacobs, *The Question of Separation*, 13.

23 Kindleberger, 'The Formation of Financial Centers,' 106–8.

24 Ibid., 108.

25 Lemon, *Toronto since 1918*, 186. (Note: this is not how we measure the wealth of cities in this book.)

26 Toronto Board of Trade, *Toronto Business and Market Guide* (Toronto: de Reus, 2001), 206.

27 Ibid., 22.

28 Data from Statistics Canada.

29 J.H. Ausubel and R. Hermann, eds, *Cities and Their Vital Systems: Infrastructure Past, Present and Future* (Washington, DC: National Academy Press, 1988), 78, table 3-1.

30 Ibid., 81, table 3-2.

31 G.L. Lankevich and H.B. Furer, *A Brief History of New York City* (New York: Associated Faculty Press, 1984), 221.

32 M. Page, *The Creative Destruction of Manhattan, 1900–1940* (Chicago: University of Chicago Press, 1999), 2.

33 Ibid.

34 Ibid., 21.

35 Ibid., 26.

36 Ibid., 28.

37 Ibid., 32.

38 Ibid., 26.

39 Ibid., 45.

40 Ibid., 46.

41 Ibid., 49–50.

42 Ibid., 25.

43 Ibid., 50.

44 Ibid., 51.

45 Ibid., 53–65.

46 The significance of the autonomous component of effective demand in driving long-term economic growth has also been argued by S. Cesaratto, F. Serrano, and A. Stirati in 'Technical Change, Effective Demand and Employment,' *Review of Political Economy* 15, no. 1 (2003): 33–52, but without mention of urban form.

47 Keynes, *The General Theory of Employment, Interest and Money*, 97.

48 Ibid., 91.
49 T.C. Barker and M. Robbins, *A History of London Transport: Passenger Travel and the Development of the Metropolis*, vol. 1 (London: Allen and Unwin, 1963), 10–11.
50 See the 1797 map of London, ibid., 17.
51 Ibid., 16.
52 Ibid., 7.
53 Ibid., 11–13.
54 H.J. Dyos, 'Urban Transformation: A Note on the Objects of Street Improvements in Regency and Early Victorian London,' *International Review of Social History* 2, pt. 2 (1957): 259–65.
55 Ibid., 262.
56 Barker and Robbins, *A History of London Transport*, 17.
57 Ibid., 19.
58 Ibid., 37.
59 Ibid., 14.
60 Steamboats are discussed ibid., 42–3.
61 Ibid., 44.
62 Ibid., 57–8.
63 Ibid., 125–30.
64 Ibid., 138.
65 Ibid., 69–98.
66 Ibid., 98.
67 Ibid., 253.
68 Ibid., 178.
69 Ibid., 199–200.
70 Ibid., 208.
71 Ibid., 200.
72 Ibid., 242.
73 Ibid., 245.
74 M. Ball and D. Sunderland, *An Economic History of London, 1800–1914* (London: Routledge, 2001), 169.
75 Ibid., 184.
76 Ibid., 141–3.
77 Barker and Robbins, *A History of London Transport*, 207.
78 Blanke, *Hell on Wheels*, 56.
79 Author's calculation based on table 353, section 15, of the 1936 Statistical Abstract of the United States, US Department of Commerce. (The index for wages per hour was 32.9 in 1900, rising to 103.2 in 1930.)
80 M. Foster, *From Streetcar to Superhighway: American City Planners and Urban*

Transportation, 1900–1940 (Philadelphia: Temple University Press, 1981), 62.

81 Ibid., 127.

82 Blanke, *Hell on Wheels*, 57, 174.

83 Foster, *From Streetcar to Superhighway*, 59.

84 Blanke, *Hell on Wheels*, 174.

85 O.D. Gutfreud, 'Rebuilding New York in the Auto Age: Robert Moses and His Highways,' in Hilary Ballon, ed., *Robert Moses and the Modern City: The Transformation of New York* (New York: W.W. Norton, 2007), 86–93. See map on p. 96.

86 K.D. Revell, *Building Gotham: Civic Culture and Public Policy in New York City, 1898–1938* (Baltimore, MD: Johns Hopkins University Press, 2003), 229–30.

87 Ibid., 245.

88 Ibid., chap. 1.

89 Ibid., 231.

90 Ibid., 232–42.

91 Gutfreud, 'Rebuilding New York,' 86.

92 T. Abeysinghe and K.M. Choy, 'The Aggregate Consumption Puzzle in Singapore,' *Journal of Asian Economics* 15 (2004): 564.

93 See ibid., 565, figure 3.

94 Ibid., 571.

95 See R. Florida, *The Rise of the Creative Class: And How It's Transforming Work, Leisure, Community and Everyday Life* (New York: Perseus, 2002); and J. Montgomery, *The New Wealth of Cities: City Dynamics and the Fifth Wave* (Aldershot, UK: Ashgate, 2007).

96 Montgomery, *The New Wealth of Cities*, 377.

97 Ibid., 69.

98 Marshall, *Principles of Economics*, 461.

99 E.D. Beinhocker, *The Origin of Wealth: Evolution, Complexity, and the Radical Remaking of Economics* (Cambridge, MA: Harvard University Press, 2006), 12.

100 A. Koestler, 'Beyond Atomism and Holism – the Concept of the Holon,' in A. Koester and J.R. Smythies, eds, *Beyond Reductionism: New Perspectives in the Life Sciences, Proceedings of the Alpach Symposium* (London: Hutchinson, 1969), 192–210.

101 I am indebted to University of Toronto professor emeritus Henry Regier for this point about the need to add more emphasis on evolution to Koestler's system. Regier also suggests that the 'H' in SOHO should stand for Holonic.

102 Odum, *Basic Ecology*, 90.
103 Dickinson and Murphy, *Ecosystems*, 116–17, 120.
104 See A. Abouchar, *Transportation Economics and Public Policy, with Urban Extensions* (New York: John Wiley and Sons, 1977), chap. 13.

Bibliography

Abeysinghe, T., and K.M. Choy. 'The Aggregate Consumption Puzzle in Singapore.' *Journal of Asian Economics* 15 (2004): 563–78.

Abouchar, A. *Transportation Economics and Public Policy, with Urban Extensions.* New York: John Wiley and Sons, 1977.

Aschauer, A.D. 'Is Public Expenditure Productive?' *Journal of Monetary Economics* 23, no. 2 (1989): 177–200.

Ausubel, J.H., and R. Hermann, eds. *Cities and Their Vital Systems: Infrastructure Past, Present and Future.* Washington, DC: National Academy Press, 1988.

Backhouse, R.E. *The Ordinary Business of Life: A History of Economics from the Ancient World to the Twenty-first Century.* Princeton, NJ: Princeton University Press, 2002.

Bairoch, Paul. *Cities and Economic Development: From the Dawn of History to the Present.* Chicago: University of Chicago Press, 1988.

Baker, T.M.M. *London: Rebuilding the City after the Great Fire.* Chichester, UK: Phillimore and Company, 2000.

Ball, M., and D. Sunderland. *An Economic History of London, 1800–1914.* London: Routledge, 2001.

Barker, T.C., and M. Robbins. *A History of London Transport: Passenger Travel and the Development of the Metropolis.* Vol. 1. London: Allen and Unwin, 1963.

Barney, J.B. *Gaining and Sustaining Competitive Advantage.* Reading, MA: Addison-Wesley, 1997.

Beckert, S.B. *The Monied Metropolis: New York City and the Consolidation of the American Bourgeoisie, 1850–1896.* Cambridge: Cambridge University Press, 2001.

Beinhocker, E.D. *The Origin of Wealth: Evolution, Complexity, and the Radical Remaking of Economics.* Cambridge, MA: Harvard University Press, 2006.

Benjamin, J.D., P. Chinloy, and G.D. Jud. 'Why Do Households Concentrate Their Wealth in Housing?' *Journal of Real Estate Research* 26, no. 4 (2004): 329–43.

Berry, B.J.L. *Long-wave Rhythms in Economic Development and Political Behavior.* Baltimore, MD: Johns Hopkins University Press, 1991.

Blanke, D. *Hell on Wheels: The Promise and Peril of America's Car Culture, 1900–1940.* Lawrence: University Press of Kansas, 2007.

Bonetti, S., and D. Cobham. 'Financial Markets and the City of London.' In D. Cobham, ed., *Markets and Dealers: The Economics of the London Financial Markets.* London: Longman, 1992.

Borio, C., and P. McGuire. 'Twin Peaks in Equity and Housing Markets?' *BIS Quarterly Review*, March 2004, 79–93.

Boyle, K. 'The Ruins of Detroit: Exploring the Urban Crisis in the Motor City.' *Michigan Historical Review* 27, no. 1 (2001): 109–27.

Braudel, F. *Civilization and Capitalism, 15th–18th Centuries. Volume III, The Perspective of the World.* London: William Collins Sons and Co., 1984.

– *The Mediterranean and the Mediterranean World in the Age of Phillip II.* Vol. 1. Berkeley: University of California Press, 1995.

Brewer, Anthony. *Richard Cantillon: Pioneer of Economic Theory.* London: Routledge, 1992.

Cameron, R.E. *A Concise Economic History of the World: From Paleolithic Times to the Present.* Oxford: Oxford University Press, 1997.

Cantillon, R. *Essai de la nature du commerce en général.* 1931. Translated by Henry Higgs. London: Frank Cass and Co., 1959.

Carosso, V.P. *Investment Banking in America: A History.* Cambridge, MA: Harvard University Press, 1970.

Carswell, J. *The South Sea Bubble.* Rev. ed. Gloucester, UK: Alan Sutton, 1993.

Cassis, Y. *Capitals of Capital: The Rise and Fall of International Financial Centres, 1780–2009.* Cambridge: Cambridge University Press, 2010.

Cesaratto, S., F. Serrano, and A. Stirati. 'Technical Change, Effective Demand and Employment.' *Review of Political Economy* 15, no. 1 (2003): 33–52.

Chartered Institute of Wastes Management. *A Resource Flow and Ecological Footprint Analysis of Greater London.* London: Best Foot Forward, 2002.

Clarke, W.M. *How the City of London Works.* 5th ed. London: Sweet and Maxwell, 1999.

Cobb, C., T. Halstead, and J. Rowe. 'If the GDP Is Up, Why Is America Down?' *Atlantic Monthly*, October 1995, 59–78.

Colinvaux, P. *Why Big Fierce Animals Are Rare: An Ecologist's Perspective.* Princeton, NJ: Princeton University Press, 1978.

Collard, E.A. *Chalk to Computers: The Story of the Montréal Stock Exchange.* Quebec: Bibliothèque Nationale du Québec, 1974.

Daly, H.E., and J. Farley. *Ecological Economics: Principles and Applications.* Washington, DC: Island Press, 2004.

Damodaran, A. *Corporate Finance: Theory and Practice.* New York: Wiley, 1997.

Davis, E.P. 'International Financial Centers – an Industrial Analysis.' Bank of England Discussion Paper, 51. 1990.

Dickinson, G., and K. Murphy. *Ecosystems: A Functional Approach.* London: Routledge, 1998.

DiPasquale, D., and W.C. Wheaton. 'The Markets for Real Estate Assets and Space: A Conceptual Framework.' *AREUEA Journal* 20, no. 1 (1992): 181–97.

Dopfer, K., ed. *The Evolutionary Foundations of Economics.* Cambridge: Cambridge University Press, 2005.

Drennan, M.P. 'The Decline and Rise of the New York Economy.' In J.H. Mollenkopf and M. Castells, eds, *Dual City: Restructuring New York,* chap. 1 New York: Russell Sage Foundation, 1991.

Dunn, M.M., and R.S. Dunn. 'The Founding, 1681–1701.' In R.F. Weigley, ed., *Philadelphia: A 300-Year History.* New York: Norton and Co., 1982.

Dyos, H.J. 'Urban Transformation: A Note on the Objects of Street Improvements in Regency and Early Victorian London.' *International Review of Social History* 2, pt. 2 (1957): 259–65.

Edwards, D.S., Earl of Cranbrook. *A Tropical Rainforest: The Nature of Biodiversity in Borneo at Belalong, Brunei.* London: Royal Geographical Society; Singapore: Sun Tree Publishing, 1994.

Ellul, Jacques. *The Meaning of the City.* Translated by Dennis Pardee. Grand Rapids, MI: W.B. Eerdmans, 1970.

Fallis, G., and L.B. Smith. 'Uncontrolled Prices in a Controlled Market: The Case of Rent Controls.' *American Economic Review* 74, no. 1 (1984): 193–200.

Ferguson, N. *The Ascent of Money: A Financial History of the World.* London: Penguin, 2009.

Florida, R. *The Flight of the Creative Class: The New Global Competition for Talent.* New York: Harper Business, 2004.

– *The Rise of the Creative Class: And How It's Transforming Work, Leisure, Community and Everyday Life.* New York: Basic Books, 2002.

Foster, M. *From Streetcar to Superhighway: American City Planners and Urban Transportation, 1900–1940.* Philadelphia: Temple University Press, 1981.

Friedmann, J. 'The World City Hypothesis.' *Development and Change* 17 (1986): 69–83.

Fu, Y. 'Hong Kong: Overcoming Financial Risks of Growing Real Estate

Credit.' In K. Mera and B. Renaud, eds, *Asia's Financial Crises and the Role of Real Estate*, chap. 7. New York: Sharpe, 2000.

Fung, M., and C.A. Kennedy. 'An Integrated Macroeconomic Model for Assessing Urban Sustainability.' *Environment and Planning, B* 32, no. 5 (2005): 639–56.

Galbraith, J.K. *A History of Economics*. London: Hamish Hamilton, 1987.

Gillen, D.W. 'Transportation Infrastructure and Economic Development: A Review of Recent Literature.' *Logistics and Transportation Review* 32, no. 1 (1996): 39.

Glaeser, E.L., H.D. Kallal, J.A. Scheinkman, and A. Shleifer. 'Growth in Cities.' *Journal of Political Economy*, Centennial issue, 100, no. 6 (1992): 1126–52.

Gras, N.S.B. *An Introduction to Economic History*. Reprint, New York: Augustus M. Kelley Publishers, 1969.

Gribbin, J. *The Fellowship; The Story of a Revolution*. London: Penguin, 2005.

Griffith-Jones, S. *Global Capital Flows: Should They Be Regulated?* New York: St Martin's Press, 1998.

Grübler, A. *The Rise and Fall of Infrastructures*. Heidelberg, Germany: Physica-Verlag, 1990.

Gutfreud, O.D. 'Rebuilding New York in the Auto Age: Robert Moses and His Highways.' In Hilary Ballon, ed., *Robert Moses and the Modern City: The Transformation of New York*, 86–93. New York: W.W. Norton and Co., 2007.

Hall, P.G. *Cities in Civilization: Culture, Innovation, and Urban Order*. London: Phoenix, 1999.

Hardy, C., and T.E. Graedel. 'Industrial Ecosystems as Food Webs.' *Journal of Industrial Ecology* 6, no. 1 (2002): 29–38.

Hodgson, G.M. 'Decomposition and Growth: Biological Metaphors in Economics from the 1880s to the 1980s.' In Kurt Dopfer, ed., *The Evolutionary Foundations of Economics*, chap. 5. Cambridge: Cambridge University Press, 2005.

Hull, C.H., ed. *The Economic Writings of Sir William Petty*. Fairfield, NJ: Augustus M. Kelley Publishers, 1986.

Hvidt, M. 'Public-Private Ties and Their Contribution to Development: The Case of Dubai.' *Middle Eastern Studies* 43, no. 4 (2007): 557–77.

Issacson, W. *Benjamin Franklin: An American Life*. New York: Simon and Schuster, 2003.

Jacobs, J. *The Economy of Cities*. New York: Random House, 1969.

– *The Nature of Economies*. Toronto: Random House, 2001.

– *The Question of Separation*. New York: Random House, 1980.

Jay, P. *Road to Riches, or The Wealth of Man*. London: Orion Books, 2000.

Jevons, W.S. 'Richard Cantillon and the Nationality of Political Economy.'

Contemporary Review, January 1881. Reprinted in *Essai sur la nature du commerce en général,* by Richard Cantillon, edited and translated by Henry Higgs. London: Frank Cass, [1931] 1959.

Jones, C. *Paris: Biography of a City.* London: Allen Lane, 2004.

Kamal-Chaoui, L., and A. Robert, ed. 'Competitive Cities and Climate Change.' OECD Regional Development Working Papers no. 2. Paris: OECD Publishing, 2009.

Kamen, H. *Spain's Road to Empire: The Making of a World Power, 1492–1763.* London: Penguin, 2002.

Kennedy, C.A. 'A Comparison of the Sustainability of Public and Private Transportation Systems: Study of the Greater Toronto Area.' *Transportation* 29 (2002): 459–93.

Kennedy, C.A., J. Cuddihy, and J. Engel Yan. 'The Changing Metabolism of Cities.' *Journal of Industrial Ecology* 11, no. 2 (2007): 43–59.

Keynes, J.M. 'The General Theory of Employment.' *Quarterly Journal of Economics* 51, no. 2 (1937): 209–23.

– *The General Theory of Employment, Interest and Money.* 1953. Orlando, FL: Harcourt, 1964.

Kindleberger, C.P. *A Financial History of Western Europe.* 2nd ed. Oxford: Oxford University Press, 1993.

– 'The Formation of Financial Centers: A Study in Comparative Economic History.' *Princeton Studies in International Finance* 36 (1974). Reproduced as chapter 4 of C.P. Kindleberger, *Economic Response: Comparative Studies in Trade, Finance and Growth.* Cambridge, MA: Harvard University Press, 1978.

Kindleberger, C.P., and R.Z. Aliber. *Manias, Panics and Crashes: A History of Financial Crises.* 5th ed. New York: Palgrave Macmillan, 2005.

Koestler, A. 'Beyond Atomism and Holism – the Concept of the Holon.' In A. Koestler and J.R. Smythies, eds, *Beyond Reductionism: New Perspectives in the Life Sciences, Proceedings of the Alpach Symposium.* London: Hutchinson, 1969.

Kostof, Spiro. *The City Shaped: Urban Patterns and Meanings through History.* Boston: Little, Brown, 1991.

Kurth, J.R. 'Between Europe and America: The New York Foreign Policy Elite.' In M. Shefter, ed., *Capital of the American Century,* chap. 4. New York: Russell Sage Foundation, 1993.

Lankevich, G.L., and H.B. Furer. *A Brief History of New York City.* New York: Associated Faculty Press, 1984.

Lee, Y. *Schumpeterian Dynamics and Metropolitan-scale Productivity.* Aldershot, UK: Ashgate, 2004.

Leff, G. *Paris and Oxford Universities in the Thirteenth and Fourteenth Centuries: An Institutional and Intellectual History.* New York: John Wiley and Sons, 1968.

Lekachman, R. *The Age of Keynes*. New York: Random House, 1966.

Lemon, J. *Toronto since 1918: An Illustrated History*. Toronto: James Lorimer and Co., 1985.

Marshall, A. 'Distribution and Exchange.' *Economic Journal*, 1898. Reproduced as chapter 14, 'Mechanical and Biological Analogies in Economics,' of A.C. Pigou, ed., *Memorials of Alfred Marshall*. New York: Kelley and Millman, 1956.

– *Principles of Economics: An Introductory Volume*. 8th ed. London: Macmillan, 1949.

Marx, K. *Capital: A Critique of Political Economy*. Vol. 1. London: Penguin, 1976.

Maslow, A.H. *Motivation and Personality*. New York: Harper & Brothers, 1954.

Masse, D. 'The Airport.' *Financial Times of Canada*, special edition, 'Perspective on Money,' 29 September 1975, 3–7.

McConnell, J.W. *Basic Teachings of the Great Economists*. New York: Garden City Publishing, 1943.

McDonald, J.E. *Fundamentals of Urban Economics*. Upper Saddle River, NJ: Prentice-Hall, 1997.

McGraw, B. 'Historians in the Streets: Life in the Ruins of Detroit.' *History Workshop Journal* 63 (2007): 289–302.

Mera, K., and B. Renaud, eds. *Asia's Financial Crises and the Role of Real Estate*. New York: Sharpe, 2000.

Michie, R.C. *The London and New York Stock Exchanges, 1850–1914*. London: Allen and Unwin, 1987.

Mirowski, P. 'Energy and Energetics in Economic Theory: A Review Essay.' *Journal of Economic Issues* 22, no. 3 (1988).

– *More Heat than Light: Economics as Social Physics, Physics as Nature's Economics*. Cambridge: Cambridge University Press, 1989.

Montgomery, J. *The New Wealth of Cities: City Dynamics and the Fifth Wave*. Aldershot, UK: Ashgate, 2007.

Mossner, E.C. *The Life of David Hume*. 2nd ed. Oxford: Oxford University Press, 1980.

Mumford, L. *The City in History*. New York: Harcourt, Brace and World, 1961.

– *The Culture of Cities*. New York: Harcourt and Brace, 1938; reprint, 1961.

Murphy, A.E. *Richard Cantillon: Entrepreneur and Economist*. New York: Oxford University Press, 1986.

Nelson, R.R., and S.G. Winter. *An Evolutionary Theory of Economic Change*. Cambridge, MA: Harvard University Press, 1982.

Nichols, A. *Discovering Aquinas: An Introduction to His Life, Work, and Influence*. Grand Rapids, MI: W.B. Eerdmans, 2003.

Odum, E.P. *Basic Ecology*. Philadelphia: CBS College Publishing, 1983.

Page, M. *The Creative Destruction of Manhattan, 1900–1940.* Chicago: University of Chicago Press, 1999.

Paine, R.T. 'A Conversation on Refining the Concept of Keystone Species.' *Conservation Biology* 9, no. 4 (1995): 962–4.

Peng, R., and W. Wheaton. 'Effects of Restrictive Land Supply on Housing in Hong Kong.' *Journal of Housing Research* 5, no. 2 (1994): 263–91.

Pollard, S., and D.W. Crossley. *The Wealth of Britain, 1085–1986.* London: Batsford, 1986.

Porter, S. *The Great Fire of London.* Gloucestershire, UK: Sutton Publishing, 1996.

Powell, E. *The Evolution of the Money Market (1385–1915): An Historical and Analytical Study of the Rise and Development of Finance as a Central, Coordinated Force.* 1915. Reprint, New York: Augustus M. Kelley Publishers, 1966.

Pred, A. *City-systems in Advanced Economies: Past Growth, Present Processes and Future Development Options.* London: Hutchinson, 1977.

Prévost, R. *Montréal: A History.* Translated by E. Mueller and R. Chodos. Toronto: McClelland and Stewart, 1993.

Rabushka, A. *Hong Kong: A Study in Economic Freedom.* Chicago: University of Chicago, 1979.

Rae, J. *Life of Adam Smith.* London: Macmillan, 1895.

Reed, H.C. *The Preeminence of International Financial Centers.* New York: Praeger, 1981.

Remini, R.V. *Andrew Jackson and the Bank War.* New York: Norton, 1967.

Renaud, B., F. Pretorius, and B. Pasadilla. *Markets at Work: Dynamics of the Residential Real Estate Market in Hong Kong.* Hong Kong: Hong Kong University Press, 1997.

Revell, K.D. *Building Gotham: Civic Culture and Public Policy in New York City, 1898–1938.* Baltimore, MD: Johns Hopkins University Press, 2003.

Roberts, D.W. *An Outline of the Economic History of England.* London: Longman, 1962.

Robinson, J. *The Accumulation of Capital.* London: Macmillan, 1956.
– *Essays in the Theory of Economic Growth.* London: Macmillan, 1962.

Rubenstein, W.D. *Elites and Wealthy in Modern British History: Essays in Social and Economic History.* Sussex, UK: Harvester Press; New York: St Martin's, 1987.

Ruskin, J. *The Genius of John Ruskin: Selections from His Writings.* Edited by D. Rosenberg. New York: Braziller, 1965.

Ryan, S., and J.A. Throgmorton. 'Sustainable Transportation and Land Development on the Periphery: A Case Study of Freiburg, Germany and Chula Vista, California.' *Transportation Research*, part D, 8 (2003): 37–52.

Sassen, S. *The Global City*. Princeton, NJ: Princeton University Press, 1991.

Scott, Allen J. *Social Economy of the Metropolis: Cognitive-Cultural Capitalism and the Global Resurgence of Cities*. Oxford: Oxford University Press, 2008.

Shefter, M. 'New York's National and International Influence.' In M. Shefter, ed. *Capital of the American Century*, chap. 1. New York: Russell Sage Foundation, 1993.

Sherrif, C. *The Artificial River: The Erie Canal and the Paradox of Progress, 1817–1862*. New York: Hill and Wang, 1996.

Silber, W.L. *When Washington Shut Down Wall Street*. Princeton, NJ: Princeton University Press, 2007.

Simon, M. 'The Pattern of New British Portfolio Foreign Investment, 1865–1914.' In A. Hall, ed., *The Export of Capital from Britain, 1870–1914*. London: Methuen and Co., 1968.

Smith, A. *An Inquiry into the Nature and the Causes of the Wealth of Nations*. 1776. London: Penguin, 1982.

Solnit, R. 'Detroit Arcadia.' *Harper's Magazine*, July 2007, 65–73.

Stewart, W. *Paper Juggernaut: Big Government Gone Mad*. Toronto: McClelland and Stewart, 1979.

Sveikauskas, L.A. 'The Productivity of Cities.' *Quarterly Journal of Economics* 89, no. 3 (1975): 393–413.

Tansley, A.G. *The British Islands and Their Vegetation*. Cambridge: Cambridge University Press, 1939.

Taylor, P.J. *World City Network: A Global Urban Analysis*. New York: Routledge, 2004.

Thomas, H. *Rivers of Gold: The Rise of the Spanish Empire*. London: Weidenfeld and Nicholson, 2003.

Thünen, J.H. von. *Von Thünen's Isolated State: An English Edition of Der Isolierte Staat*. Translated by C.M. Wartenberg, edited by P. Hall. Oxford: Pergamon, 1966.

Toronto Board of Trade. *Toronto Business and Market Guide*. Toronto: de Reus, 2001.

Trevelyn, G.M. *Illustrated History of England*. London: Longman, 1956.

Veblen, T. *The Theory of the Leisure Class: An Economic Study of Institutions*. 1899. Rev. ed. New York: B.W. Huebsch, 1918.

Vogel, D. 'New York as a National and Global Financial Centre.' In M. Shefter, ed., *Capital of the American Century*, chap. 3. New York: Russell Sage Foundation, 1993.

Welsh, F. *A History of Hong Kong*. Rev. ed. London: HarperCollins, 1997.

Wilson, A., and J. Boehland. 'Small Is Beautiful, U.S. House Size, Resource Use, and the Environment.' *Journal of Industrial Ecology* 9, nos. 1–2 (2005).

Wright, R.E. *The First Wall Street: Chestnut Street, Philadelphia, and the Birth of American Finance*. Chicago: University of Chicago Press, 2005.

Wrigley, E.A. *People, Cities and Wealth: The Transformation of Traditional Society*. Oxford: Blackwell, 1987.

Xenophon. 'On the Means of Improving the Revenues of Athens.' In *Xenophon's Minor Works*. Translated by J.S. Watson. London: George Bell and Sons, 1905.

Index